INDIAN MONOCRACY

INDIAN MONOCRACY

Perspectives and Challenges of 21st Century

Joginder Singh

GYAN PUBLISHING HOUSE
New Delhi - 110002

Indian Monocracy : Perspectives and Challenges of 21st century

Rs. 540

ISBN : 81-212-0917-X

Published in 2007 in India by
Gyan Publishing House
5, Ansari Road, Darya Ganj, New Delhi -110002
Phones: 23282060, 23261060, fax : (011) 23285914
E-mail : books@gyanbook.com
Website : http:// w.w.w.gyanbooks.com

Laser Type Setting by: Mega Graphics, Delhi
Printed at: Salasar Imaging System, Delhi

Contents

Preface

If men were angels, no government would be required. If angels were to govern men, neither external nor internal controls on government would be needed. But since human beings are governing and no human being is without infirmities, aberrations and that also serious aberrations take place.

Despite the brought spots and the country doing well, and economy booming at least for the richer and middle class, things for a vast majority are far from rosy. Our country is passing through vitalizing and bristling times. The present description almost fits the current epoch in India, what Charles Dickens once said; "It was the best of times, it was the worst of times, it was the age of wisdom, it was the age of foolishness . . . it was the spring of hope, it was the winter of despair . . . in short, the period was so far like the present period . . ."

This book is a journey through such times, lived in not only by the author, but his generations. Every book is written with an objective, which in this case, being to involve the rulers and ruled in good governance. Good or bad governance affects us all. In the case of some, it is in smaller degrees, and in the case of others by larger degrees.

History does not long assign the care of freedom to the weak or the timid. Both the past and future will always belong to the bold and brave.. Let us be clear on one fact that it is not the for the government to keep the citizen from falling into error. No Government does it. On the contrary, it is the job of the citizen to keep the government from falling into error.

This book seeks to examine and raise some of the issues, facing the Nation, Government and Citizens, so that the citizens should at least get the fruits of democracy. Agreed, that it is not the best form of Government, but unfortunately, all those tried before, have proved worse. Happy readings.

1
Mayhem of Minorities

The hot spot of insurgency and infiltration is strife torn Kashmir. The worst in the gory achievements of the terrorists has been, the massacre of 35 Sikhs at Chattisinghpora. The causality graph is rising so steadily that deaths in single figure do not cause even ripples either in the public mind or in the Government. Obviously, foreign mercenaries and trained terrorists have been pushed in a big way in the aftermath of Kargil. According to one official estimate about 5000 militants had sneaked into the valley in 1999 alone. More than 1500 were believed to be foreigners. Every time there is a major killing, action is taken to induct more forces, announce new strategies or create new areas of operational responsibility. Still the suicide squads have been killing Majors, Colonels, and DIG's with impunity. The terrorists have attacked more than 25 establishments belonging to military, para military, and police in 1999-2000. Some of the prominent targets are Headquarters of 15 Corps, based in Srinagar, Special Operation Group Headquarters of Rashtriya Rifles near Khannabal, Sector Headquarters of the Deputy Inspector General of Police at Bandipore and many more. It appears that despite loud proclamations, matters have been drifting in valley.

Figures tell a grim story. Between 1990 and February 2000, 365 AK rifles, 8,825 pistols, 958 UMGs, 757 RPGs, 308 sniper rifles, 615 rocket launchers, 1,687 rocket boosters, 75 LMGs and 25,000 kg of RDX were recovered. In the same period, the death toll has been 7,284 civilians, 9,864 terrorists and 2,579 security personnel. Political parties too have not been spared. 205 members of the National Conference have been killed. The Congress Party has lost 49 persons, the BJP 9, the CPI (M) 5, the Janata Dal 10, and the Awami League 5.

Violence is being imposed on the valley for the political objective of severing it from India. According to one report, the Pakistani Government and the terrorist organisations have trained two Lakh terrorists called Mujahideen. The terrorists during the training are brainwashed that terrorism in the name of Jehad is not the means for their end, but an end itself. Merciless and ruthless terrorists are being trained rigorously on the military lines in Pakistan. It is for this reason that terrorist have been engaging the security forces in long drawn gun battles, with a sophisticated arsenal. On the day of the visit of the President of the United States on 21st March 2000, the terrorists stormed a BSF camp in Sirinagar. Long drawn 18 hours battle culminated in the elimination of the terrorists. The Border Security Force used an IED to blast a building along with the terrorists. A few days later, there was another gun battle for over 21 hours in Kupwara District (Dudipora). In all these actions, the security forces had the upper hand. The low intensity proxy war has been going on for the last seventeen years in the valley. Three full-scale wars or conflagrations (1947, 1965, and 1999) have taken place between India and Pakistan over Kashmir. Pakistan tried the military option in the past, to wrest Kashmir from India, on the sole ground that there is a Muslim majority in the valley. Its second option to create disturbance in the valley and destabilise India through ISI activities has not succeeded. India has no interest in hitting Pakistan through military means, except to the extent of preserving its integrity and unity. India had to fight for the Independence, whereas Pakistan was born out by carving it out of India. It was given on a platter to the Muslim communalists, who had stoked religious brawls in undivided India. For currying favours with the Western Nations, it joined various alliances like SEATO, CENTO, primarily directed against the Communists belonging to the Soviet Bloc. During the Afghan war, it supported the American policy and strategic goals of turning that country into a Vietnam. When they withdrew, a lot of mercenaries and sophisticated weapons were acquired by it to reinforce Mujahideen.

Five days visit of the President Clinton convinced the United States, that, "India is the largest, strongest and indeed the dominant player in the sub-continent". The United States has given a clear message to Pakistan that it will not bail it out of any trouble. If it is aggressive towards India, the USA will side with India. Clinton said: "This moment in history poses some hard choices (for Pakistan). For, this era does not reward people who struggle in vain, to redraw borders with blood... Pakistan must also help create conditions that allow the dialogue to succeed. The stark truth must also be faced - there is no military solution to Kashmir". Cross border terrorism is a violation of the Line of Actual Control. Even the United States President was convinced that the terrorism is led by certain elements supported by Pakistan Government. Pakistan is continuing to bleed India, with continued militancy and using Kashmir as a place for its military misadventures. It has threatened to use its nuclear capability for expanding the present conflict. Pakistan's President said in a speech in Karachi that even solving Kashmir problem would not dispel hostilities, being inherent in Indo-Pakistan relationship. In other words, Pakistan would continue to create problems and work against India, even when all possible irritants are removed. There is a grave competition in between political parties and groups in Pakistan to be branded as the most rabid anti-Indian outfit. Successive regimes in Pakistan have stoked anti-India fire to stay in power there.

Security forces perform the most difficult and dangerous tasks in the most trying circumstances. If any force is required to be used, it is to protect the human rights of the silent vast majority, who do not wish to get involved in anything, which may endanger their life. In this vitiated atmosphere, even for genuine encounters and killings, people under the threat to their lives, are compelled to take out procession to support the terrorists cause. Recovery of weapons is not held as evidence. In Kashmir, the terrorists use mosques as sanctuaries, reducing our security forces to sitting ducks. Religious places, whether they be temples, Gurudwaras or Churches are meant for religious work and not as sanctuaries for the terrorists. Battles lines and rules of the game are slighted in favour of those wrecking the country. The country is bleeding at nose.

The terrorists use all tactics to gain their objective. One achievement was to open fire on the Security Forces in Anantnag, from behind the protestors' alleged protesting against some killing of terrorists, whom the former considered to be innocent. The more noise a person makes, the more likely he is to be heard and still more likely to be believed, if there is no official rebuttal. It is an old tactic by Pakistan and its henchmen to use civilian population. While dealing with a similar procession in 1990, I noticed that only old ladies beyond 70 years of age were put in the forefront of the procession. They were not ready and amenable to listen to the Security Forces not to act as a shield for such activities in which they might suffer harm. Inquiries were made and one of the old ladies told me that terrorists were needed at their houses. Every time, there was a need to use somebody as a shield, they along with small children were forced to participate in such processions. They did not even understand the cause for which or against which they were protesting. Any major killing of the infiltrators and terrorists is given the colour of innocent killing and human rights violation. Terrorist or their supporter are portrayed as innocent victims. Unfortunately, nobody talks about the human rights of 3.50 lakh Kashmiri Hindus and Sikhs who had to leave Kashmir valley against their wish due the mayhem created by the terrorists. No body talks about the killings of the whole marriage parties of minorities in Doda District or the killing of 35 Sikhs in Chattisinghpora or the violation of their human rights. Human Rights are welcome and should be respected. It should not be used only to tom-tom human rights of the terrorists, but for their innocent victims also.

Many times a question has been raised whether Pakistan is a failed State? Certain specific features point out a sorry state of affairs. There is a Constitutional Provision Section 63 (1G) for disenfranchising a person from the voting, if he is "propagating any opinion or acting in any manner prejudicial to the ideology of Pakistan". Every new ruler of Pakistan changes it and enforces his own ideology. Any criticism, which the ruler of the day, may not approve, can be construed as prejudicial to the ideology of Pakistan. No ideology is immutable. The ideology and approach of one ruler is bound to be different from the other. In this process, where people have always to look for the frowns and smiles of the rulers of the day, the question of voicing any public opinion contrary to that of the establishment, hardly arises. A breakthrough in relations with our neighbours depends more on their deeds rather than words. Relationships with Pakistan depend on substantial reduction in its support to the terrorists and its help to end cross border terrorism. This is the crux of issues between the two countries, before any meaningful dialogue can be started. The ultimate sufferers are the common people of J&K, who have no respite from violence. Even when the Government is keen for peace initiatives, the terrorists response has been in the form of renewed increase in the level of violence. The terrorists by selectively crafting their attacks, have almost completed the ethnic cleansing from the valley. Almost the entire Hindu population was forced to leave there hearth and homes in the valley. The biggest strike of the terrorists after the Centre's extension of three months' cease fire till May, 2001, was ambush, which led to the killing of 17 Police men and injuring of another 4 on 1st March, 2001 near a village in Rajouri District. Earlier in February, 2000, six policemen had been killed in the terrorists attack on the Police Control room, apart from the loss of life of 11 policemen in a bomb explosion in Srinagar in August, 2000. The strategy of the terrorists also changes. After laying ambush, they started human bombs fallowed by grenade throwing through their tacit associates. They are now targeting those, who stand for the country. The bigger aim is to demoralise and tie down all security forces, so that they can have a run of the valley. It may look madness. But there is a method in this madness.

Though the Government and the Security Forces were keen to keep their guns silent, in view of the unilateral extension of cease fire by the Government of India, till May, 2001, the terrorists or at least some of their groups interpreted it as a sign of weakness and not a desire on the part of India, to go all out to give a peace chance in J&K. People in strife torn parts of the world want peace and Kashmir is no different. But unfortunately, the local media give the impression to the terrorists and common people there, that their victory is in sight and they need to throw a few more grenades or blow up a few more building and to kill a few more army officers. The first major strike on March 1, 2001, killed a Col. and two soldiers and seriously injured a brigadier near Anantnag. Whether it was the kidnapping of the daughter of a former Home Minister, other relations of highly placed Kashmir politicians or getting the hostages of IC 814 hijacked from Nepal to Kandhar, the easy way was, to surrender and release the dreaded terrorists, on the conditions set by the perpetrators of the crime.

India is taken as a fertile training and experimental action ground by Pakistan. Recovery of RDX, AK -47 Rifles, detonators, hand grenades and fuse wires, originated from Pakistan, is something, which routinely happens, in our country. Pakistan has reportedly recruited 21000 Indian spies. In the terrorists activities prone State of Jammu and Kashmir, terrorists, equipped with light weaponry, latest frequency hopping communications, missiles, night visions devices have entered from the long and porous hilly border, for creating trouble. Recovery of a pneumatic boat, 15 hand grenades, 10 gelatine pipe bombs, 10 IED switch boxes, 2100 rounds of AK 47 Rifles and 440 rounds of sniper rifle ammunition from a cave in Kakua in Nogam in early 2000 was only a trailer of the subversive activities to follow. One of the long term plan of the terrorists is, to bury large quantities of explosives at various places for convenient retrieval in times of need. The weapons, explosive materials and the ammunition are stored in a special material, which will ensure their long-term preservation and kept for ready to use at the first opportunity. In this way, a terrorist does not have to carry the explosive with him. He can be directed, by his higher formation, to dig the same from a particular place. The attacks on the military and para military headquarters are intended to, to tie up these forces in defending themselves, rather than launching offensive to flush them out. Such attacks are not confined only to India. Russia is fighting a similar battle against mercenaries in Dagestan. Moscow had vowed to stamp out the rebellion by radical, self-proclaimed Wahahabi Muslims before it spreads to the neighbouring Muslim regions. The Russians stormed the rebel stronghold in Dagestan, to crush an up-rising which had left more than one thousand Muslim insurgents dead. Chechen based rebels had proclaimed an independent Islamic State. The rebels are seeking to establish Islamic rule in Dagestan. Pakistani religious leaders have supported the efforts of Chechen rebels. Russian foreign Ministry has already issued a warning to the Islamic countries against aiding the rebels. China is also not oblivious to the possibilities of problems in the Muslim state of Xinjiang. The nursery for training and providing rebels is Pakistan. Through its army and Madarsas, the recruits of Jehad fighting Pakistan's battles in the name of Islam are prepared for. It is these Madarsas or fundamentalist schools, which churn out religious fanatics. They are reared on religion. They are brainwashed for Jehad and their mindset is fixed. Pakistan was only one of three countries in the world, which recognised Taliban Government in Afghanistan. The worst victims of Talibans are the ancient Buddha statues in Central Bamiyan province of Afganistan. There is no limit to which the fundamentalists will stoop.

Pakistan and its front organisations in the name of Jehad, have been indulging and committing suicidal attacks with a view to tie down the security forces. The attacks on para military and military establishments like the one on Red Fort or on Corps Headquarters in Kashmir, are publicised by a section of the media, in such a way as to give a larger than life image to the capabilities and the acts of the terrorists. It is beyond the acceptable limits and national interests. Even if terrorists are killed one kilometre away from Srinagar Airport, it is publicised as an attack on the airport. The Sikhs were targeted again, in Kashmir after the earlier killing of 35 Sikhs in Chitttisinghpora. The objective behind the latest Sikh massacre is to complete the ethnic cleansing, which was substantially completed with the exodus of Kashmir Pundits in 1990s.

The terrorists had struck, in another big way, on February 16/17, 2002, killing eight members of three Hindu families, including children and girls, while they were sleeping. The incident happened, in a hamlet called Narla (near Rajouri). Terrorists killed 17 persons, in Kotli village in 1999, in Rajouri. Terrorists have been, having a free run of the remote areas, in J&K, because of almost no or very thin presence of the security forces there. We have a sizeable presence of security in J&K, to deal with the terrorists in the disturbed areas. The question arises, why despite the security forces, the gruesome incidents, continue to happen almost with impunity. One thing, which needs a closer look, not by the top brass of the concerned force but by an independent group, is the pattern of deployment. There is a mindset, about deployment. The only flexible force for deployment is the Central Reserve Police Force, which agrees to be deployed in one section or even half section strength. Roughly there are 11 persons in one section. Whereas all other forces, deployed anywhere, whether it is the Border Security Force or Army, do not work at any spot with less than one platoon (32 men) or one company strength (99 men). Their deployment level in this strength is unquestionable. In Army, Section commander is only a Naik with no authority to order fire. In the Army Platoon Havildar only can order shoot to kill in insurgency. CRPF being a batton charging Police Force, cannot fight terrorists weilding latest self loading automatic hidden weapons. Consititutionally, CRPF, a riot control force, is not designed to fight modern terrorists. The Army is dynamic in its combativeness.

2

Contours of Islamic Fundamentalism, the Jehad

As long as the terrorism was far off from the shores of America, it felt its pinch in a kind of academic way, even when its owns national were the victims, as the following incidents will show:

Nov 4, 1979 – Islamic students storm U.S. embassy in Teheran, holding 52 Americans hostage for 444 days.

April 18, 1983 – Suicide car-bomber blows up U.S embassy in Beirut, killing 17 Americans.

Oct 23, 1983 – Shiite suicide bomber blows up U.S marine barracks in Beirut, killing 241 marines.

Dec 12, 1983 – Shiite extremists set off car bombs in front of the U.S. and French embassies in Kuwait city, killing five and wounding 86.

Sept 20, 1984 – Car bomb at U.S. embassy annexe in east Beirut, kills 16 and injures the Ambassador.

June 14, 1985 – Shiite gunmen seize a TWA Boeing 727, forcing it to Beirut. They demand the release of 700 Arabs held by Israel. A U.S. Navy diver is killed and 39 Americans are held til their release on July 1 after Syrian mediation.

Oct. 8, 1985 – Crippled American Jew, Leon Klinghoffer, killed by Palestinian terrorists who seized the Italian cruise liner, Achille Lauro.

Sept. 5, 1986 – Hijackers seize Pan Am jumbo jet, carrying 358 people at Karachi airport. Twenty people killed when security forces stormed the plane.

Dec. 21, 1988 – Pan Am Boeing 747 explodes over Lockerbie, Scotland, on a flight from London to New York, killing 270 people, including residents of the town.

Feb. 26, 1993 – A bomb explodes in a parking garage below the World Trade Center in New York, killing six people and wounding more than 1,000. Six Islamic terrorists were convicted in the bombing and sentenced to life in prison.

April 19, 1995 – Bomb rips through the Alfred P. Murrah Federal Building in downtown Oklahoma city at 9.02 a.m., killing 168 and wounding more than 500. Former U.S. soldier, Timothy McVeigh, is convicted of carrying out the attack; he was executed.

Sept 13, 1995 – Rocket-propelled grenade pierces wall of U.S. embassy in Moscow, but causes no injuries.

Nov 13, 1995 – Car bomb detonates at U.S. military headquarters in Riyadh, killing five American service personnel.

June 25, 1996 – Truck-bomb explodes outside the Khobar Towers, Dharan, eastern Saudi Arabia, killing 19 American servicemen and wounding hundreds of various nationalities. Member of a little-known Saudi militant group, Hezbollah, were indicted for the attack.

Aug 7, 1998 – Car bomb explode outside U.S. embassies in Nairobi, Kenya, and Dar-es-salaam, Tanzania, within minutes of each other, killing 224 people and wounding thousands of others. Osama is again blamed.

Oct 12, 2000 – Terrorist bombing kills 17 U.S. sailors aboard the USS Cole as it refuelled in Yemen's port of Aden. U.S. says Saudi exile, Osama bin Laden, is prime suspect.

The mighty nation, United States of America, had to eat a humble pie, when the terrorists in a daring and an innovative way, used two hijacked aircraft of the American Airlines on 11th, September, 2001 and used them as missiles with almost fully loaded passengers to destroy the World Trade Towers. In this suicide mission, the first of its kind under the leadership, support, guidance and help of Osman Bin Laden, America lost its outstanding symbol. The latest incident, also shows that the terrorists will go to any length to achieve their objective.

Terrorism feeds on those, who fan it. Osma Bin Laden and Afghan Talibans were the creation of USA, who funded and armed them with weapons worth over $4 billion to fight the Russians. Having not known any other way of living, the same fundamentalists have turned against the USA, whom Osma Bin Laden has called The Great Satan. The investigation done by the FBI has led to some arrests and the arrested have been linked to the master terrorist. It still remains to be seen, how far America will discharge its functions, being a self appointed Policeman of the world to control terrorism, despite its proclamations that attack is war. While India has offered full help in dealing with the terrorism, Pakistan wants a price for fighting against the terrorism and co-operation with America. It is to be in the form of $30 billion equivalent of what Pakistan owes international community and active intervention in Kashmir against India. In other words, there is a price tag for helping America in nailing the supporters, aiders and abettors of those who wreaked a tragedy on the USA. It wants to co-operate only in fighting U.S. limited war and not against international terrorism. In fact, it does not consider either the Talibans or the Kashmir terrorists as terrorists. It euphemistically calls them Jehadis. Pakistan wants its terrorist activities to be separated from the international terrorism. It does not want either India or Israel to be associated with the action against terrorism on international level. Pakistan has also sent a signal to America, that there are no free lunches even for its friends. They have to pay for safeguarding their own interests. A question also arises, how could an incident of this kind happen, without anybody knowing about it or at least getting a wind that some big strike was planned. It may be legitimately asked, if there was a failure of intelligence. Intelligence is different from the hard evidence and quite often the two are mixed up and one is misunderstood for the other. In America, there has been an over-dependence on the gadgetry and less on human factors. In India, we mostly depend on human intelligence, which also has failed at times, as in Kargil, which the Kargil Committee report showed. A mix of the two is ideal. It is also time for the intelligence agency in America, to have a look at itself and do some introspection. No intelligence, like any operation can be successful. It is certain that America will take suitable steps to ensure that it is not caught napping again. It has settled down after punishing the terrorists and rehabilitation. American Congress has voted $40 billion for dealing with the massive tragedy and Pakistan wants 7 per cent of this amount. If America yields to any of the demands of Pakistan, it would not only be soft pedalling war against terrorism, but also letting down the biggest democracy, which unhesitatingly offered its support and co-operation. If Pakistan wants to prove its bonafides, it should help in curbing the terrorists in Kashmir, who are having safe sanctuaries, hiding places and terrorists training camps in its territories. It has obeyed USA for the lure of dollars in America's aerial bombing of Afghanistan. America's invasion of Afghanistan was a signal to the terrorists all over the world, to "Keep off USA."

Even the countries not involved would have to pay in the form of higher costs of goods and services to keep their economies running. President Bush has said, he wants Osma Bin Laden dead or alive. There is no doubt that there would be some trade off to Pakistan, should the master terrorist be handed over to America.

At home, India's experience has been no different. Indira Gandhi reared fundamentalist and propped up Bhindrawala. The events took an ugly turn and led to the operation Blue Star and assassination of Indira Gandhi. Later on, LTTE according to the Press report was trained and funded during late Rajiv Gandhi tenure as Prime Minister. It is they who assassinated him. India has been crying hoarse to declare Pakistan as a terrorist State, but with no effect on the USA or the world conscience. Even if they declare Pakistan a terrorist State, it hardly affects the health of Pakistan or its rulers. USA could not care less, what happens elsewhere as long as it and its interests are safe. We have to fight our own battle and we need not depend on the goodwill and sympathy of others. We also have to rein in our own Mullahs, who are proving more loyal than the king. Fortunately all parties have supported the stand of our Government against the terrorism. Our Security Forces have done a remarkable job, despite the loss of civilian lives and their own loss, as the following figures will show:

Period 1990 - July 2001 In J&K	
Terrorists killed	13,326
Terrorists surrender	3148
Civilians killed	9319
Civilians injured	13,368
Civilians killed in grenade attacks and blasts	1113
Injured	9458
Grenade attacks	4727
Explosion	4541
Civilians killed in securitymen-ultras encounters	946
Injured	2893
Abductions	4124
Casualties (police & security forces)	3053

Pakistani fundamentalism has been rearing its head, from time to time and ducking when it finds that the price of confrontation would be heavy. In fact, it suits the ruling Colonels and Generals to have fundamentalists raising a hue and cry periodically, so that they can encash the same in dollars from their American Masters. Pakistan's main fundamentalist Islamic party, Jamaat-I-Islami, which is a key member of the hard-line alliance with MMA, has demanded that Pakistan should get rid of FBI agents and that its air and military bases under the control of the Americans forces should be taken back. It has also demanded that Pakistan Government should submit the US visitors, to stringent checks and registration requirements, in reciprocation of the new US requirements for Pakistani visitors. It is estimated that there are nearly 50,000 Pakistanis living illegally in USA, who may be deported as a result of the latest USA drive against terrorism.

Unfortunately, Sikhs living in USA and UK have become the subject of attacks and humiliation as they are being confused with Muslim fundamentalists. It is for the leaders of Sikh community to enlighten the people of these countries that they are distinct from Muslims and they follow a religion of their own.

Pakistani fundamentalism had percolated to Kashmir, despite so called claims of a liberal Kashmiriyat. All kinds of wide-ranging and assorted groups, had issued diktats, as to how the Muslim women should live. Their commands ranged from wearing of burqas, to getting married as soon as they cross 15 years of age and giving up their jobs, In fact they carried out their threats by killing three young girls in December, 2002, in Hasiyot.

Fundamentalists have also raised their head, in the erstwhile Talibanised Afghanistan, where the Chief Justice of that country had shut down licensed cable services in Kabul and Jalalabad, on the ground that what they were airing was unislamic programmes. The cable firms mostly aired Western and Indian music and movies and were very popular.

In London, the Police recovered weapons and explosive from a mosque in January, 2003. India has given to Afghanistan, in the form of aid of over $ 100 million including some aircraft and busess. Terrorism has been breeding ground in the countries, where coups, bloody power struggles and military take overs are common. US Ambassador to Pakistan felt constrained to warn Pakistan on 24th

January, 2003 that "Pakistan must ensure that its pledges are implemented to prevent infiltration across line of actual control in J&K and the end use of Pakistan as a platform for terroris". Pakistani fundamentalist party, Jamaat-e-Islami, a mouth piece of Mushraff, on the contrary observed: "America itself was the biggest terrorist and involved in cross border terrorism against various countries like Libya, Sudan and Afghanistan". Incidentally, all above countries are either Muslim fundamentalis are run in a dictatorship or semi dictatorship fashion like Pakistan. No greater proof is required to brand Pakistan as a terrorist State, than the fact, that USA's FBI will collect complete information about three million Pakistanis in USA, which includes criminals, politicians, industrialists and businessmen, who might pose a threat to US interests.

Pointing out that the US is 'the last remaining superpower', late President Nixon had said: "No crisis is irrelevant to our interest." It is being fiercely attempted in the Western constituencies of Egypt and Algeria and even Bosnia. As the Russians stormed Chechnya, Mujahideen from Afghanistan, Abkhazia, Azerbaijan, Pakistan and Ukraine rallied behind the Chechnyans. The Russians claimed that the war in Chechnya was not being fought by the locals but by the mercenaries from outside. The message is clear. Islamic fundamentalists will intervene wherever they perceive, they have an obligation. The same has been happening in Kashmir.

The atmosphere has changed to threaten the very survival of all moderate, pro-West governments in West Asia. Privately and in whispers, some are openly ruing the decision of agreeing to 'the request of the US' to help the Afghan resistance and later on, join the coalition for war against terrorism. Jack Blum, a former US Congressional investigator, told a Canadian Broadcasting Corporation programme. "Once you train people in these techniques for some kind of insurgency, you can't untrain them and you then have what we in the United States refer to, as a disposal problem."

Pakistan pushed by the fundamentalist tide, has become the nerve-centre of Islamic terrorism. It is the US policies and help that have made Pakistan a reckless State, making it clearly one of the premier terrorist rogue states of the world. Pakistan has tried to take the credit for winning the war against Talibans, in the hope that America will throw some more crumbs in its way.

In a major policy speech delivered by Robin Raphel in early 1994, when she was US Assistant Secretary of State for South Asia, stated that the conflicts in Afghanistan and Kashmir "challenge our conscience and our imagination." The statement was made, after the US had initiated the Afghanistan War in 1994 and aggravated the Kashmir problem by allowing Pakistan to divert sizeable quantities of arms from Afghan pipeline to Kashmir.

There is an inescapable link between the fall of Soviet control over Afghanistan in 1994 and the beginning of terrorism in Kashmir in 1989. Pakistan had all the knowledge, experience, expertise, manpower and equipment to export terror to Kashmir, which it gleefully did. All those, so called Mujahideen, with their arms intact, were suddenly without any work to do on Pakistan's bidding. There was no better way to keep them gainfully occupied than to divert them to new theatres of terrorism in Kashmir.

A Washington-based Human Rights Watch in its report entitled *India: Arms and Abuses in Indian Punjab and Kashmir*, said that 'the massive proliferation of small arms and light weapons in South Asia is directly linked to the Soviet invasion of Afghanistan in 1979 and the subsequent creation by the US, of a system commonly known as the Afghan pipeline, to funnel weapons covertly to the Afghan resistance'. It added, 'The deliberate efforts by the US to evade accountability for the diffusion of arms and the US's continuing silence regarding its responsibility, has also been an element, contributing to abuses'. The report called upon the governments of Pakistan and US to 'formally investigate' the matter, make public the results of these investigations and initiate appropriate action. Nothing of the sort was ever done. While Washington's protestations and support is welcome in the war against terrorism in Kashmir, we should read too much in between such statements. USA would not take with Pakistan the fight against terrorism on behalf of India to the point, where it annoys the former. Coalition against terrorism is principally to neutralise the criticism from other countries against the USA, for any action it may take in its own interests.

The U.S. war on terrorism, really started after September, 11, 2001 attack on World Trade Centre in New York. Operation Enduring Freedom in Afghanistan, has achieved only limited success, as compared to the objectives set after 11 September 2001. The U.S. was able to capture, some important members of the Taliban-Al Qaeda networks. It also managed, to destroy their infrastructure in Afghanistan and to a limited extent has hacked the flow of finances to the terrorist network. Even by U.S. assessments, only about 20 to 25 per cent of Taliban-Al Qaeda operatives were killed in action and another 15 or 20 per cent captured. This indicates a likelihood of 50 to 60 per cent of the network's total estimated strength, including the leaders Mullah Omar and Osama bin Laden still at large and probably hiding in Santh Wazirstan.

However, the U.S was able to dislodge the Taliban from power and establish a broad-based friendly Government. The U.S strategy to combat terrorism and violence of the Taliban-Al Qaeda and Iraqi variety has difficulties, including from its own allies and friends like France and Germany. Pakistan is no doubt part and parcel of the problem, as the deposed Taliban-A1 Qaeda leadership and cadres have found safe havens in Pakistan. The U.S campaign starting from north to south Afghanistan, gave enough time to the Taliban-Al Qaeda cadres, to cross quickly over Pakistan, with the connivance of Pakistani Army, which has had good relations with them.

The U.S. has not underestimated the Pakistani armed forces' involvement with the Taliban-Al Qaeda network. It has acquired 54,000 acres of land, on a 99-year lease in the NWFP Wazirstan and Baluchistan for establishing bases to direct operations against the Taliban-Al Qaeda forces, with or without the help of Pakistan's armed forces. Pakistan advent is that, whenever the U.S. expresses its displeasure, a small fry of the Talibans or Al Qaeda is arrested by it and deported to the U.S. Pakistan has been hoodworking to distance itself from the original charge that it was part of the Taliban-Al Qaeda network.

The U.S perceives that a crime against America or Americans, is a crime against humanity. This argument does not sell anywhere, when the rest of the world keeps quiet. The intelligentsia all over the world, is well aware of the fact that in spite of their best efforts, U.S and its allies' heavy dependence on Persian Gulf crude oil is still continuing. Their crude oil imports from the Middle East is a very critical component of their energy requirements. Therefore, countries such as Saudi Arabia and Kuwait are treated with kid gloves. The U.S war on terrorism or to be very precise for guarding its own interests, is not going to end soon. If anything, it will be a prolonged affair, going from one country to another, who resist US interests. US banking is upon the spectacular results achieved, through air power in Operation Desert Storm in Iraq in 1991. However, now it is counter productive in Iraq.

The war on terrorism cannot be fought and won, with fighter aircrafts and armoured personnel carriers only. The ground operations and the participation of the people equally matter. The war on terrorism has to be handled politically, with a certain amount of dexterity and subtlety; without being abrasive or authoritarian. India has been facing terrorism, which is organised, engineered and carried out by Pakistan, with the help of mercenaries under the cloak of religious brotherhood. Having failed in direct confrontations, Pakistan has chosen to bleed India, with a low-intensity campaign, with the help of quisling and misguided elements. A Turkish saying fits the problem in Kashmir: "When the axe came into the forest, the trees said, the handle is one of us". This way, Pakistan wants to find out the handle and make use of the axe – so that Indian body politic is amputated.

India has made its stand clear that terrorism is terrorism and there are no two brands, one of so called freedom fighters, who can be considered good terrorists and the other of bad terrorists like Talibans, the Pakistan's blue eyed boys. America, though keeping Pakistan in good humour, is very clear about its own security concernsn. Under the National Security Entry-Exit Registration System (NSEERS), nationals of 25 countries, out of which 23 are from Muslim countries, including Pakistan are required to be registered and finger printed. Upto 2 Lakh Pakistanis could be involved by the new law.

No amount of security forces can end terrorism, if the affected nation, including India, does not go whole hog after them, their cells and networks. The only way to deal with terrorism, is to strike it before it batters you. Terrorism is no more conventional. It comes in different shapes and form. It may be a burqa clad woman, a taxi driver or a teacher, a petty shopkeeper. The old conventional means have outlived their utility. They cannot successfully tackle unconventional threats. The terrorism requires unconventional response, backed by an unwavering political will and good intelligence.

A Union Home Minister, admitted that the terrorists have looked upon India as a soft target. This needs to go. It is so because, we have not sufficiently paid them back, by their own methods.

When it comes to taking a tough stand, all the Governments, have so far been buckling down and following the easier option of surrendering to the demands of the extortionists and intimidators. This would not do now. Many Western analysts think that the emerging geopolitical scenario, is a conflict between the North and the South between what Professor Robert Keohane of Harvard defines as the

Zone of Peace, represented by the Western countries and the Zone of Conflict, consisting of the South. The Zone of Peace, is threatened by terrorism, unwanted migration, proliferation of nuclear weapons and ecological damage posed by the Zone of Conflict. It is also perceived as an economic conflict between the haves of the North and the have-nots of the South and between the poor and disorganised nations against rich organised nations. There are more than four billion people in the Southern nations, against one billion in all of the North. It is a situation, where it would not always be possible to 'tell the good guys from the bad' according to Marenches and Andelman. In these conditions, Pakistan pushed by self generated fundamentalist tide, has become the nerve-centre of Islamic terrorism, notwithstanding President Bush describing it as "One of our strongest allies against terrorism". Our country needs to become strong both economically, politically and militarily. It is important to remember that reciprocity walks hand in hand with our capacity and power. Our good intentions to safeguard our Nation, must clothe itself with power. The best way to do so is, to break the back of terrorism, with higher fire power and bigger and better strategies.

The issue of oppositional terrorism first made its appearance on the international scene in 1972, with an attack by the Black September organisation on Israeli athletes at the Munich Olympic Games. Regrettably, the United Nations has not been able to define terrorism since that time and for the last 34 years. Terrorism in actual practice, is the use or threat of violence against a small number. Its objective is to put larger numbers in fear, with a view to obtain a set objective. Terrorists use violence to coerce officials and public in doing things against their will. The immediate by-products of terrorism can be publicity, extorting of money and political blackmail. Long term dividends from political terrorism embrace destabilization of the government of the day, erosion of public confidence and provoke over reaction. Very rarely has terrorism succeeded in actually overthrowing government, especially a democratically elected one. The major terrorism incidents all over the world, where hostages were taken and people killed are as under:

August 1978: Nicaragua, Managua parliament, 400 hostages and 14 killed.

Nov 1985: Colombia, Bogota courts of justice, 400 hostages, approx. 100 killed.

February 1981: Spain, Spanish Parliament, Madrid, Putschists take deputies hostage.

Oct 1985: Mediterranean, Italian Luxury liner Achille Lauro hijacked, 450 on board. 1 killed.

June 1995: Russia, Chechen action at Budennovsk, 1,500 hostages. 166 killed

Jan 1996: Russian Caucasus, Chechen action in Degestan, 2,000 hostages. 50-100 killed.

Apr 1996: Liberia, Monrovia, 600 hostages.

Dec 1996: Apr 1997: Peru, Japanese ambassador's residence, Lima, 700 hostages. 17 killed.

Jan 1999: Phillippines, School near Cotabato, 570 hostages including 500 children.

Jan 2000: Thailand, Ratchaburi Hospital, 500 hostages. 9 killed.

May-July 2000: Sierra Leone, 500 hostages (UN peacekeepers).

Oct. 26, 2002: Russia, 700+ people freed after 3 days in a Moscow theatre.

1979-2004: Maximum attacks on people, public men, places and properties were committees in India.

When Americans fight terrorism or do anything, they do it with single-minded attention; unlike many countries, which believe only in taking half measures. They no longer believe in willing to strike, but afraid to wound. The Bush administration has prepared a list of terrorist leaders, whom the Central Intelligence Agency is authorised to kill, if capture is impractical and civilian casualties can be minimised. The previously undisclosed CIA list includes key Al-Qaeda leaders like Osama bin Laden and his chief deputy, Ayman al-Zawahiri, as well as other principal figures from Al Qaeda and affiliated terrorist groups. The name of about two dozen terrorist leaders are now on the lethal force list. The Americans claim that it is a list of the worst of the worst. American President George W. Bush has provided written legal authority to the CIA to hunt down and kill the terrorists without seeking further approval each time the agency is about to stage an operation.

Despite the authority given to the agency, Mr Bush has not waived the executive order banning assassinations, officials said. The presidential authority to kill terrorists defines operatives of Al Qaeda as enemy combatants and thus legitimate targets for lethal force.

Mr. Bush had issued a Presidential Order in 2001, after the September 11 attacks on New York and Washington, providing the basic executive and legal authority for the CIA to either kill or capture terrorist leaders. Initially, the agency used that authority to hunt for Al Qaeda leaders in Afghanistan. It is also the basis for the CIA's attempts to find and kill or capture Bin Laden and other Qaeda leaders during the war in Afghanistan. The US President is not legally required to approve each name added to the list, not is CIA required to obtain Presidential approval for specific attacks, although the President is kept well informed about the agency's operation.

The international community including the USA and Western Nations adopt double standards on the question of fighting terrorism, when it affects them and India. Pakistan has been harping on good or bad terrorists. For Pakistani Colonels, terrorists fighting on its behalf in Kashmir are good terrorists, whereas it now regards Talibans, its erstwhile blue eyed boys as bad terrorists as its Master, the USA bids it.

Under pressure from USA, the Pakistani President in his address of January 12, 2002. assured of the following steps against terrorists: He banned Lashkar-e-Taiba and Jaish-e-Mohammad Sipah-e-Sahaba, Tehrik-e-Jaffria and Tehrik-e-Nifaz-e-Shariat (Mohammed) well known ISI's terrorist outfits. Says no organisation to be allowed to indulge in terrorism in the name of religion. He also said that he will not allow Pakistan's territory to be used for terrorist activities and offered fresh dialogue with the Indian Prime Minister on Kashmir. He also said that any group found involved in December 13, 2001 attack on Indian Parliament and October 1, 2002 attack on the Jammu and Kashmir Assembly to be dealt with severely. But all these promises have turned out to be an eye wash. Pakistan continues to be the hotbed of terrorism, not only against India, but also against USA. An American journalist,was killed in Pakistan. It was a full Christian Church, which faced terrorist attack in 2002. The claims of Pakistan Government that it is against terrorism, can not be sustained in view of the open and instigated terrorist activities. It is not known, whether Pakistan has ever called any such terrorists as good terrorists. The war between India and Pakistan appeared almost certain in January, 2002, after the Pakistani sponsored attack on Indian Parliament and Kaluchak incident in which terrorists methodically targeted and killed, for the first time, more than 20 family members of Indian Army personnel. USA, UK and other Western Nations pressurised Pakistan to take some concrete steps, which it announced on January 12, 2003 but in actual practice discarded the same later on.

In actual practice, wily Pakistani President General Musharraf goes off and on. His theory seems to keep the pot boiling and go back on his word. The international community by this time also knows, that Pakistan's word cannot be swallowed. It would look the other way when India objects. During September-October, 2002 Assembly elections in Jammu and Kashmir, Pakistan used every trick possible to disrupt the polls. The elections held were hailed as "free and fair". However, Mussarraf called the elections as a farce. He suitably forgot his own farcical referendum, where he was the only candidate. He arrogated to himself the job of Paki President for another five years to begin with.

India's problem with terrorism is of hardly any concern to the USA. In a twenty one days war, coalition forces led by USA crushed the 24 year tyrannical rule of Saddam Hussein on 9th April, 2003. In a scene reminiscent of the fall of Berlin War in 1989, Iraqis took a sledge hammer to the marble plinth of the statue of Saddam Hussein. Youths placed a noose around the statue of Saddam Hussein and pulled it down marking the symbolic end of the rule. USA is gunning for support for war against Iraq's Saddam Hussein whom he considers evil, forgetting that the greater evil is in neighbourhood of India. Saddam's only crime is that he has no nuclear weapons and has not become the lackey of USA, unlike Pakistani President, who is licking up the American shoes all the time. One cannot really find fault with USA, being the most powerful country in the world, both economically and militarily. Power occasionally brings with it an attitude of condescension and arrogance. In an academic sort of way, the great are entitled to some amount of it. It is only us, who are to be responsible for our National Affairs. We cannot trust our neighbour Pakistan. Shakespeare aptly said: "Trust not him that hath once broken faith."

The purpose of terrorism depends upon the terrorists. It can range from coercing a group of people, or even a government, into yielding to some of a variety of demands; extracting revenge for a perceived wrong and to harassing a government. These days the terrorists have an incredible armoury at their disposal. Not only they can commandeer an enormous number of weapons of annihilation and devastation also but are well versed in the use of mobile telephone technological advances to capture society's normal air, road and rail network and communications to their benefit. This facility enables terrorist groups to organize, plan, recruit and augment their strength. Several terrorist groups, both in Kashmir and Pakistan operating against India, have used the Internet in their operations.

Bombs made of common fertilizer and gasoline loaded into a truck can be driven to the door of a target structure to cause massive destruction. The leaning in crushing terrorism over the last 25 years is moving towards attacks which can result in, as many fatalities as possible. For instance, in 1998 more than six thousand people were the victims in the bombing of two U.S. embassies in African countries, one in Kenya and the other in Tanzania.

It is essential for India, not to neglect, what is happening elsewhere on the ground that, all these happenings are, far from it. In our neighbouring Pakistan, there is no division in their objectives between Pakistan Army and Jihadis or terrorists. Pakistani Army uses terrorists, masquerading as Jihadi, to further its objective of destabilising India and create trouble. Despite international action to contain the Al-Qaida, terrorist network with worldwide presence, is "fit and well" and poised to "strike again at its leisure". This warning comes from a UN expert panel group which, in a report released in New York in October, 2002 says: "Members of the Al-Qaida and their associates, are deployed in many countries across the world and given the opportunity, they will have no compunction, in killing as many people as they can, from those nations, that do not conform to their religions and ideological beliefs and which, they perceive as, their enemies."

There is no doubt that despite being a lackey of the U.S. Pakistan continues to harbour the Al-Qaida terrorists. The capture of Al-Qaida's No. 3 man, Khalid Shaik Mohammed, in the first week of March 2003, has shown what was known earlier that Pakistan was playing a double game. It was only a pious hope, which has been futile expectation that intelligence and evidence gleaned from documents, laptop computers and mobile telephone; taken from the house where Mohammed was apprehended, may lead to the discovery of Osama bin Laden.

A prominent Yemeni cleric, apprehended in Germany, on charges of financing terrorism used a mosque in Brooklyn, New York, to help funnel millions of dollars to Al-Qaida; had boasted that he had personally delivered $20 million to Osama bin Laden. US federal officials said this in this March, 2003. In New York, police Commissioner Raymond W. Kelly said that Al-Qaida operatives "did their fund raising right here in our own backyard in Brooklyn."

The three well coordinated suicide bomb attacks on May 12, in 2003 in Riyadh, have once again turned the spotlight on Al-Qaida. The attacks have all the hallmarks of an Al-Qaida move. 34 people, including at least 12 nationals of the United States were killed in the suicidal bombers attacks, on three residential compounds, housing mainly foreigners. Two hundred people were reportedly wounded in the attacks. Nine terrorists involved in the mission were also killed. The blasts took place a few hours before U.S Secretary of State Colin Powell was to reach Riyadh on an official visit. The U.S. State Department had issued a warning on May 1 that terrorist "may be in the final phases of planning attacks" on U.S. targets in Saudi Arabia. The attacks came soon after 19 suspected militants had escaped arrest, from the Saudi Arabian security authorities who raided their hideouts. The suspects, 17 of whom are said to be Saudi Arabian nationals, had fought in Afghanistan and Chechnya. Saudi Government had claimed that the mastermind of the attacks was Al-Qaida supremo, Osama bin Laden, who had given the green signal to target foreigners and members of the royal family. Five bomb attacks tore through the coastal Moroccan city of Casablanca on 16th/17th May, 2003, killing dozens and damaging a Jewish community centre and two western targets. The official death toll was at least 40, including engineers, while nearly 60 people were injured in the attack. The attacks occurred nearly simultaneously, a possible Al-Qaida involvement was suspected as Al-Qaida maintains a presence in Morocco.

Al-Qaida's new military chief, a sharp terrorist mastermind Saif Al-Adel of Egypt, carries a reward of $25 million on his head. He succeeded, in keeping Osama Bin Laden safe from the manhunt. These changes were reportedly necessitated because of the capture of Khaled Sheikh Mohammed, who is supposed to be the mastermind behind 9/11/2001 attack on Twin Towers, in USA.

Presently, both Bin Laden and other Al-Qaida members are believed to be hiding in the Pakistan-Afghanistan border region. There are reports of regrouping, of Al-Qaida, in Pakistan, Chechnya, besides Kenya, Bangladesh and Sudan. The Al-Qaida is aiming to attack new targets, within the United States. A senior American Embassy official in Pakistan described in the first week of June, 2003, the latter as the epicentre of terrorism. It is not India, but Americans, describing Pakistan as the epicentre of terrorism. Despite the American coalition against terrorism, Islamic terrorism is not far from India. No country is safe from it, not even Russia, where 17 Russian Air Force men were killed and 12 injured on 5th June. 2003, when a female suicide bomber walked upto their bus and detonated explosives strapped to her body in Mozdok on the Russia-Chechnya border. India has been warning the world against the dangers of terrorism and Talibanisation of the world. Now is time for the world to realise that you cannot allow terrorists disguised as your friends to cry hoarse that they are against terrorism, when actually they hunt with the dog hunter and run with the hare. Sooner or later, the world would have to deal with Pakistan as it has dealt with Iraq.

The trend in terrorism, over the last two decades, has been shifting towards brutalities and cruelties that cause as many fatalities as possible. The problems of definition of terrorism are many. One dilemma is; how to differentiate political terrorism from other forms of activity which may attract the terrorist label. However, criminal terrorism can be singled out, as systematic use of terror for material ends, which may be connected to political terrorism. The most legal definition of political terrorism identifies it with the use of violence for political objectives. However, Wardlaw classifies political terrorism as the use or threat to use violence by an individual or group, whether acting for or against the established authority, when such action is designed to create extreme anxiety and/or fear-inducing effects, in a target group, larger than the immediate victims, with the purpose of coercing that group into acceding to the political demands of the perpetrators.

This definition, however, raises the question of differentiating legitimate violence from illegitimate violence of the terrorists. Many would question the legitimacy of the state's use of force unlawfully, as by staying away, the police or armed forces automatically become terrorists. The justification for official violence must, therefore, rest upon the wider legitimacy of the incumbent regimes. However, there is a some moral relativism, implicit in Yasser Arafat's speech delivered to the General Assembly of the United Nations: "one man's terrorist is another man's freedom fighter". The modern technology, faster means of communication and Internet, have brought a sea change in the situation, enabling the availability of faster means of communications between members of terrorist organizations, for fund raising and changing strategies. The faster means of new communication and new weapons, are not only available to the Governments, but also to the terrorists, who can completely change their modus-operandi in different situations.

The terrorist incident in Russia which saw more than 150 people dead, many of them children and 310 wounded on 3rd September, 2004, has beaten all records of savagery. Russian commandos stormed a school in southern Russia in Beslan, where hundreds has been held hostage, by the rebels strapped with explosives for three days. Russian officials had negotiated on and off with the militants, shortly after the crisis began. They added that the hostage takers had repeatedly refused offers of food and water. "They are very cruel people, we are facing a ruthless enemy", said Leonid Roshal, a paediatrician involved in the negotiations. "I talked with them many times on my cell phone, but every time I asked to give food, water and medicine to the hostages they refused my request."

Two major hostage taking raids by Chechen rebels outside their country have forced Russia to take action. Earlier, the seizure of a Moscow theatre in 2002 ended, after a knockout gas was pumped into the building. At that time one hundred and twentynine hostages and 49 rebels died when Putin sent troops to overpower Chechen rebels. The terrorists cum hostage takers had demanded Russians troops to leave Chechnya, as they felt that they could pressurise Russia.

Hardly any country in the world is free from terrorism. Nearer home, the President of the great terrorist factory, that is Pakistan's unelected President Pervez Musharraf, had two attempts made on his life within ten days around Christmas time in 2003. His near brush with death, twice in December, 2003, and narrow escape and the failure of Pakistani intelligence to detect and pre-empt the threats to his life underscore the problem that, if you rear a Frankenstein, you might be gobbled by it. Since 1990s, the focus of international terrorism has shifted to Middle East and South Asia. Terrorism has grown up, including the conflicts in Sri Lanka between the LTTE and Government of Sri Lanka. Terrorists struck in a big way in Bali, Indonesia, where in 2002's bombings, 202 people were killed. Again there was an explosion of a powerful car bomb outside a luxury hotel in Jakarta in August, 2003 which, led to the killing 13 people and wounding 149.

Russians in the context of the school children hostage have observed that so called "Holy worriors" from the Middle East have long supported fellow Muslims fighting in Chechnya. According to Russian officials, nine or ten Arabs were among the militants killed on 3rd September, 2004. Enlightened Muslims also realise this. Abdul Rahman al-Rashed, General Manager of Al-Arabiya television said in his daily column published in the Pan-Arab Asharq Al-Awsat newspaper, under the headline: "The Painful Truth: All the World Terrorists are Muslims!"... He also added, "Our terrorist sons are an end-product of our corrupted culture". He recounted the attacks by Islamic extremist groups – in Russia, Iraq, Sudan, Saudi Arabia and Yemen. He added that "Most perpetrators of suicide operations in buses, schools and residential buildings around the world for the past 10 years, have been Muslims. ... Muslims will be unable to cleanse their image unless we admit the scandalous facts, rather than offer condemnations or justifications". Another Egyptian Islamist, Ahmed Bahgat, wrote in his column in Egypt's leading pro-government newspaper, Al-Ahram, "that hostage takers in Russia as well as in Iraq are only harming Islam. If all the enemies of Islam united together and decided to harm it ... they wouldn't have ruined and harmed its images as much as the sons of Islam have done by their stupidity, miscalculations, and misunderstanding of the nature of this age. The horrifying images of the dead and wounded Russian students showed Muslims as monsters who are fed by the blood of children and the pain of their families."

This unusually forthright self criticism followed the end of the hostage crisis, along with warnings that such actions inflict more damage to the image of Islam than all its enemies could hope for.

So far as International Community is concerned, it is hardly distressed or disturbed, as to what is happening to or in India. The maximum, it does is, to brand an incident as unfortunate, condemnable or inhuman. It hardly affects the health of the terrorists, who care two hoots for the view of other nations.

3
The Talbani Turf

Gun culture promotes itself, as it is a double-edged weapon. The United States had decreed ban on US Trade with Taliban ruled Afghanistan. It had frozen the assets of the Afghan Airline in USA country. It was in retaliation to Afghan refusal to hand over the top Islamic fundamentalist terrorist Osman Bin Laden. A draft document of the United States National Security Council Staff says: "Due to our military superiority, potential enemies, whether nations or terrorist groups, may be more likely, in the future to resort to attacks against vulnerable civilian targets in the United States, instead of conventional military operations abroad... Foreign intelligence agents, are trying to glean U.S secrets, at an unprecedented pace and foreign Governments and terrorists are creating sophisticated, well-organised capabilities to launch cyber attacks on strategically information networks. The threat from foreign intelligence services, is more diverse, complex and difficult to counter than ever before."

India is taken as a fertile training and experimental action ground by Pakistan. Recovery of RDX, Ak-47 Rifles, detonators, hand grenades and fuse wires, originated from Pakistan, is something, which routinely happens, in our country. Their objective is to tie up security forces, in defending themselves, rather than launching an offensive to drive terrorists out. Out of the, terrorist killed between 1990 and 1998, were from 1073 mercenaries belonging to Pakistan (400) Afghanistan (190) Bangladesh and Sudan (Five each) Turkey (2), Bahrain, Chechenya, Iraq, Iran, Kazakhstan, Saudi Arabia and Yemen (One each) and 48 to Pakistan Occupied Kashmir. Amongst the arrested mercenaries Pakistan topped the list with 59, Pakistan Occupied Kashmir (30), Bangladesh (24) Afghanistan (11), Burma (5). Kazakistan (1).

India being an open society and a democratic country, has all the handicaps. Whatever is to be done, is done as per the rule of the law. Arrest of terrorist with 50 KGs of RDX, eight grenades, three pistols, 24 electronic detonators and 141 rounds of ammunition on 20th August, 1999 on Delhi-Karnal Road, did not mean that they were punished straightaway for their lapses. The interrogation, cross-checking and legal formalities had to be gone through before the final orders could be passed by the court, may be after a few years. There is a lot of floating RDX. It might be used to subvert the development as well as the elections. There have been many cases of explosion of the rail link connecting Jammu and Kashmir and North East with the rest of the country. The Capital of the Nation, Delhi is the prime target, as 120 KGs of RDX, enough to blow a major part of it, was recovered from here only. As a Nation, we have to live with the fact that our prime neighbour and enemy, Pakistan would do anything to stoke communal fires, encourage infiltration of its spies, create disturbance, spread fundamentalism and weaken India. With the tightening of the security in Punjab, and Rajasthan, the porous border land of 1093 kilometers with Bangladesh, offers a tempting opportunity. Only a part of the above border in West Bengal is fenced with Bangladesh. The infiltrators and illegal migrants manage to mix with the local population.

The Government has banned an organisation called SIMI or Students Islamic Movement of India. One of its office bearer, a Bihar Zonal Secretary says: "The Quran is our Constitution. If the Indian Constitution clashes with the Quran, we are not bound by the Constitution". India is fighting a life and a death battle with terrorism and international terrorists and has proclaimed its intentions to join the war against the international terrorism. One of SIMI's office bearers proclaims: "If a battle breaks, it will be a fight between the Satan and humanity". A self- proclaimed Shahi man of a Delhi Mosque has called upon the Muslims all over the world to support the master terrorist Osma Bin Laden, a creation of the USA to fight the Russians in 1980's the latter carries an award of $30 millions announced by the USA, for which a number of bounty seekers have jumped into the letter fray. Indian adherents of Osma Bin Laden are exactly being more loyal than the King. Pakistan's military dictator is reported to have paid the Mullahas and Chiefs of Jamaat. e- Ulemma, Saami-ur-Haq and Jamaate-e- Islami, hefty sums in a deal stuck with them, for keeping a low profile on street demonstrations against his regime's decision to back America in its war against the Talibans openly supporting terrorist mastermind, Bin Laden. It appears that as the news of the deal between Mushraff and the important clerics spread, a number of small organisations also wanted to be paid for keeping silent and have made similar demands as such. There is nothing unusual about such deals in the political world. Only thing is the creation of a new class of religious mercenaries who can be bought with cash and gifts. Pakistan is also not helping American, out of revulsion to terrorism. It is a simple pure interest in Dollars. Pakistan, according to Washington Post, is seeking a trade off or rewards in Kashmir, for its assistance to kill Osma Bin Laden and its own creation Talibans. It has already managed it with America, for opening purse strings, to purchase its co-operation. A serious problem, which India will face in the days to come is that, over three lakh, estimated newly entered Afghan refugees in Pakistan, along with the earlier three million would, most likely be pushed to further boil the hot cauldron of J&K. The 1st October, 2001 saw another day of a bloody massacre in Srinagar, when terrorists attacked the State Assembly complex, with the help of a car suicide bomb strike. The RDX filled vehicle killed 30 people and injured another 95. A spokesman of the Pakistan based terrorist outfit, Jaish-e. Mohammad confirmed the participation of a North West Frontier activist in the attack. Probably he did not want to confirm that Pakistan is asking the Afghan refugees entering Pakistan to go straight ahead to the Kashmir and foment trouble there.

Most people, including Muslim priests, indulging in rabble rousing in India to support the terrorists, need to realise that, neither terrorists nor terrorism has any religion. In a democratic country like India, the aggrieved citizens could approach the judiciary for the redressal of their grievances. The ludicrous part of the entire episode is that in America, many Indians and Sikhs are being targeted with threats and intimidation and attacks, under the belief of mistaken identity of being Muslim terrorists. Especially the Sikhs wearing turbans and sporting flowing beards or beards, are the victims, for a similar appearance, as fundamentalist Talibans.

For understanding the terrorism and Jehad, which in the common parlance, have become interconnected, and in some cases synonymous, it is essential to understand the background of Islam. Islam has been more sinned against than sinning by Jehadis, who are using it as all comprehensive term to cover a multitude of their sinful and anti-Islam activities. Probably, prophet Hazrat Muhammad, would be aghast at what has been happening in his name, which was not definitely his intention. No Prophet has yet taught intolerance and neither did Muhammad Sahib peace upon him. Jehad in simple terms means fighting for protection of religion. All religions have passed through this stage. Christianity was itself persecuted by people who rebelled against their then existing traditions. Executions, burning at the stake of the non-believers, like the Joan of Arc of France, were not an infrequent occurrence. Protestants were the target of attack and atrocities by the Catholics.

Religion is a sensitive issue. Irrespective of any religion, it has been seen that the orthodox or fundamentalists of all religions have a sway and carry the day of whatever they demand or command. Religion is an accident of birth. We happen to be Muslims, Hindus, Sikhs or Christians, because our parents were so. It is not a matter of choice for most people, though some do convert to other religions. It is difficult to accurately assess, what impact any teaching would have on the generations to come. Conversion is an article of faith for Christians. During the last visit of Pope to India, he had expressed a hope that the new millennium would see Asia embracing Christianity. Similarly, it is the converted population of India, which has become Muslims or Christians. Sikhism waxed aside Hinduism. The Muslims have been enjoined to raise a Jehad against the non believers. The recent attack of 11th September on USA has once again focused the need to examine the issue again and the impact, it is going to have on the world. In my understanding of the Islam, Jehad was a call given by prophet Muhammad to fight against those, who did not want him to live; believe and pray as he wanted. It is correctly said that devil can cite scriptures to suit his cause and case. Using the name of Islam to attack and destroy non Muslims, whom the Jehadis would call non believers, would have been far from Hazart's mind. Jehad has become an industry. There is Jihad factory run by the Taliban and the Inter Services Intelligence (ISI) of Pakistan. It has recruited volunteers from all Islamic nations and Muslim populations to fight disparate or different causes. It was initially funded by the Americans to fight the Russians and supplied it with weapons worth over $4 billions. Other sources of financial contributions to run Jehad are, world wide donations from individuals, narcotics and drugs trade of Afghanistan and Pakistan, the estimates of which, vary between $ 5 and $ 9 billion. Besides, some Saudis also provides a major chunk of money. Jehad is the very antithesis of the sovereignty of nations, which is based on a specific territorial limits of a state. Jehadis made in Pakistan, supported by fundamentalist Islamic regimes, have created troubles in Kashmir, Afghanistan, Chechnya, Dagestan, Bosnia and Xinjiang. Bin Laden and the International Islamic Front, have new vowed to destroy the United States, Israel and India. Bin Laden has declared: "The International Islamic Front for Jihad against the US and Israel has, by the grace of God, issued a crystal clear fatwa [decree] calling on the Islamic nation respectivily to carry on jihad (holy war) aimed at liberating holy sites. The nation of Muhammad has responded to this appeal. If the instigation for jihad against the Jews and the Americans in order to liberate al-Aksa Mosque and the Holy Ka'aba (Islamic shrines in Jerusalem and Saudi Arabia respectively) is considered a crime, then let history be a witness that I am a criminal. Our job is to instigate and by the grace of God, we did that and certain people responded."

When asked, whether he knew the men who had been arrested for these attacks, he replied: "What I know is that those who risked their lives to earn the pleasure of God, are real men. They managed to rid the Islamic nation of disgrace. We hold them in the highest esteem... The fact of the matter is that America and in particular the CIA, wanted to cover up their failure in the aftermath of the events that took place in Riyadh, Nairobi, Dar-es -Salaam, Capetown, Kampala-and other places". He was also asked for his reaction to the December attack on Iraq by US and British forces and he replied: "There is no doubt that the treacherous attack has confirmed that Britain and America are acting on behalf of Israel and the Jews, paving the way for the Jews to divide the Muslim world once again, enslave it and loot the rest of its wealth. A great part of the force that carried out the attack came from certain Gulf countries that have lost their sovereignty. Now infidels walk everywhere on the land where Mohammed was born and where the Koran was revealed to him. The situation is serious. The rulers have become powerless. Muslims should carry out their obligations, since the rulers of the region have accepted the invasion of their countries. These countries belong to Islam and not the rulers."

To another question, as to what can the US expect from him, the acquisition of nuclear weapon, efforts by USA to stop the flow of funds for his activities and the impact of his Islamic Message, Bin Laden replied: "Any thief or criminal or robber who enters another country in order to steal should expect to be exposed to murder at any time. For the American forces to expect anything from me personally reflects a very narrow perception. Thousands of millions of Muslims are angry. The Americans should expect reactions from the Muslim world that are proportionate to the injustice they inflict. Acquiring weapons for the defence of Muslims is a religious duty. If I have indeed acquired these weapons, then I thank God for enabling me to do so. And if I seek to acquire these weapons, I am carrying out a duty. It would be a sin for Muslims not to try to possess the weapons that would prevent the infidels from inflicting harm on Muslims. The US knows that I have attacked it, by the grace of God, for more than 10 years now. The US alleges that I am fully responsible for the killing of its soldiers in Somalia. God knows that we have been pleased at the killing of American soldiers. This was achieved by the grace of God and the efforts of the Mujahideen from among the Somali brothers and other Arab Mujahideen who had been in Afghanistan before that. America has been trying ever since to tighten its economics blockade against us and to arrest me. It has failed. This blockade does not hurt us much. We expect to be rewarded by God. Winds of change have blown in order to lift the injustice to which the world is subjected by America and its supporters and the Jews who are collaborating with them. The time will come, sooner rather than later, when criminal despots who betrayed God and his Prophet, and betrayed their trust and a their nation, will face the same fate."

When questioned that many Muslims who do not agree with his kind of violence and his reaction to American regarding him as enemy number one, Bin Laden replied: "Fighting is a part of our religion and our sharia [an Islamic legal Code]. Those who love God and his Prophet and this religion cannot deny that. Whoever denies even a minor tenet of our religion; commits the gravest sin in Islam. Those who sympathise with the infidels, such as the PLO in Palestine or the so-called Palestinian Authority, have been trying for tens of years to get back some of their rights. They laid down arms and abandoned what is called violence and tried peaceful bargaining. What did the Jews give them? They did not give them even one per cent of their rights. Hostility towards America is a religious duty. We hope to be rewarded for it by God. To call us Enemy No I or 2 does not hurt us". Osama bin Laden is confident that the Islamic nation will carry out its duty. "I am confident that Muslims will be able to end the legend of the so-called superpower that is America."

The plain truth is that, Jehad means different things to different people and not necessarily what is obvious or whatever may be the truth? The simple and plain Jehad, which is also encouraged by Geeta, is to stand up and fight for your right. There can be no dispute on that score. The problem arises, when the right of one set of Jehadis clash with the rights of Jehadis, professing different convictions or faith. The world has become an inter-dependent one and no one man, can impose his will or faith on others. If it was the intention of the Lord Almighty, that there should be one set of religion for the whole world, then He would have seen to it that there is only one religion professed by human beings. Bin Laden, carrying the highest reward of $ 30 million on his head, as announced by the USA, is free to profess his religion, like others in the world, but within the confines of Holy Quran, which preaches, love and brotherhood for all fellow human beings. He is committing a sacrilege and misleading by citing scriptures to run his terrorist shop, for which, at least at present there are no takers, not even his former mentors in Pakistan and America.

Bible says, there is a time for everything, and a season for every activity under heaven:

2 a time to be born and a time to die,
a time to plant and a time to uproot,

3 a time to kill and a time to heal,
a time to tear down and a time to build,

4 a time to weep and a time to laugh,
a time to mourn and a time to dance,

5 a time to scatter stones and a time to gather them,
a time to embrace and a time to refrain,

6 a time to search and a time to give up,
a time to keep and a time to throw away,

7 a time to tear and a time to mend,
a time to be silent and a time to speak,

8 a time to love and a time to hate,
a time for war and a time for peace.

It is also time to reming that those who live by gun, will die by gun only. Talibans in Afghanistan, when pressed, the possibility of their debut in Kashmir, can not be ruled out.

4
Trained Terrorists

The shoot out in Bangkok between the gangsters of Indian origin, Chota Rajan and Dawood's hitmen has again focussed the problem on the empires that gangsters wish to control and the territories they wish to command. The names, Chota Rajan, Bada Rajan or Ibrahim Dawood are only the religious labels, indicating their birth in particular families. A newspaper of Mumbai went to the extent of saying that the attempt on the life of Chota Rajan was an ISI plan to eliminate 'Hindu Goonda'. In the world of gangs, goondas or criminals, the label of religion is only of very marginal interests. It is used by the gangsters to suit the gangsters their greater and bigger objectives. The only interest of a gangster is the colour and amount of money he can make out of his activities. Any excuse or plank is good enough for him.

In the Dons gallery, names like Shakeel, Chota Rajan or Dawood have been doing the rounds in the country. In many places, their name is enough to fork out millions as the price of continuing to live. A disturbing menace of the present times is the growth of criminal gangs and the inability of the police to nail down their master brains. Since the boss is never on or near the scene of crime, the investigating officer is left with no option but to establish the guilt of the persons directly involved in the crime. As much, the main dramatis personae is left out.

No legally acceptable evidence is available against the gang leader. What is available, is only unconfirmed rumours and hearsay evidence, collected through unconfirmed sources.

What comes to public notice is only the tip of the iceberg of the vast hidden danger they face. Gang activities range from settling property disputes to extortion for ransom or contract killings. In big cities, extortion is done to ensure labour trouble free operations in factories or obstruction free construction of commercial and residential complexes. Otherwise, the builder will rue the day, he did not submit to the blackmail. Some gangs levy a one-time charge based on square foot area. Depending upon the locality, the price fixed can be anything between Rs. 50 and Rs. 200 per square foot. More often than not, only a verbal threat is enough to achieve the gangster's objective as crores tumble out of income tax evaded chests, stashed away carefully. These gangs or private armies usually have a well-defined command structure. They have ruthless killers on their roll. The easiest target of the gangs is, a one-time operation for extorting money. It is indulged with relative immunity, as the intended victim in most cases pays up on threats rather than get involved with legal procedure. The victim knows that once he gets involved with the police, he and his family are likely to become fixed targets.

Settling disputes is another favourite vocation of these gangs. Killings perpetrated by them are generally of their rivals or their associates. Sometimes, their disloyal members, defectors or potential defectors are also the target. Rivals in business, often commission contract killings but sometimes it is done in politics as well. It is not necessary for the hit man or the hit-team to know the targeted victim. One way of solving the problems of the gangs is, let them kill each other to settle their scores, without shedding too many official tears. All over the world sometimes, moles are used to penetrate the gangs. But rarely this strategy has succeeded and that also to a limited extent and a limited time. The country gains nothing except the headache in bringing Chota Rajan back to India. It is doubtful, if anybody can give any evidence against him in the court of law. It is better to use him abroad, as any case of extradition is a tortuous and unending process.

Normally ordinary people, do not know much about gangs. Only when there is a shoot-out in a public place or some criminal gets killed in a gang war outside the courts, in a hotel or in his house, is the public indignation expressed through the columns of various newspapers. After sometime, it is forgotten history. As for police records, the entire incident is reduced to an individual crime and not projected as the work of a gang. The question arises as to what police and public should do so that the gang war does not bring to halt commercial and social life. One way is that, the police itself should be above-board. There are frequent complaints even in the National Capital of low rung policemen getting mixed up with the gangs. The police themselves have found their members participating in gang wars and arrested them. This needs to be done on a constant basis. The gangs have the latest gadgetry and weapons. Old ammunition or the vehicles of the police cannot cope with any contingency requiring speed and lightening reaction. This aspect needs attention of the Central Government. It is doubtful, if any member of the public will place his neck on the block, by giving evidence in the court of the law. The law in the case of a gang should place the onus on the criminals.

There was point of difference, while dealing with terrorism in Punjab between the Para Military Chiefs and Punjab Police in 1980's & 1990s, wherein I was the Chief of the Central Reserve Police Force. One of the Forces, always used to keep back some people, as Reserve, when the State was burning. This was raised in a joint meeting, with the Governor of Punjab. But still, that particular Force Chief, did not agree, either to give the reserve or deploy people in less than a platoon strength. When questioned, about unsatisfactory deployment, the standard reply from the Forces was that, you give us the task and it is upto us, how we complete it. I have seen the same reply and the same thing said for the last three decades. With such mindset, even on the methods of deployment, the result is that, the situations remains the same despite the heavy deployment.

On the other hand, a single policeman of the State Police, would handle most of the problems himself. But those, who have noticed carefully, it is not so with the Central Forces. As they are deployed in groups, the tendency to exchange notes, on men and situations, and even being careless at times, is there. It is not so only in India, but in all the areas, including Pakistan, where the British, have left their same legacy.

The Government is a system of checks and balances. Nobody can be a repository of all information of intelligence. While professionalism is good and should be encouraged, it should not turn into an obduracy, with the result that wood is missed for the trees. New situations call for new strategies and new planning methods. The solution does not lie, in creating new forces or new agencies, but in making optimum use of the plenty of existing resources. The biggest single problem in dealing with terrorism, is that of making all agencies, to view the whole problem as a whole, without bringing their personal egos in between.

Despite having a multiplicity of intelligence agencies, it is doubtful if the intelligence is shared at the ground level. The first effort of the operatives on the ground, is to show their bosses, as to how active they are and what tremendous amount of work, they are doing. It does not matter for them, whether in the process, a so called predicted incident takes place. Moreover, the tendency to make vague generalisations, about the incidents, which might happen, needs to be discouraged. Most agencies, have a habit, of painting a ghastly scenario of the things, which might happen. A senior officer, who was heading Special Protection Group, to guard the Prime Minister and later on headed an Intelligence Agency told me that, he himself was the victim of the Intelligence. At midnight, whenever the PM had to go out of Delhi, he would get a double sealed covered from Intelligence, informing him as to what might happen to the Prime Minister. He said that this was done, only to safeguard their turf, so that if later on, even if some small incident happened, they could claim that 'We told You'. If nothing happened, they would take credit, that it was their timely intelligence, which enabled the local security agencies to take precautions and prevent the happenings of the incident. Such general alarm should be subjected to justification.

It is true, that no intelligence, can be hundred percent accurate. But in the absence of accurate intelligence, no operation can be successful. Hence we have had, too many serious incidents happening, giving a bad name to the country. The incidents include the attack on Red Fort, Parliament House, attack on Corps Headquarters in Srinagar and the Kargil intrusion by Pakistan in 1999. Subramaniam Committee looked into Kargil attack, mentioned obliquely, about too many cooks spoiling the broth. Everybody is keen to build his own empire. Army wants a separate Defence Intelligence Agency. Army's job is, to fight and defend the country. There is, a psychological chasm, between the civilians and the people in uniform. An army man, by his thinking and training, is not going to make a good intelligence man, unless he has spent a lifetime doing intelligence work. Intelligence is not everybody's cup of tea. In any case, the intelligence at the ground level, is collected by comparatively junior functionaries of the level of Constable to Deputy Superintendent of Police or in the case of army from Sepoy to Captain. Everybody above, only analyses what has been collected and put up to him or them. The solution lies, in redesigning and restructuring the existing institutions. The standard request for meeting any new challenge, is more staff. But nobody keeps a track, as to how many of the existing ones, are idle or are doing nothing. British Intelligence had infiltrated in all political parties, religions bodies, trade unions and all organisations pasing threat to their rule.

Two solutions are urgently required. There should be a Permanent Security Commission, with a minimum tenure of two years. It should consist of only eminent public men, journalists, analysts and a sprinkling of knowledgeable politicians. As far as possible, all retired Government officials, especially those, who have worked in such organisations, should be kept out. It is strange that when an Intelligence, security organisation or Defence Chief, does not do one penny's worth of work when in service, is called upon after retirement to advise the Government, as to how to improve the Intelligence or the organisation or organisations he had worked with. The only way country can progress, is to follow the Singapore Model, where the ruling party, makes use of the talent, whether in or after Government service, or in private sector.

According to a Chief Minister of Rajasthan about, 12,000 ISI agents are operating in that State. The border districts of Jaisalmer, Barmer and Jalore have turned into havens for their activities. He also said that the "traitors", who had helped the Pakistani Army in the 1965 and 1971 wars, were active again in the border areas. 240 Madarsas operating in the border areas were hotbeds of fanaticism. Pakistani agents were teaching students there, who have started wearing clothes like those worn by the Taliban. The source of funds received by these Madarsas has not been disclosed.

People detained under the National Security Act for smuggling and helping Pakistani intelligence agents had managed to get themselves elected Zila Pramukhs and Sarpanches in the past two years. The situation in the areas along the 1,044 km long international border today is the same as before the two wars fought with Pakistan. This is a grave threat to the country's security. The Chief Minister also added that a large number of people had occupied the land falling in the inner line area, declared so after the 1965 and 1971 conflicts. Land allotment near the border violated the law and the Border Security Force (BSF) had objected to this. The population increase was the maximum in Jaisalmer and Barmer districts due to above factors. Over 19,000 people had migrated to Pakistan during the two wars. The present ownership status of the land owned by them, which should have vested with the Government, is not clear.

The incidents of violence increased in Jammu Kashmir in the post cease fire period, which was announced on 19th November, 2000. The violent incidents against Defence and para military forces increased from 36 in July-September 2000 to 55 in October-December

2000 with 113 causalities. The terrorists incidents were 3071 in 1999 and 3074 in 2000. In 1999 security forces lost 408 persons. The ratio of terrorist killed as against security forces works out from 1 to 3.3 to 1 to 4, which is one of the highest in the world. There is a similar increase in terrorist violence in North East. It (terrorist violence) was 451 in Assam in 1999 and rose to 536 in 2000. Similar figure for Tripura was 616 in 1999 and 826 in 2000. 220 civilians were killed in violence in Assam in 1999 and 419 in 2000.

India has been facing problems from its neighbours not from nineties but almost from the time of independence. Even Bangladesh, which could not have come into existence but for India's active moral and material support, has been both disdainful and distrustful of us. The problem is further compounded by the fact that there are 111 Indian enclaves in Bangladesh and 50 Bangladesh enclaves all along the no man's land which stretches across 4000 km. In a skirmish on April 18, 2000, India lost 19 persons, including 4 civilians and Bangladesh Rifles lost two of its men. Enclaves connected by a small stretch of land, but surrounded by either Bangladesh or India are the prime areas for such conflicts. The problem gets acute, when there are election times in Bangladesh, because the opposition parties there always indulge in using India as a whipping boy to garner votes. Incidentally, as per the statement of a late Home Minister of India, there are over 2 crore illegal Bangladeshi migrants staying in India. Where is the question of showing restraint by India, in not throwing out those, who are not even the citizens of this country?. Where is the question of remaining friends and even not raising the matter strongly, when our soldiers are tricked and executed in cold blood? It is almost fooling a gullible public. In the tougher game of preserving life, honour and independence of the Nation, there should be no holds barred. Adventurism continues at the border and quite often it is not possible to put the border incidents behind. The only solution lies in the maximum alert on our borders with other countries. India baiting rhetoric goes on both in Pakistan and Bangladesh. The greed of power makes people there blind. Any excuse whether it is outside danger or the security of their countries, will be exploited by the politicians there with phoney promises. Double standards are nothing new either in Bangladesh or in Pakistan. The problem is that for most rulers any crutch, which can continue them in power is good enough. In the interest of keeping good neighbourly relations, we are being exploited by our smaller neighbours. It happened with us in Kargil, where the bodies of our dead soldiers, handed over to us, clearly indicated inhuman treatment by Pakistan. Now Bangladesh, picks up our border security forces personnel, murders them in cold blood and returns their bodies in mutilated conditions. Every time, such an incident happens, we haw, thaw, mourn, register a so called protest and then every thing is forgotten till the next incident. India bashing and anti Indian proclamations, in the perceptions of politicians in Bangladesh, Pakistan and Sri Lanka get them both popularity and votes. Bangladesh has obviously picked up the threads where Pakistan left in treating our soldiers. Lives of the Indian soldiers are not cheap and neither they are, the doormats to be trampled by any country. None of these countries would have dared to behave, in a similar way with an American citizen. Why should India bother about Bangladesh Government? What for is this appeasement policy? With the fourth largest Army in the world, what are our politicians afraid of? Others will try your Lakshman Rekha and see how far they can take you for granted and what is the level of your patience. India should be proud of Indians but the senseless and deliberate humiliation of the Indians is something which should be totally unacceptable to any Government in power. The perpetrators of such crimes, whether the Governments or the individuals should not go unpunished at any cost at any time. This is both a challenge and opportunity for the Government to show that it cares and is sensitive to Indian lives.

Terrorism is unlawful or threatened use of force or violence by a person or an organized group against people or property with the intention of intimidating or coercing societies or governments, whether for ideological or political reasons. However, it must be made clear that despite debating terrorism and terrorist incidents, United Nations has not been able to evolve any universally acceptable definition of terrorism. Terrorists these days are technological savvy and not illiterate ruffians, having at their command an incredible arsenal. They make use of enormous number of weapons of destruction available at a price. Nuclear materials are much easier to procure and process. Seen in the light of above development, America woke up to a shock on September, 11, 2001. The scene was captured alive by a TV Camera man who happened to be around and it haunted the world for some months. American President declared that America was under attack. 9/11 rudely aroused the most powerful nation of the world. Dealing with terrorism was not a mice and cat show, he added. India has been facing terrorism for the last over two decades.

Communication is now so inexpensive and easy that it is a much simpler task for terrorist groups to organize, plan and recruit. Several terrorist groups have been known, to use the Internet in their operations, either as a means of communication or as another arena for terrorism. Through large-scale communication, some groups are able to recruit new members and find financial backing.

In September 2003, at least 153 persons were injured and 53 killed in the powerful bomb blasts, in front of the Mumbadevi Temple in Zaveri Bazar, the heart of Mumbai's diamond business and in a parking lot, next to the Gateway of India opposite the Taj Mahal hotel on Monday, 25th August, 2003. Both bombs were kept in the boots of two taxis. Bombs can be made by use of common fertilizer and gasoline. They can be loaded into a rented taxi as was done in Mumbai to cause massive destruction. However, in the Mumbai blasts, the deadly RDX was reportedly used.

Terror has been haunting Jammu and Kashmir for over two decades with the people feeling insecure and terrified. The terrorists now seem to have found another soft target in the Commercial Capital of India. The latest bomb blasts, are an indicator, that sinister forces are better organised and would leave no opportunity untapped to create trouble. Obviously, some people may make all efforts to communalising the latest incident. This needs to be combated by a vigilant state and Central government, to ensure that the atmosphere is not vitiated and terrorists' effort does not succeed to divide the people, and undermine the secular and democratic basis of the Constitution. The terrorists goal is to strike terror and create conditions, that will further their agenda. Too many deaths naturally point out at the inefficiency of the Government and particularly the intelligence and local police. Police is a State subject. The responsibility of whatever happens in any state, is the responsibility of the State Government. Two boms blast in Mumbay and Srinagar in July 2006, killed hundred of people and injured forteens more.

The easy availability of the means of communication and weapons of destruction is equally an asset to the terrorists. Things become much worse, when our neighbour encourages, recruits, trains and deploys terrorists. Obviously terrorist operations, like the one done on 25th August in Mumbai, could not have been done, without a firm base of support. Core issue between India and Pakistan is that of terrorism and not of molly coddling and paying lip service to the people to people friendships, between the two countries.

Even the most die hard democracies like the USA, UK and France have been compelled to enact laws, for dealing effectively with the threats of terrorism. Having stringent anti terrorism laws to protect the integrity of the country, is not inconsistent with the democratic values. Dealing with terrorists broadly involves identifying the terrorist organisations, their members, sympathisers, supporters, infrastructure, methods of funding and command and channels of communication. Since all organisations including the terrorists, depend upon individuals or small groups to carry out their operations, the next step entails dealing with them. Unlike the terrorists, who are not inhibited by any limitation or requirements of working within the confines of the laws, the counter terrorists agencies, whether police or other security forces, are required to act within the parmetres set by law, courts and the Government. It is not within the ambit of the security agencies to punish any terrorists or their sympathisers. This lies within the purview of the judiciary, where ultimately the case has to be filed for prosecuting the terrorists. The present Indian laws were framed in 1863, when there were no crimes like terrorism, hijacking, threat to the security of the State, assassination of Prime Ministers and Chief Ministers. The terrorist these days are also very adept in the use of information technology. They use improved communication methods like Internet for effective links with followers, fellow terrorists, potential donors and recruits, who may be located over a large geographical area.

Pakistan has reportedly recruited over 31,000 Indian spies. Over 10,000 Pakistani and other foreigners have infiltrated into India. Between 1990 and 2000, 30,071 civilians and 6077 defense personnel, were killed in the country, by the different militant groups and more than 3,50,000 rendered homeless. The normal laws of the land, which exist on the statute book, are hardly or not at all adequate to deal with terrorism. Hence, to deal with terrorism, India had first introduced TADA, later POTA and now Unlawful Activities Act.

In France and USA, not only the executive and the legislature but even the judiciary have recognised the need for special powers and special procedures to deal with terrorism. In August, 1994, Carlos, a notorious terrorist, was allegedly drugged and kidnapped by the French external intelligence from Khartoum with the help of the Sudanese intelligence. Carlos' contention that this method vitiated his prosecution and trial, was rejected by the judiciary. In the USA, the judiciary had upheld in 1980s, the right of the US Counter

Terrorist agencies to kidnap an international terrorist, wanted for terrorism offences against US nationals and/or interests and found in foreign territory, if in the assessment of the agency, there was no other way of bringing him to justice. On the other hand, we in India, keep on tinkering with the statutes to deal with terrorism and go on endlessly debating, whether the defence rights of the terrorists are being violated. It is a well known fact, that the first effort of the terrorists is to leave no track and try to survive another day; to continue to create problems.

5

Implement of Silent Invasion

Terrorism is threat to the country, as it is a continuing one. Small organised gangs also use terrorism to wage war against established nations. A terrorist war is dissimilar to a conventional war, between two countries or nations. A conventional war has well defined battle lines, battle fields in which, trained professionals in the military skills take part. It is a do or die affair. A conventional war, like the one in Iraq in 2003 or Kargil in 1999, has a commencement, middle and conclusion.

A terrorist war or terrorist act, like the attack on Indian parliament on 13th December, 2001 on the other hand, is random act of violence, which can be against the civilians, defence and political personnel, generally at places, where they live or work. The purpose of terrorism, depends upon the objectives of the terrorists. It can range from coercing a group of people or even a government, into yielding some demands or for extracting revenge for a perceived wrong.

Terrorists generally use destructive violence by stealth, rather than openly on public buildings, political figures, military and police officials, primarily for creating dramatic effects. Explosives and incendiary devices, sniping, kidnapping, hijacking and biological agents, have been used by terrorists. Individual terrorists groups may not have any atomic weapons. But some terrorists or terrorist supporting States like Pakistan, do possess nuclear weapons.

Modern day terrorists are also well versed in technological advances. The profile of modern terrorist is, of one, who is highly educated, an MBA, an Engineer, capable of even flying an aircraft or a Professor in some institution. The trends in terrorism, over the past few decades, have been towards attacks, which can result in as many deaths as possible. For example, about six thousand people were the victims in the bombing of two U.S embhassies in African countries in 1998, one in Kenya and one in Tanzania. Perhaps the most extraordinary and striking form of creating spectacular effect is that of airline hijacking.

In Pakistan, Brigadier Imtiaz Ahmed, once head of the Pakistan Intelligence Bureau and a protégé of Nawaz Sheriff in his term as prime minister, was arrested by the Benazir Bhutto government in 1994 July on the charge that he had in 1989 played an active role in purchasing members of the Pakistan National Assembly to oust the then government of Benazir Bhutto. It had appeared in the Pakistani media that as director of Pakistan's Intelligence Bureau, Brigadier Imtiaz Ahmed had planned riots, launching fake intelligence operations, indulging in large-scale tapping of telephones of Nawaz Sheriff's rivals and even setting up a private parallel intelligence agency with official secret funds.

CIA Director, in a testimony to USA Senate on 10th February, 2003 informed that "Pakistan continues to support the groups that resist India's presence in Kashmir, in an effort to bring India to the negotiating table. Frustration with continued terrorist attacks has prompted India, to reject any suggestion of resumption of dialogue with Pakistan. Al-Qaida continues to find refuge in the hinterlands of Afghanistan and Pakistan, apart from establishing a presence in Iran and Iraq. Osama Bin Laden's network is living in the expectation of resuming the offensive". Nearer Home, Pakistan and its agency ISI have left no stone unturned to create mayhems in India. Apart from freely providing arms and other support to the terrorists, which it has been doing for the last two decades, it is now directly providing cash and foreign exchange to support the terrorists in India. Pakistani High Commission, which is the hub of the terrorists sponsoring and supporting activities on behalf of Pakistan in a brazen way, was caught with its pants down; after it had passed on a few lakhs to a woman for sustaining terrorism on 6th of February, 2003. The diary of the woman conduit, through whom the money was to passed, clearly indicated that the money was to be passed on to Lashkar-e- Toiba, Jaish-e-Mohammad, Jammu and Kashmir Liberation Front (JKLF), Jammu and Kashmir Islamic Front, Al-Badr, Hizbul Mujahiddin and Al-Umar. The conduit herself was to keep some money for the services rendered. The direct involvement of the acting Pakistani High Commissioner, in sabotaging activities left no choice for Government of India, except to ask him to leave the country. For our country to be strong, we need to stand united and not take a partisan stand. At present there is no effective Federal Agency which can tackle crimes, international in character, crimes that are federal in nature, such as terrorism, drugs trafficking, illegal migration and organised crime. The Chief Ministers, in a meeting convened by the Government of India on 8th of February, 2003 had again rejected the proposal to have such an agency, which only shows that petty personal interests and desire to streamline in the national interest are far from the thoughts of the state heads. However, the Chief Minister, agreed on the desirability of deporting illegal migrants from Bangladesh. It does not mean much, unless it is matched by actions of throwing out the undesirable aliens, without being swayed by the vote bank politics. Bangladeshis have treated India as a Dharmshala, wherein they can walking into at will. The result is that there were 25 million Bangladeshis, illegally staying in India in 1996.

December 13, 2001 was a black day for India, when the country witnessed the most audacious terrorist attacks on our Parliament. Five well-armed terrorists, not only mocked at India, but at its intelligence agencies, which had no wind of their actual operation. Their plan was to take as many MPs and other leaders as possible hostages and place demands before the Government. If in the process, some MPs had been killed, the terrorists would not have shed any tear. Had their plan even partially succeeded, both killings and kidnappings would have been adopted, depending upon what suited the terrorists. The suicide squad of five terrorists had on their persons, grenades, two 9 mm pistols, 4 AK 56 Rifles also called Kalashnikovs as well as RDX. At the end, all five terrorists were shot dead. Six security personnel and a gardener also lost their lives in the gruesome encounter. Eighteen others, including 12 security staff and a TV cameraman, were injured.

The 13 December attack on Parliament was telecast almost live by most private LTV channels, as September 11 attack on the World Trade Centre, was captured alive by the American television.

The chronology of the events is as under :

11.41 a.m - A white Ambassador car, bearing number DL 3CJ 1527, with a red beacon entered the complex from the Parliament Street end. It sped past the main gate and the porch towards the gate on the Vijay Chowk-Raisina Road end. Sitting inside were the armed terrorists. The car swerves to the right. It attracts the attention of Security Officer J.P. Yadav, who asks it to stop. The car rushed past him near gate 12 and he raised an alarm over the walkie-talkie. Terrorists fire at Yadav and kill him. The car, loaded with 30 kg of RDX, as discovered later on, speeds on. Terrorist's car finds its path blocked by a number of other cars, parked outside gate 11. These cars were a part of the Vice-President's convoy. There is an exchange of fire with Late Vice–President, Krishan Kant's security. The terrorist's Ambassador, forced to brake hard, veers sharply, striking one of the cars. There is a wall that prevents further progress of the car.

11.42 a.m –The terrorists rush out firing. They scale the wall. The firing alerts security staff and they close the doors of the building. Security men quickly shut all entrances to the Parliament so that the armed men do not enter the main building.

11.44 a.m –One terrorist breaks away from the group. He rushes towards the main gate. He lobs several hand grenades and shoots indiscriminately from his assault rifle. He is shot by the security staff. Terrorist detonates the RDX tied around his body near the gate.

11.50 a.m –Four other terrorists run towards the other gates of Parliament House. Three terrorists fire at the security forces, killing four policemen and a gardener. But they are killed between gate 8 and 9. Obviously they were looking for an entry point into the building.

11.55 a.m –The last surviving terrorist tries to climb to the first floor with the help of TV cables. He fails in his efforts and hobbles towards gate 5 normally used by the Prime Minister. He is shot dead by the security forces. In this open attack, a CRPF woman constable posted near the iron gate at Vijay Chowk, is killed. A TV cameraman, while taking shots alive and seeking cover is hit by a bullet.

My information is that all the security gadgetries required for the security of the Parliament were not in position. After my command of more than one para military force during my service period, things have not changed much. I noticed a totally lackadaisical bureaucratic approach to equipping or training in the forces. The only way we can have the better of terrorism is, to give the best of equipment to our forces, so that they can finish the problem at the entry point itself. This is something, which the attack on Parliament points to a trend among terrorists, of deliberately seeking out targets, which will not only give them mileage, but also tremendous publicity. Such glare of publicity would show them as dare devils, who would be willing to go to any extent to achieve their objectives. The objective of the terrorists, anywhere in the world, including our country, is to frighten the public and by their sheer audacity boost the morale of those supporting them which needs to be monitoral at the Home Minister's and the prime Minister's level.

Prime Minister Vajpayee said on TV on 13th December, "battle against terrorism had reached its last phase and that we will fight a decisive battle to the end. By the attack, the terrorists have yet again flung a challenge at the country. The nation accepts the challenge. We will liquidate the terrorists and their sponsors, whoever they are."

The question arises as to what should be the response of the Government of India to such activities?

1. Should we cross the LOC in a full-scale military operation? If so we have to be clear in our own thinking, whether the objective of such an exercise is to destroy the terrorist training camps in Pakistan-occupied Kashmir (POK) or merge POK with the rest of Kashmir?

2. Should we undertake covert operations to destroy the training camps?

3. Is our objective to replace the Pakistani government with one, which will see reason and would not allow any anti terrorist activities as USA has done in Pakistan?

4. Should we use nuclear weapons to teach Pakistan a lesson for supporting terrorism?

5. Should we press US President to move hard against Pakistan, on the same lines as he had done against Al Quaida and other terrorist groups in Afghanistan?

6. What is going to be the cost of the war and how long both the countries can sustain it? What will be its effect on our economy?

7. What will be the result of such a war on the world community and how many countries would stand by us?

While answering the first question, about hot pursuit and crossing border to attacks, we certainly have the sovereign right to protect our country and to attack the source of terrorism, as USA has done in Afghanistan. It must not be forgotten that central objective of the attack on Parliament was to incite a strong reaction, in the form of an attack from India. This would help, the so called Jehadis, masquerading as terrorists in their objectives. We had 4 wars with Pakistan. There has been no change in the status quo and neither the fifth war, if it comes about, is likely to change the scenario. War does not seem to be solution. If we use our force to cross the borders, Pakistan would do so at a time and place of its choosing. It could lead to a full scale or a low intensity war. Instead of addressing the problem of terrorism, we would have started another war, without eliminating terrorism. A terrorist is an invisible entity. Training camps for terrorists are not fixed training institutions. What you need for a training camp is a target, a few rifles and a place for lectures even if it is open. It can be wound up and shifted anywhere. Military action was ruled.

Answer to question number 2 is that, we should give back to Pakistan exactly in the same measure and to the same extent the trouble it is giving us. Wherever the agencies of the country need upgradation or other support, the same should be extended. We should keep on talking peace but not let go off, our guard. About replacing the Government of Pakistan, with one which is more friendly to us, we should be clear that it is the internal affair of Pakistani nation. If they are happy with dictators, why we should interfere in their happiness. We have to deal with, whoever is in power in Pakistan.

About question number 4, the nuclear weapons are more for self confidence of the nation and a deterrent. Since both Nations possess it, the use of nuclear weapons is out for the moment. About question number 5, it is very clear that we have to fight our own battle, as America is doing its own. Moral support and other tokenism is all we can expect from others, including the USA.

About question number 6 and 7, Indian economy has faced wars in the past and it can face in the future also. Generally, others are not interested in us or our problems. The investment from the developed countries would be affected, because nobody wants to invest in any country facing war and other problems. About weaponry, most of the arms, ammunition and aircraft are imported. May be, we could sustain the war for a few weeks, according to Defence Magazine Jane and Pakistan not even for a week. The best bet appears to be to fight terrorism, on our own soil and especially at the entry points of our porous border. The cost of entering India needs to be made, extremely prohibitive for the terrorists, who are invisible enemies. But they are very much visible, when crossing the Line of Control. It is clear that terrorists, whether of Pakistani or Afghani brand understand only the language of the booming gun. Nowhere in the world, terrorism has been vanquished by laws. It has been the guns, which have silenced terrorism. The only language which Pakistani trained/supported and abetted terrorists will understand is the loud and clear message of the bigger and booming guns trained on them. It is the success of the security agencies, who killed the terrorists, before they could wipe out the political leadership, as per their plans.

It is time to show that India is not a soft State. Frederick, the Great said, "Don't forget your great guns, which are the most respectable arguments of the Rights of the Kings". The same is true of all countries as of China and India.

Managing the internal security of the country and dealing with the several terrorist groups, in different parts of the country requires a very high degree of preparedness and quickest possible response. There is no limit to the kinds of weapons, and tricks, which the terrorists may use. Apart from the conventional weapons like rifles, grenades, there is no knowing as to when the terrorist groups may use nuclear, biological and chemical weapons. The problem is that, governments traditionally respond slowly and many a times, well after a disaster has struck. There is a classic case of the United States of America, which despite all the technology and resources at its command, could not even imagine, what to say of anticipating a disaster, like September, 11, 2001. Technology is a double edged weapon, which is available both to the criminal, the victim, the Governments and the crooks all over the world.

However, in the final analysis, the problem boils down as to how one should tackle terrorism and terrorist attacks. Of all the countries in the world, India and some of its State Governments have been most exposed to terrorism. We have the dubious record of the largest number of hijackings of Indian Airlines. There have been as many as a dozen hijackings and the Mumbai bomb blasts, which shook the country unnerved.

The September, 11 attack on the United States as well as December, 13, 2001 attack on Indian Parliament, have highlighted a new form of terrorism. It is suicide terrorism, where the perpetrator, knows well in advance, that he would not live to see the end result of his actions. There have been hundreds of suicide terrorist attacks all over the world. The first suicide terrorist attack in October 1983 in Beirut killed more than 250 American and French peace-keepers. An analysis of these attacks reveals the following aspects: Most of the suicidal attacks have been carried out by groups like the Hezbollah, the Amal, a Shia terrorist organisation, Hamas, Kurdistan Workers' Party (PKK), Palestinian Islamic Jihad (PIJ), Egyptian Islamic Jihad, Gama'a al-Islamiya and Al Qaida. They are all followers of Islam's professed Islamic faith, Sunni. However, LTTE in our part of the world, has also at times, adopted the techniques of suicidal extermination. It was the suicidal squad and members of LTTE, which killed Rajiv

Gandhi, a Former Prime Minister of India. Though the majority of the organisations involved in suicide terrorism, are Muslims, their primary objective of the attacks, has been political and not religious. Most of these groups use Islam religion to secure religious legitimacy for their actions, which are far from being religious.

The question arises whether the Indian state is fully prepared to deal with the challenge of terrorism of twenty first century. For using the services of Central Forces like the Central Reserve Police Force, Border Security Force and Central Industrial Security Forces, the Central Government bills the States and expects them to pay for using the Central Forces for fighting the terrorism. This is based on the constitutional distribution of subjects, wherein the Law and Order, Investigation and Prosecution of Offences, including terrorist offences, is the responsibility of the State Government. Each time there is a major terrorist attack in any region, the Central Government's response is, to provide more security forces there. It is time to have a second look at this approach of treating terrorism as only a law-and-order problem. It is in this way, the terrorists bleed the country. It suits them, if only a half hearted, a sporadic attention or unsustained attention, is paid to their activities.

The cost of compensation paid to victims of terrorism, border fencing, raising of local anti terrorist forces is more than Rs. 18,500 crore. The estimated expenditure on Army and paramilitary forces deployment is about Rs 9000, crore. Automatic and other sophisticated weapons, including AK 47/56 and other brands, rocket launchers, grenades etc. reportedly smuggled into India number 61,000 of which 47,700 were recovered up to 2001 end.

Some of the Major Strikes of terrorists in J&K are as under :

July 3l,1988: First bomb explosion outside Central Telegraph Office in Srinagar.

Jan 25,1990: Five Indian Air Force men gunned down at Rawalpora in Srinagar by JKLF men.

Jan 24,1992: Police HQ blasted - two killed. All top police officials including then DGP JN Saxena and IGP CRPF MK Singh critically wounded and had to be shifted to the All India Institute of Medical Sciences, New Delhi.

Jan 26,1995: Serial explosions in MAM stadium Jammu during Republic Day Parade when then Governor, Gen (retd) K V Krishna Rao escapes - nine dead and 100 others wounded.

April 19, 2000: First suicide bombing in Kashmir outside cantonment in Srinagar. Besides suicide bomber Afaq Ahmad Shah, 12 others killed.

Dec 25, 2000: Second suicide bombing in Kashmir outside cantonment, 11 killed.

Oct 1, 2001: Suicide bomber strikes at the State Legislative Complex in Srinagar, 40 dead.

Terrorists have been having a free run of the country, as well the National Capital, as the details of the following blasts in Delhi will show:

2001 Red fort Assault and Killings.

Arrests of Pakistan's ISI's operatives on a number of occasions, which are too numerous to be recounted.

2000, June 18: Two killed and 12 hurt in twin explosions near Red Fort.

2000, Mar 1: Seven hurt as a low-intensity bomb explodes in Sadar Bazar.

2000, Feb 27: Eight injured in a high-intensity explosion in a guest house in Paharganj.

2000, Jan 6: 25 persons hurt in an explosion at the Old Delhi Railway station.

1999, June 3: 37 persons injured after a explosion in Chandni Chowk.

1999, April 16: A powerful bomb explodes inside a train at Holambi Kalan railway station, killing two and injuring five.

1998, Dec 19: A crude bomb explodes inside a Bhajanpura temple at night. No one hurt.

1998, Aug 31: One killed and 17 hurt as bomb explodes in the crowded Turkman Gate area of Central Delhi.

1998, July 26: Two killed and three hurt after a high-intensity blast ripped apart a bus parked at Kashmere Gate inter-state bus terminus.

1998, June 27: Two injured after a bomb, thrown from a moving Gypsy by men in police uniforms, explodes outside a club in Greater Kailash-I.

1998, January 9: One killed and 55 injured in an explosion 50 metres from the police station.

Thousands of Hindus are migrating from Bangladesh to India after risking their lives and leaving their property, as well as kith and kin behind. A migrant said, "The true picture is not known to the outside world. It is a free for all, so far as it goes, to torturing minority. Women and property are the prime targets. Hundreds of Hindu women are hospitalised. Many women have been killed after being raped... It is a war against the minorities". India has lost over 55000 lives in terrorist violence.

Britain has already brought new tough anti-terrorism law into force. Eventually, every country takes a decision, guided by its own security perception. Until now, no action could be taken against any group including self-confessed extremist outfits, so long as they did not break any British laws. The result was that Britain had become a haven for terrorist organisations, including those which were openly engaged in raising funds and recruiting volunteers for waging guerrilla wars against foreign countries. Under the latest British Law for tackling terrorism, raising funds, organising meetings and recruiting Jehadis, would be deemed an offence, if it is established that these activities are intended to export terrorism. Once a group is banned, then any association with it — direct or indirect — would be deemed to be an offence and punishable.

In Doda (J & K) terrorists attacks 1993 and 2001 reported to be :

14 August 1993: Terrorists drag 14 people out of a bus an Sarthal Link Road in Kisthwar and kill them.

5 January 1996: Heavily armed Pakistan-trained terrorists, massacre 15 people of Hindu community, 8 kilometres from Thatri near Kishtwar.

8 June 1996: A group of 14 terrorists kill eight members of Hindu community including five family members of one Jagan nath Sharma, Senior Superintendent of the State Forest corporation, in kamlari Village.

4 May 1998: Nine shot dead in Dessa village.

6 May 1998: Five more people killed in Dessa Village.

19 June 1998: Terrorists gun down 25 members of two marriage parties including both bridegrooms and critically wound seven people at Chapri, 8 kilometres from Doda.

4 August 1998: In Kalaban village on the Chamba-Doda border 37 migrant labourers are killed.

3 September 1998: Sixteen members of Hindu community gunned down in two villages of Thukarie-Keshwan in Kistwar.

22 July 2001: Ten killed at Cherjee Village.

3 August 2001: Fifteen massacred on Rakshabandhan-eve at Sharhoti Dhard, village in Atholi, Padder.

International co-operation is based on the convergence of interests of Nations. India faces real danger from Nuclear Terrorism, as the master terrorist Bin Laden, has already branded India, Israel and USA as his enemies and declared Jihad against them. Considering that his terrorism is religion based, it is inconceivable that in the unlikely event, of his possessing a nuclear device, he will use it against a Muslim Country, like Pakistan or Iran in the neighbourhood of Afghanistan. It is beyond his capacity, if at all he possess a nuclear device, to have a delivery system to use, such a weapon, against America. India is the obvious target.

Pakistan has become a haven for terrorist organisations, including those which were openly engaged in raising funds and recruiting volunteers for waging guerrilla wars against foreign countries.

Under the latest British law for tackling terrorism, raising funds, organising meetings and recruiting Jehadis, would be deemed an offence, if it is established that these activities are intended to export terrorism. Once a group is banned, then any association with it – direct or indirect – would be deemed to be an offence and punished.

6
Crusade in Kashmir

In negotiations and settlements, many proposals some wild and some sensible are thrown on the table. Each party invariably asks for more, fully convinced that if you ask for Mars, you are bound to land up at least on Moon. Various proposals made in international negotiations are aimed at different audiences. Sometimes, the proposal are floated, to gauge reaction of people and other concerned political parties.

Pakistani President once suggested a new formulation to resolve the vexed Kashmir issue but has been careful to call it not a proposal but a food for thought. He said: "Take Kashmir in its entirety. It has seven regions across both sides of the Line of Control. Two of the regions are in Pakistan and five are in India. In my view, identify a region, whether it is the whole or seven or part; I do not know. They are to be demilitarised, granted independence or joint control or put under a UN mandate". He also said that he has never spoken like this before. "It is a debate of options for finding out a possible solution to Kashmir imbroglio. The whole debate of options will be based on this. We have to find a way out". Elaborating further, he said: "The status can be independence, condominium where there can be a joint control or there can be UN mandate which has to be defined by legal people. We have to consider the options in a purposeful manner going towards a solution. I strongly believe that there are options and there is a solution."

Keeping a way out, Musharraf said since both India and Pakistan agreed to consider options to resolve Kashmir after his meeting with Prime Minister Manmohan Singh in New York, in September 2004, he wanted to suggest a solution as a "food for thought". Sugar coating his suggestion he said, if there is a way out both countries could claim victory and Kashmiris too will be happy as they would acquire some authority to manage their affairs. When making this proposal, Pakistan President had in his aim, the international community, to whom he tries to appear to be reasonable. This is his way of scoring brownie points. A fundamental problem with Musharraf's idea is that is violat the understanding with Prime Minister Manmohan Singh that any new proposal should not lead to the redrawing of boundaries or the re-partition of India. These are the fundamental flaws in Musharraf's proposal.

President of Pakistan, despite being a benevolent dictator, is not that free agent, which other may feel he might be. Pakistan was created on the basis of fundamentalism and Muslims being separate from Hindus. Education in Pakistani Madarsas, has sown fairly deep roots of hatred against India. Pakistani school books still paint Hindu India, as a cowardly Nation, which lost all its battles with Pakistan, including that of 1971. There has been a talk of people to people contacts and confidence building measures. Suspicion is sown at young age in the mind of the citizens of Pakistan, that a secular India, which has Muslim population is renegade, apostate and permanent enemy of Pakistan. It is the Government, everywhere, to decide as to which country is hostile to them and which is their enemy. Pakistan has largely been governed by the army Generals and Colonels, right from 1958. General Musharaf is instrumental is the fourth Army take over of Pakistan. General Ayub opened the door to the takeovers on 7th October 1958. He ruled Pakistan for nearly 10 and half years. General Yahaya, who was in office for 2 and three fourth of years, replaced him. When Pakistan lost its war with India on the creation of Bangladesh, he handed over the power to Zulfiqar Ali Bhutto. Bhutto lost his job to General Zia-ul-Huaq on 5th July 1977. General Zia hanged Bhutto and was himself killed in an air crash on August, 17, 1988. Neither the enemity nor other evils disappeared with the Army Generals and Colonels having ruled Pakistan for over two decades. Neither have they improved anywhere in the world, with the army in command.

Democracy briefly returned to Pakistan, with Benazir Bhutto and Nawaz Sheriff alternating as Prime Minister. General Musharaff deposed the elected Prime Minister, Nawaz Sheriff on 12th October 1999. Senator Ackerman of the United States aptly described the coup: "When a fired general overthrows a duly elected civilian head of the Government, it looks like a coup and it walks like a coup, because it is a coup. It is a military coup in Pakistan and not a military take over."

The immediate provocation for the army stepping in, was the replacement of the Chief the of Army Staff, General Parvez Musharaf by the Director General of Inter-Services Intelligence, Lt. General

Ziauddin by the Prime Minister. Pakistan has a tradition of Army being lionized and even its junior level Generals being cultivated by the politicians. Nawaz Sheriff had earlier sacked the Chief of The Army Staff, Jehangir Karamat, only 90 days before his retirement. For the present ruler, General Musharaf, it was a question of saving his own job or bowing meekly to the orders of the Prime Minister, enabling Nawaz Sheriff to retain his job. It was a choice of 'his job', for the two actors involved. The excuse for such an action was given, as wide spread corruption, malpractices and rising prices under the regime of Nawaz Sheriff. Public anger at corrupt activities of successive civilian governments has been a favourable factor for public response. In any case, nobody, except the mad and foolish will dare to criticize the Army rulers anywhere in the world and least in Pakistan. Musharaff has a proverbial cat's nine lives, having survived almost deadly attacks around Christmas in December, 2003. Musharaff is wily where India is is concerned, but has ably served his country. He, deserted his protégé Talibans, when he found the going tough for them and joined the American band wagon for nearly 5 billion Dollars, which Americans paid as the price of his cooperation in throwing out the Talibans. He despite his record, as the architect of Kargil war with India, bided his time during Clinton's time and mended his fences with his successor, Bush. Confident that during his summit with Vajpayee, he would be able to bring about a diplomatic coup in Agra, he had to return empty handed. It looks that it has finally dawned on Musharaff that living in peace with India, is the only viable option for him. But his present proposal suffers the greatest flaw that it wants India to resile from the position that there can be no compromise on the integrity of India. Accepting the proposal even partly, would mean encouraging separatism. If Pakistani President is that sincere, then why not he first try the same scheme in POK and agree to end the cause of tension between India and Pakistan due to infiltrators. Moreover, Musharaff has the fundamentalists and Jehadis to tackle with and appease before he can seriously talk to India.

The second largest party in India after the ruling Congress, that is the BJP, has already lashed out at the General's proposal. It believes that it implies virtual dismemberment of the State of Jammu & Kashmir. However, the General's proposal shows that there is some realization on Pakistan's part that the position it had hitherto held on Jammu & Kashmir, is neither practicable nor sustainable. Moreover there is a need to go to still greater lengths by Pakistan, before a realistic and mutually acceptable solution can be found.

Musharaff's proposal, supported by his being both Army Chief and President till October, 2007, at least indicates that the Pakistani leadership realizes its past policies on Kashmir, based on promoting terrorism: are no longer effectual. Meanwhile, Musharaf's utterances on the solution of the Kashmir problem have evoked mixed response in the Valley, as a window of opportunity for the resolution of the main issue. Some terroritst organizations have called it as "stage-setting" for a sell-out on Kashmir. However, no Indian or Kashmiri would be averse to talks to any proposal that can bring about peace and settle the Kashmir imbroglio. At the sametime, the outcome for both parties should be such that they go away with the feeling that both have won. At the bottom of any dialogue, both the sides need to remember that peace has its victories no les than that of war.

Suicide attacks is the latest weapon, in the armoury of the terrorists. After Kargil, there have been mere than 100, so called fidayeen, or suicidal attacks. The terrorists have spread themselves in the Valley and reportedly, are waiting to strike. Their detail are as under:

Waiting to strike Group	*Area of Influence*	*Strength*
Hizbul Mujahideen	Kashmir, Poonch, Rajouri & Doda	800
Harkat-ul-Jehad e-Islami (HUJI)	Kashmir, Poonch, Rajouri & Doda	350
Lashkar-e-Tayeba (LET)	Kashmir, Poonch, Rajouri & Doda	300
Al Badr	Srinagar	300
AL Barq	Kupwara & Baramulla	60
Al Jehad	Pulwama, Baramulla, Srinagar & Anantnag	50
JKLF	Srinagar, Budgam and Baramulla	60

It is also reported, that the terrorists have highly modern and lethal weapons in their armoury. Their inter-terrorist group linkages have grown. President Bush of USA has laid down first strike strategy, for dealing with the terrorists. This policy broadly says that, if you are convinced that they are going to attack, get them, before they get you. This policy is based on the belief that, no homeland defense, however comprehensive, can stop all conceivable terrorist attacks, whether carried out by the states, with weapons of mass destruction, or by an armed group, with the same capacity. US Defense Secretary said in May 2002 that, USA had a good deal of intelligence from people, who say they believed that Al Quaida men were in Kashmir.

Although low intensity war and widespread terrorism, have been going on for decades, in 2002 only the Government declared its will, to finish cross border terrorism once for all.

Prime Minister Vajpayee addressing a strong massive public rally on 18th April, 2003 in Srinagar, said: "We once again extend our hand of friendship to Pakistan, but the desire ought to be on both sides". The Prime Minister once again extended his hand of friendship, with the condition of reciprocation. It was the first ever rally, ever addressed by our Prime Minister, in the last fifteen years in J&K. In continuation of the offer of Vajpayee, India and Pakistan broke the political ice on 28th April 2003 and moved closer towards a resumption of the long stalled bilateral dialogue when the two Prime Ministers had a telephone conversation.

It was the first direct bilateral political contact at the highest level in more than a year. Mir Zafarullah Khan Jamali, then Prime Minister of Pakistan telephoned Atal Behari Vajpayee and invited him to visit Pakistan. This move was in respons to Mr. Vajpaee's decision during his visit to Srinagar, to extend the hand of friendship to Pakistan. Obviously Pakistan has been, undergrowing pressure from the international community to respond positively to Mr. Vajpayee's initiative. A radical change had appeared in the tone and tenor of Pakistan. India had sent indication that Mr. Vajpayee would be willing to travel to Pakistan to attend a postponed SAARC summit, if the leaders could sign concrete economic agreements.

Mr. Vajpayee, reportedly emphasized the importance of economic cooperation, cultural exchanges and people-to-people contacts between the two countries as well as the importance of reviving civil aviation links. A visit to Pakistan by Mr. Vajpayee was a small price to pay, if Pakistan agreed to end its opposition to normal trade and people to people relations with India. The two prime Ministers agreed to consider these measures as the first step towards restoration of normal bilateral relations. Pakistani Prime Minister Jamali also believed to have affirmed Pakistani opposition to terrorism.

Pakistani Foreign Minister said, "Pakistan is neither sponsoring nor encouraging anyone venturing into the Indian side of Kashmir. It does concede the possibility, of some making it despite vigil." Once bitten twice shy was natural for Indian side, to insist on seeing the affirmations of Pakistani Prime Minister translated into deeds on the ground. A similar commitment by the Pakistani President on January 12, 2002, was honoured more in breach.

Under Anglo-American pressure, Pakistan gave strong verbal commitments to end terrorism. It had the effect of defusing the military tension between the two countries, when the armies of the two countries, had eye ball to eye ball confrontation. Pakistani Foreign Minister, Khurshid Mehmood Kasuri, said on the infiltration issue that Pakistan was ready to appoint foreign observers, including from the U.N. He had named seven countries for consideration by India for 'joint monitoring' of the Line of control. The countries identified were France, Russia, the United kingdom, the United States, China, Saudi Arabia and Iran.

This proposal is not new. It is for the first time Pakistan has actually gone ahead and named the countries whose representatives could form part of the proposed joint panel. India has rejected as 'self-serving and impractical' Pakistan's proposal for international monitors on the issue of cross-border infiltration. Islamabad consistently denied charges. On the contrary, India has been proposing joint patrol of the LoC by forces of India and Pakistan. The offer was repeated by prime Minister A.B. Vajpayee at the Almaty summit in USSR in June 2002. Pakistan rejected the proposal on the plea that it was not feasible, because of the distrust and mistrust between India and Pakistan. It considered the proposal as unworkable. The matters stand there.

The annual report of the Union Ministry of Home Affairs for the year 2002-2003 shows that the chief areas of concern remain terrorism in Jammu and Kashmir and especially the "incremental use of suicide bombers". There were 10 suicidal attacks in 2002 and that 60 to 70 percent of terrorists operating in the State are from outside, "under the direct control of Pak ISI" with local people "playing the role of porters and guides."

In his interaction with an Indian politician, in March 2003, Gen. Musharraf has washed his hands off, of Pakistan sponsoring terrorism in J&K by describing those crossing over as "freelance Jehadis". He also said that the decade-long Afghan war, in the eighties, had given birth to so many of them that it was beyond the control of the State to keep a check on them. He also said that it is worth pondering, whether it was correct to expect a relatively smaller Pakistani force, to seal the porous border, when a larger Indian contingent could not do so. It is not clear whether Pakistani President wants the meance of 'freelance Jehadis' to be collectively dealt with by India and Pakistan or it is a ploy to win international sympathy. India, however, feels that it is Pakistan's game to internationalise the issue and bring in third parties. It is true that India has been faced with terrorism right from its inception. All over the world the mischief makers and discontented groups, with or without the support of rogue Governments, seek the attainment of their cause through barrel of gun. A total of 33,132 persons lost their lives in the war of terrorism both in Punjab and Kashmir, apart from sporadic acts of violence like the Mumbai blasts in March, 1993 which claimed loss of life and injury to hundreds and Coimbtore terrorist bombing in February, 1998, which left fifty dead including 35 men and ten women and two hundred injured in 13 bomb blasts, out of which 11 happened at places, within a twelve kilometer radius. In January, 1998 on the Republic day, the terrorists killed 23 Kashmir Pundits in Wandhama village near Ganderbal. The terrorists repeated their performance of killing almost similar number in Nandimarg in J&K in March, 2003. Other incidents like the attack on Army headquarters, BSF and other units are too numerous to be recounted. We should take Musharaff at his words with a pinch of salt and make the price of terrorism in India so prohibitive that, anybody should think twice before any such act. Army wanted to buy scooter mobiles, which could be used on snow. The number of queries asked were out of the blue and simply absurd. The proposal was sanctioned only after the Defence Minister had ordered the bureaucrats to go and see things for themselves and spend a few weeks with the troops. The uniformed Services, whether Army, BSF or CRPF are too disciplined, to take their grievances to the press. The result is that, bureaucrats sit tight on proposals for ages. In the absence of the equipment the fight against terrorism gets affected adversely.

Vajpayee faced opposition from the hawks in the country for talking to Pakistan. But all over the world, talks had led to solution. The talks will be more fruitful, if they are backed by heavy casualties of the foreign mercenaries, who are operating in our country. Talks with international pressure, massive elimination of the mercenaries and presses of US may persuade Pakistan to see reason and fall in line to actually fight terrorism along with India, instead of exporting it to India.

7
Illegal Migrants

Illegal migrants from Bangladesh have become vote Bank. It is delayed action of throwing out the undesirable aliens. Bangladeshis have treated India as a Dharmshala, wherein they can walking into at will. The result is that there 30 million Bangladeshis, illegally staying in India. We need to strengthen and empower our intelligence and enforcement agencies, apart from fencing 4100 kilometer long border with Bangladesh. What Burke said about the statesmen and pseudo is worth repeating here: "The great difference between the real statesman and pretender is that the one sees into the future, while the other regards only the present and acts on expediency; the other acts on enduring principles and morality...... in the true interests of the country and morality."

Our Government has held that the illegal overstay of Pakistani nationals and Bangladeshis posed a serious threat to the national security. It has asked State Governments to launch special drives to detect and deport them. As many as 11,500 Pakistanis have come into the country with regular papers and passports but have overstayed and nobody knows where they are. It also urged launching of immediate steps to identify, locate and throw them out. The powers of the Central Government to detect and deport illegally residing foreign nationals have been delegated to States. This call has not come a day too soon. In fact, the neglect of this aspect of policing and indifference of the State Governments to this subject is, proverbial and well known.

I was Superintendent of Police, Bidar District in Karnataka from 1965 to 1968. I was keen to leave a personal touch to the policing in the District. As a part of this drill, I would move around in my office and find out as to what was happening. I noticed a couple of middle aged men with burqa clad women in the office, with the officers of the Special Branch. I asked an officer as to who were the visitors. He said that they were Pakistani nationals and had come to register themselves with the Police, as per the law.

The law requires that every foreign national and especially a Pakistani national has to register himself with the local police on arrival. The spirit behind the law was, that all foreigners should leave India, after the expiry of their visas. I did not realise that it was a part of my duty, to throw out the foreigners, who had defied the visa rules. It was for the simple reason that Foreigners Act was taught to us during our training, as a minor act. Since the marks assigned to a plethora of minor acts, including the Foreigner Acts were few, no body at that time and even now bothers much about it and thinks far less of implementing it.

As an SP I felt that if a person has chosen another country as his place of abode, then he better go away after his social visit was complete. I started making inquires about the number of illegals overstaying Pakistani citizens in my District. The figure came as a shock to me. I asked my office as to whether the Government or the IG's office had called any explanation, comments or conveyed its unhappiness, over non-performance of Foreigners Act. I was told that it had never been done and in fact, no District Police Chief had shown any interest in this item. I said it would not do. I launched a drive to throw out the illegal migrants and in a rare gesture Secretary to the Government of Mysore, sent me the following communication. "The Inspector General of Police has brought to the notice of Government that you have been responsible for launching a drive to trace Pak nationals who had evaded leaving India after the expiry of their permits and that you have made untiring and praise-worthy efforts in tracing Pak nationals. I am directed in this connection, to convey to you the appreciation of Government for the excellent work carried out by you, in spite of serious handicaps and difficulties met with in handling such work."

It is true that sometimes, migrants whether illegal or legal come to India, in search of better opportunities of livelihood. Even Indians have been going outside India to Russia, Russian, Western and Baltic countries, as illegal migrants. But unfortunately, it is not so, in the case of people coming from our neighbouring countries. Illegal migrants who have disappeared have done so, with a view to create riots and disturbances in India, at the bidding of Pakistan. It is not a good policy to close your country to any body. But it is the lesser of the two evils, to deny entry to such people, who are going to devastate it. It would be wrong to deny that some of these overstaying Pakistanis are a part of proxy war with India.

Unfortunately, a lot still needs to be done in this direction, like the preparation of a National Register of Indian citizens and issuing to them Multi-Purpose National Identity Cards, which could serve as Ration Card, Passport, Driving License and a credible individual identification system. Everybody knows all members of his family. But as a nation we do not know, who are ours and who are not. The Government has proposed introducing a scheme for National Identity Cards, covering 13 states that is Delhi, UP, Rajasthan, Assam, Jammu and Kashmir, Gujarat, Andhra Pradesh, West Bengal, Tripura, Tamil Nadu, Goa and Pondicherry. The Government has clarified that the National Identity Card would be different from the Voters Identity Card issued by the Election Commission. It needs to be examined as to why can we have one card, for dealing with all the facets of the Government. It will also lead to a lot of economy and create less confusion both for the citizens and the Government. Most illegal migrants from Bangladesh live only in the low cost areas or even slums. They naturally eat into the resources and the jobs meant for our citizens. In an empirical way, we have sympathy with the poor in the world. But our first duty is to our own people and our own citizens. National parties need to evolve a consensus on this issue and not politicise the same for vote bank politics. One way is that, since we cannot control slums, we can consider following Hong Kong model, which has licensed slums, with all the modern facilities. But let not the Government make it obligatory for itself, to provide land to every illegal encroacher of Government land. Most illegal migrants manage to start ghettos or start living in slums and then enlarge their size. Delhi High Court held such a policy as illegal. India has very generous citizenship laws. For instance, in Germany citizenship is linked with nationality and is based on biology. In France, citizenship is linked with nationality and foreigners cannot be citizens, however, their children can apply for citizenship rights and status. It is based on notion of ethnicity and foreigners are not entitled to citizenship rights.

Experts of the Monitoring Committee of the UN Security council, which oversees the implementation of the UNSC Resolution No. 1373, say that despite the freezing/seizure of terrorist funds and other assets worth US $112 million since 9/11, Al-Qaida and its allies in the International Islamic Front still have at their disposal about US $ 300 million. Replenishments continue to flow into their funds. The spate of terrorist incidents since December, 2001, in different parts of the world, including attack on Indian Parliament, Akashdham and Raghunath temples and the sweeping victories of pro-Al-Qaida and pro-Taliban fundamentalists in the recent Pakistan elections show, that the terrorists do not as yet feel any shortage of funds for any of their overt and covert activities. They would not hesitate to use a part of it, through 11500 overstaying Pakistani nationals, who officially entered India, apart from millions of illegal migrants. Any foreign national who overstayed his visa and thus broke the law of the land, must be deported without second thoughts, any political or religious consideration.

Bhutan was a reluctant host, to terrorists groups of North Eastern States of India. They had imposed themselves on that country. On May 17, 2003 Bhutanese Foreign Minister Thinley had announced in Dhaka, that his government had warned that, it would expel ULFA rebels by force, if they refused to withdraw peacefully. Thinley had said that the Bhutan Government had held two meetings with senior ULFA leaders and asked them to fix a date for another meeting, probably the last, to fix a deadline for withdrawal. "We cannot wait indefinitely. We are getting ready to expel them by force if needed. Their (ULFA's) presence is a direct threat to our security and sovereignty". India had, of course been requesting Bhutan to take action against them, so that they do not use that country as a base of terrorism activities in India.

Royal Government of Bhutan served notices on the three militant groups ULFA, NDFB and KLO, on the 13th December, 2003 through the national newspaper Kuensel, saying that it was left with no option but to entrust Royal Bhutan Army, with the duty of removing militants from its soil, in accordance with the decision of the 81st session of National Assembly. After lapse of 48 hours, from the time of issue of notice, The Royal Bhutan Army (RBA) started operations on 15th December, 2003. The crack down was on three insurgent groups - the United Liberation Front of Assam (ULFA), the National Democratic Front of Bodoland (NDFB) and the Kamtapur Liberation Organisation (KLO). These groups were using Bhutanese soil for their subversive activities in the North-East of India, for the 12 years. There were at least 30 to 40 well fortified camps, sheltering over 3000 heavily-armed militants of the three outfits along the entire stretch of southern Bhutan bordering the states of West Bengal, Assam and Arunachal Pradesh. Of these camps 13 of ULFA, 12 of NDFB, and 5 of KLO were dismantled and destroyed. Some terrorist leaders were arrested. It is reported that RBA had arrested some terrorists and more than 160 of them were killed in the flush out operations. Of the dead, 100 belong to the NDFB, 38 to ULFA and 12 to the KLO. The Royal Bhutanese

Army also suffered losses. About 34 personnel were killed and many injured. Bhutanese operation led to the recovery of 500 AK 47 rifles, over 100 Pistols and other sophisticated weapons like anti aircraft guns, 60 mm mortars, Self Loading Rifles besides 150000 rounds of ammunition and 80000 rounds of ammunition for AK Series of Rifles. Bhutan also took action against its own citizens, who were collaborating, aiding and abetting the terrorists. Top ULFA Leaders as well as KLO chief had surrendered, as a result of operations. So much was the pressure of Bhutanese Army action that its top brass had appealed, to the King of Bhutan to call off the operations

It is also a fact that ULFA cadres, some of which are based in Bangladesh had been asked by the Inter Services Intelligence (ISI) of Pakistan, to retaliate and strike targets in India for the operations in Bhutan. ULFA had given a call to the Bhutanese living in North East to leave. It called for a bandh, as a protest against the Bhutanese military action, which flopped. It is also a matter of concern that North Eastern Terrorists had managed to enter Bhutan from Indian States. Obviously there was failure, in checking and preventing the entry of the North Eastern terrorists to Bhutan. West Bengal's Jalpaiguri district has 150km long border with Bhutan. An octogenarian ULFA leader and one of the founder-members of the outfit, Bhimakanta Buragohain, popularly called "Mama" (uncle), who ULFA had said was killed, was presented before media persons along with three others to the Corps Commander on 27th December, 2003. He is the senior most founder member of ULFA; had made an appeal from Army custody to the rank and file of the outfit to lay down arms and hold discussions with the government for a peaceful solution to the problem in Assam. 76 persons, including 45 women and 31 children, were handed over to the State Government. Of these, 37 women owed allegiance to the United Liberation Front of Asom and the rest to the National Democratic Force of Bodoland. The Assam Chief Minister, had said that the State Government would provide amnesty only to militants who surrender by 31st January, 2004.

As a result of the pressure of Royal Bhutanese Army and Indian Army, terrorists ran away from Bhutan. Over 20 new camps of Ulfa and NDFB, anti-India terrorists came up in Bangladesh, especially in the Chittagong, Sylhet, Habibganj and Sherpur areas. While Bangladesh foreign minister Morshed Khan had denied the existence of these camps, the Indian agencies have irrefutable evidence in this regard. Our neighbors continue to harbour terrorists. Action by Bhutan is a majer contribution to fight against terrorism by India. It is the best action by a neighbour, whose population is just Lakh and an army of only 12000. It is not the end of the terrorism. The following groups are still operating in North East, which are, nevertheless, a threat to the unity and integrity of our country:

The Kukis have settled in Myanmar, Manipur and Nagaland. In Myanmar, they are known as the Kuki Chin, In 1987, the Kuki National Organization (KNO) demanded an autonomous state within Myanmar. A similar group, the Kuki National Front (KNF), demanded a "Kukiland," comprising parts of Myanmar and Manipur in India. They are operating in Manipur and Nagaland.

National Socialist Council of Nagaland (NSCN) was founded by one Angami Zapu Phizo, who began his secessionist movement for an independent homeland for the Nagas. NSCN is still active and Government is having talks with it to bring peace to Nagaland. The NSCN based in Nagaland (Muivah faction) demanded Greater Nagaland, a cross-border entity which would comprise parts of Arunachal Pradesh, Nagaland, and Manipur.

All Tripura Tiger Force (ATTF), an insurgent group is most dreaded in Tripura. It carries out ambushes against the Tripura State Rifles. It has established links with the NSCN and the ULFA. ULFA has provided arms to the National Liberation Front of Tripura and the ATTF. In 1986, they established contacts with Kachins in Myanmar to receive arms and arms-training. Subsequently, the ULFA cadre were trained by both factions of the NSCN. From 1990, they have been in touch with Pakistan. Some of its cadres have undergone intensive training, with the Mujahideen under the supervision of ISI agents. Bodo Security Force looted the armouries of central paramilitary forces, including the Central Reserve Police Force and the Border Security Force. It wants a separate Bodoland. Bodo Security Force is allied with the National Socialist Council of Nagaland (NSCN) and the United Liberation Front of Assam (ULFA). It is reportedly linked to the Kachin Independent Army (KIA) of northern Myanmar (Burma), bordering Arunachal Pradesh. Bhutanese December, 2003 operation is not the end of terrorism in the North East.

8

Indo-Pak Relations

India has been facing the proxy war from Pakistan literally from 1947, due to pathological hatred of India. Pakistan has lost no opportunity, to show India down, whether by sponsoring terrorism by the foreign mercenaries or by its own troops, disguised as Jihadis. The first sign of foreign mercenaries' role came to light, when they burnt the Charar-e-Sharief on May 10 1995.

Getting fed up with Pakistan's bleeding India, through the slow poisoning, low intensity war or sponsored terrorism, India naturally administered a strong warning that, this matter had to be finished one way or the other. This warning had woken up the Western World to the danger of India-Pakistan war, which would affect their war against the hidden terrorists and their mastermind Osma Bin Laden, in NWFP. It also woke up the world's super powers to the double standards, that Pakistan was adopting in the fight against terrorist in Kashmir.

To continue its pathological hatred of India, Pakistan was camouflaging its designs behind the smoke screen of Jihadis. Strong diplomatic offensive by India, coupled with the massing of the troops on the border, had the desired effect. Pakistani dictator Pervez Musharaff was forced to do an about turn, on the policies of Pakistan towards terrorism. Military Colonels and Generals are trained, to do Left Turns, Right Turns and About Turns. The General of Pakistan, is doing About Turns on the Talibans in Afghanistan. As Pakistani co-operation against terrorism, had been purchased by dolling out dollars, there was no way for Pakistan, not to listen to His Masters and become His Masters Voice. In a broadcast, supposedly targeted at Pakistan, but with eyes and ears open that his masters would be watching his every move, Musharaff, made the following main points in his speech on, January 12. 2002:

He banned Lashkar-e-Toiba and Jaish-e-Mohammad, Sipah-e-Sahaba, Tehrik-e-Jaffria, Tehrik-e-Nifaz-e-Shariat (Mohammedi). This had earlier been done by USA and it was also the Indian demand that he take action against the terrorists operating against India from his country. He said that no organisation would be allowed to indulge in terrorism in the name of religion. There was no way out for him, except to use these words, as 98% population of Pakistan is Muslim. The rest are Christians and Ahmedias. Ahmedias are Muslims, who are also followers of Islam. But Pakistan regards them as non-Muslims. He also said he will not allow Pakistan's territory to be used for terrorist activities. It means nothing on the ground. He also added that any group found involved in December 13 attack on Indian Parliament and October 1 attack on the Jammu and Kashmir Assembly, would be dealt with severely. He offered fresh dialogue with Atal Behari Vajpayee on Kashmir. He also promised, considering taking appropriate action against non-Pakistanis, wanted by India. He ruled out handing over of any Pakistani wanted by India. He cautioned India against crossing border. He pledged to continue moral, political and diplomatic support to Kashmir cause. He said that all madarsas will have to be registered by March-end 2002 and no new madarsa will be allowed to be opened without Government permission.

Foreign students for admission in madarsas will have to seek permission of Government. Musharaff admitted and said "Madarsas should not be used for spreading religious fundamentalism. It is humiliating for all Muslims that mosques are being used for jihad". Apart from other pressure, the strong anti-terrorism declaration endorsed by the SAARC Summit, could not have been forgotten by the Pakistani dictator. Very appropriately, India had utilised the September 11 events, Ist October attack on J&K Assembly and the December 13, 2001 attack on the Indian Parliament to highlight the external nature of the terrorism, Kashmir has been facing since 1989. It must be said to the credit of the N D A Government, that despite the handicaps of a multi-party government, they were able to project forcefully India's case of a terrorist victim. However, the Western world considers Pakistan's usefulness, as immediate neighbour of Afghanistan, in its war against terrorism in the latter. The war against terrorism does not come cheap. The US Congress has provided more than $60 billion since September, 2001 to combat terrorism at home and abroad and to rebuild from the attacks on New York and Washington. This is more than five times what the United States spent to fight terrorism in the previous one year. Provision for 45 billions dollars is being sanctioned each year.

Incidentally, the British Muslims, reportedly donated over 2 million pounds last year to either the Lashkar-e-Toiba or the Jaish-e Mohammad. British Muslims were Lashkar's second biggest benefactors after the Mirpuri Kashmirs of the Middle East. Lashkar sources in UK also said that while some of the donation was for charity, most of it was used to attack Indian military targets. "We receive millions of pounds from the UK. British Kashmiris are very patriotic. Some mony is for charity but the rest, for attacks against military targets" a Lashkar man told the Telegraph.

The question arose what the future scenario holds, after the declaration of Musharaf on 12 January, 2002 and what will be India's response. The reply has been articulated by the Government, which feels that the words spoken by Mushraff are only words, till they are followed up by deeds. Fortunately, Chinese Prime Minister Zhu Rongji during his visit to India in January, 2002 has said: "Co-operation against terrorism is ... top of the agenda. China and India have agreed to jointly counter this menace". De-escalation will depend on the will of Pakistan, to deliver what it has proclaimed, all over the world. Pakistan has fought four wars with India and came out badly worsted. It is rightly said that those, who do not learn from history are condemned to repeat it. Pakistani General and his Colonels know where they stand, as against India's standing and military might. Both countries need to fight poverty, illiteracy, ill health and many times over to overcome those scourges. If the Pakistani General, has really changed his mindset, it is time for him to show that he has jettisoned his past baggage. He will be judged by his deeds and not his words, by the world and India. India's post-De. 13, 2001 strategy of putting diplomatic and military pressure on Pakistan, is yielding results. The result is that, USA had to tell off Musharaff and clear his stand on terrorism. General, naturally could not say no to his Paymasters, as he, who the piper, calls the tune.

One cannot choose one's neighbours, due to the fact of geography. It is reported that Pakistani army had mobilised its nuclear arsenal against Indian in 1999 during the Kargil war, without the knowledge of the then and now exiled Prime Minister, Nawaz Sheriff. American came to know of it in advance and so the then President Clinton asked Sheriff, if he knew how advanced the threat of nuclear war really was. Did Sheriff know his military was preparing their missiles. Intelligence officer had assessed that the flight times of the missiles fired by the either side would be as little as three minutes and that Pakistani strike on one Indian city Mumbai, would kill 1,500000 to 8,00000 persons. The total killed in the nuclear war can be any number going upto 100 million people. It is reported that the Pakistani Premier was in darkness. First of this myth needs to be blown out. Army no doubt is a strong institution in Pakistani. But it will be naïve to believe, that a Pakistani Chief Executive, whether Prime Minister or President would be so stupid as not to know through his own intelligence sources as to what was happening in the country. Pakistan is the fountain head of terrorism, as admitted by General Aziz, Chief of the General Staff to General Pervez during Kargil war that "The Army controls the Mujahideen tap."

The supreme interests of a country are supreme for it and not for its neighbours or friends. Kashmir has been turned into a major problem for us by Pakistani infiltration. It has been aggravated by the induction of fundamentalist Afghanis, courtesy Pakistan. In the first instance, it is worthwhile to recall that it was the CIA of the United States of America, which encouraged Islamic groups from all over the world to come to Afghanistan. The USA provided $ 3 billion for building up these Islamic groups. USA also accepted Pakistan's demand that it would decide, as to how this money would be spent. An American security expert Mr. Selig Harrison said: "General Zia-ul- Haq spoke to me about expanding Pakistan's sphere of influence to control Afghanistan, then Uzbekistan, and Tajikistan and then Iran and Turkey. The old association between the intelligence agencies continues. The CIA still has close links with ISI. That money and those weapons helped build up the Taliban. The Talibans were not just recruits from Madarsas but drew sustenance from Pakistani. Talibans who made a living out of terrorism, are now the enemy number one of United States of America. The original objective of the CIA was to prepare severe fanatics in Afghanistan, so that they could more fiercely and savagely fight the Soviets. Terrorist ranks in J&K have swelled, after end of America's fight against the Talibans. The present situation has become grim and alarming, with battle hardened militants building their bases within towns and hearly populated villages, besides the city of Srinagar. The estimates of the terrorists vary from 6000 to 10000, with at least 70 per cent being foreign mercenaries, who are using land mines, IED, Rifle Grenades, Rockets and Bombs to launch attack on the security forces. This has resulted in a strange situation, where unwilling people have been forced to live under the shadow of the terrorism. Out of fear, they do not distance themselves from the militants. It is the scare amongst the people even in far-flung areas, which has led to the migration of the minorities from the valley to the comparatively safe areas.

It will be wrong, to expect anything else from Pakistan, except to foment trouble in Kashmir in particular and India in general. It is wrong either to hold Pakistan responsible for the present situation or expect it to help us. Jammu and Kashmir is a part and parcel of India and it is our problem there. It is for us, to bleed Pakistan, as it is doing to us. Militants have changed their strategy and targeting only the security forces and managing to inflict heavy causalities.

Unilateral cease fire is declared by winner like China in 1962 or negotiated on intervention. Hiter overrule Goebbles for cease-fire and was got overpowered, ending the Second World War. The Vietnamese guerrillas never declared unilateral cease-fire, as they were winning. The war stopped there, only after the Americans had pulled out. Causalities in Kargil war were only a fraction of what security forces have lost in J&K during the fight against terrorism. The terrorists had issued a warning in March, 2001 through the local newspapers, asking the contractors, working for the Military Engineering Service and Army Service Corps to stop working for the army.

In the reply to the appeal of the contractors, the terrorists said that the contractors, should seek alternative avenues of livelihood, failing which they would be treated as enemies of Islam and dealt with accordingly. Oral condemnation by the international community or the visiting Assistant Secretary of State, Christina Rocca calling any activity barbaric, inhuman, ignominious and fanatical, does not affect the health of the terrorists. Writs of the terrorists backed by the gun, naturally lead to the eclipse and almost rejection of the moderates and intellectuals, who want the terrorists to see the reason. The terrorists by their propaganda and killings, have been able to turn the protagonists of peace, into villains. Margret Thatcher used to say that publicity is the oxygen of terrorism. In fact that oxygen is being liberally extended to the terrorists by the media and especially the local press. An impression has been given that all Human Rights belong to the terrorists and not to their innocent victims. A stage has reached, where as if every terrorist killed in encounter is portrayed either as a martyr or an innocent bystander. Diplomacy and aide memoirs do not solve problem of cross terrorism. Those who use guns, understand the languagc of guns only whether a Hitler or the home grown terrorists of Punjab, North East or Jammu and Kashmir. It looks now, that peace will also come from the barrel of used guns and not, guns used by Security Forces which outnumbered guns with terrorists in Punjab ending the menace for ever.

After September 11, 2001 assault on WTC towers in New York, 13th December, 2001 attack on Indian Parliament and the promulgation of the Prevention of Terrorism Ordinance (POTO) in our country, there has been a great deal of discussion, as well as, action to curb terrorism. Every country has its objective and reasons for fighting the terrorism. In the case of the USA, according to President Bush, it is to "bring (Al-Qaida) to justice". This objective suits us. It is in accordance with our policy to eliminate terrorism and terrorists from Indian soil. Legal Pundits quibble over the difficulty of clear legal definition. President Bush described the WTC attacks both as a "criminal act" and as an "act of war". POTO by definition recognizes 'terrorism' as a crime and it includes "overthrowing the government established by law."

The legal luminaries feel that there is fundamental difference between a crime and an act of war. A crime is investigated and finally adjudicated by the judiciary. In a war, the perpetater is shot dead or captured for trial by military court. These two systems operate on different premises. But whatever it is, terrorism aims to kill and intimidate. In Kashmire, the terrorists are clearly operating on communal lines, with the sole objective of ethnic cleansing of Hindus and Sikhs, who have almost vacated the valley under the fear of the gun.

There is no doubt that Pakistan has been masterminding terrorism in J&K as well as in the rest of India, with a view to annex Kashmir being a Muslim majority state. When India threatened to fight this proxy war and a thousands cuts strategy of Indian polity by a conventional war, Pakistan brandished nuclear weapons. Its representative to the United Nations stated that Pakistan would resort to nuclear weapons, even in a conventional war with India. U.K. pressure forced Pakistan to change its track. Americans as well as other world leaders have put pressure on Musharaff to do end, what he had promised on 12th January 2002, to end the cross border terrorism. India has made it clear that a dialogue with Pakistan will succeed if the terrorist infiltration across the valley is stopped. Pakistan has been clearly told by its mentors and its masters that it better take steps to permanently end infiltration across the Line of Control and disband and dismantle its terrorist training camps. India knows it very well that Pakistan is capable of reneging on its commitment to keep the terrorist tap off.

Prime Minister, Shri Vajpayee refused to meet Pakistan President at a summit in June 2002 in Kazakhstan nor did he indulge in any social pleasantries with him though the two were sitting only a few feet apart. Belief in Pakistan's right over Kashmir runs in the Pakistani blood, as proclaimed by Mushraff. For the Pakistani rulers this is one way to show their patriotism. This approach has been accompanied with anti India stance by the Pakistani rulers over fifty years of history. The terrorists operating in Kashmir are hit men, thugs and mercenaries hired to cause holocaust in the valley and kill the innocents both Hindus and Muslims. There is no doubt that Musharaff is their accomplice.

A release of classified documents of the British Government reveals to the delight of India, that the then US Secretary of State, George Marshall, was of the view that the accession of J&K to India was final. It was unchallengeable and the issue was muddied by the rogue British Minister of commonwealth Relations, Philip Noel Baker, who defied his own Prime Minister and British Cabinet to favour Pakistan. We should be clear on one thing that as a Nation, we should not negotiate with terrorists, who are criminals and guilty of the most heinous crimes. Terrosim is a disease, which needs to be removed from the societies. War many times is which would have been only the continuation and culmination of terrorism by other means. The danger of war is still there as it is confirmed that a number of Al Qaida operatives have entered Pakistan occupied Kashmir as well as the rest of Pakistan. They are being provided shelter and assistance by the Lashker-e-Toiba and other terrorists groups, which were banned by Musharaff.

He has pleaded with the USA, that he could not be held responsible for every Jihadi in Pakistan. He has also claimed, mistakenly that "Heightened international concerns of a nuclear conflict in South Asia and the hesitation, frustration and inability of India to attack Pakistan or conduct a so called limited war, bear ample testimony to the fact that strategic balance exists in South Asia and that Pakistan's conventional and nuclear capability together deter aggression". He conveniently forgot to add that he has almost abjectly surrendered to the Indian pressure and the international demands to stop giving aid and assistance to the terrorists in cash and kind. For the first time, the world has started saying whatever is happening in J&K is not a freedom struggle but terrorism. It is strange that on the one hand Pakistan professes to close all the terrorists camps and stop all cross border infiltrations and on the other hand he goes on trumpting that he will give only moral and diplomatic support to the cause of the terrorists, killing innocents in Kashmir. It is either a case of mental block or mental breakdown, when the Pakistani dictator talks in double language. Because of ditching the Talibans, he does not want to ditch the terrorists in Kashmir. May be he cannot control the rogue elements in the ISI, Army or in his Government. Musharaff claims that has banned infiltrations, but he has not disbanded the Jihadi groups, as he looks upon them not only as proxies but also as strategic assets in case of war with India. Pakistan has been supporting cross border terrorism with training, men and material for over 15 years. It is rightly difficult for India to believe that Pakistani leopard has changed his skin. We cannot afford to let off our guard. A dwarf (Pakistan) is small, even if he stands on a mountain peak. A colossus (India) keeps its dignity and height, even if he stands in a well.

General Musharaf's bluff is nothing new to India, that in the event of a war in 2002, he would have used the nuclear weapons against India. He, as usual, had denied it and said he was misquoted. Musharaf is the fourth Army Colonel or General, who by sheer force, threw out the democratically elected Government of Nawaz Sheriff, in October, 2000. It was not for love of Pakistan, but to save his job, from which he had been dismissed in absentia.

Smarting under the successive defeats by India, Pakistan has always nursed ambition to it cow down, both in military might and in international forums. Nuclearisation of Pakistan is the only step in that direction. The Indian missile programme for self defence, is not only transparent but also by and large is indigenous. India's nuclear doctrine clearly lays down of no first use but is also emphasis building and maintaining a minimum deterrent. It also warns adverturists that nuclear retaliation to the first strike will be massive and designed to inflict unacceptable damage. Unlike the countries ruled by Colonels, so far as India is concerned, nuclear retaliatory attacks can only be authorised my mature civilian political leadership, through the nuclear command authority. Both India and Pakistan have a ballistic missile capability to hit each others targets. India announced its indigenous integrated guided missile development programme in 1984. Pakistan suddenly claimed possession of ballistic missiles in 1989. It will be interesting to compare Indian and Pakistani missile programmes as reported in a USA publication.

Missiles	Payload (kg)	Max Rage (km)
India		
Prithvi-I	1000	150
Prithvi-II	500 – 750	250
Prithvi-III	500 – 750	350
Agni-IA	1000	700
Agni-I	1000	1500
Agni-II	1000	2000
Agni-III	1000	5000
Pakistan		
Hatf-I	500	80
Hatf-IA	500	100
Hatf-II (M-11)	500	300
Haft-III	500	600
Ghauri I (Nodong I)	600	1000
Ghauri II (Nodong II)	700	1500
Shaheen-I	1000	700
	1000	2000

All above missiles can deliver nuclear warheads. Pakistan has conducted the third test of its Ghauri missile, primarily for the benefit of its domestic audience. Pakistan's programme is dependent on China and North Korea. All ballistic missiles with solid propellant have come from China, while those with liquid propellant owe their existence to the North Korean Nodong missile. In a fusion of interests, Pakistan provided North Korea, with many of the designs, for gas centrifuges and much of the machinery, it needed, to make highly enriched uranium, for nuclear weapons project.

The Central Intelligence Agency told members of US Congress that North Korea's uranium enrichment programme, which it discovered only in the summer of 2001, will produce enough material to produce weapons in two to three years. Previously the CIA had estimated, that North Korea probably extracted enough plutonium from a nuclear reactor to build one or two weapons. It halted in 1994 in a confrontation with the United States. It is strange that one of the world's poorest and most isolated nation puts together its new and complex uranium project. The relationship between North Korea and Pakistan is much deeper and more dangerous than the United States and India ever suspected.

Even after Gen. Musharraf sided with the United States in ousting the Taliban and hunting down Al Qaida leaders, Pakistan continued its murky relationship with the North Korean military. It is a partnership, involving an insecure Islamic Pakistan and a failing poor Communist country, both in need of each other.

Pakistan in its desperate desire to counter India's superior military force and due to years of American-imposed sanctions, turned to North Korea. As North Korea, was increasingly cut off, from Russia and China, it tried to develop nuclear weapons, based on uranium. Incidentally North Korea has plentiful supplies of Uranium. The US had put tremendous diplomatic pressure on North Korea, to abandon the project and also cut off oil supplies to the country. USA has never publicly discussed the role of Pakistan or North Korea in nuclearisation. The Bush administration in its wisdom, has decided, at least by implication, that Pakistan's cooperation in the search for Al Qaida is so critical, that it better ignore the federal statues that require President Bush to impose stiff economic penalties on any country, involved in nuclear proliferation or alternatively, to issue a public waiver of those penalties, in the interest of national security. Mr Bush earlier removed sanction and penalties that were imposed on Pakistan, after it set off a series of nuclear tests in 1998.

Any move, which will bring two neighbours, bound by history and geography together and reduce tension between the two nuclear powers, which have been having wars and other border skirmishes, is welcome. The fact remains, that we do not know, what will end Pakistan's pathological hatred of India. Pakistan respects only those nations which are economically and militarily stronger than it. The only way to deal with Pakistan is to be stronger than it in all ways, which we are, in any case as at present. It is equally important to remember that it is the force and money power, which rules the world. Power will come to us, if we are determined to be powerful. While we should stick to the doctrine of no first use, let us not be caught unaware by a wily General. We should not allow the bluff of the

Pakistani General to get better of us. In the view of Kim Jong Il of North Korea, the difference between North Korea and Iraq is that Saddam does not have nuclear power and what is happening to him is due to absence of nuclear power.

The game of mouse and cat goes on between the Nations. India and Pakistan have fought four wars. But there is an agreement between them to exchange nuclear information, which they have been doing periodically. It is a part of a 10-year-old agreement between the two nations. It binds them, to share information on nuclear facilities. Delhi and Islamabad have been following the agreement for the last 10 years. The agreement was signed in 1988. It came into effect in 1991. These exchanges of information take place through diplomatic channels. The information includes, the information about the old and new installations and facilities. Under the agreement of the prohibition of attack, between India Pakistan, the two countries are supposed to inform each other on January 1 of every calendar year of their nuclear installations and facilities. The latest exchange of information was on 1st January, 2006?

The two neighbours have been implementing the agreement about exchanging information, even as their relations pass through a period of grave turmoil. Both the countries have carried out nuclear tests in the last decade. After Indian tested a nuclear device at Pokhran, Pakistan conducted similar tests, in the Chagai Hills. There has been no other interaction, with each other since the Kargil crisis. It is because of Pakistan's supporting terrorism and encouraging disruptionists in India. It is futile to hold a dialogue with military government in Islamabad to resolve impending issues, including Kashmir. Kashmir is at the cross-roads and Pakistan's mindset is well known. Hence India feels that it is futile and waste of time, efforts and labour to talk to somebody, who wants only a solution acceptable to it. There is no problem in talking and listening to anybody as the alienation of a people begins when they start feeling that the government is not interested in listening to their problems. A solution to the vexed Kashmir problem is possible only through dialogue and discussion. Some good can come out only of free expression of views.

9
Unworsted Pushtuns

War is cruel reality. It brings devastation and misery, after the dust has settled down. The war on the terrorists, disguised as Talibans (or students) in Afghanistan, would have been a distant dream but for the September 11, 2001, attack and demolition of the twin towers of World Trade Centre in New York. It was the most dare devil scheme, to send a signal to USA, that it might consider itself, world's only superpower, after the literal demise of USSR, yet there were people, who could find chinks, in its amour and use its armoury against it. Naturally, USA looked upon the September 11 incident, as a slap on its face. It was the shaken to the reality, as the saying goes in Punjab and Hindi, *Tera Joota Tera Sirr* I will use your shoe to thrash you, on your head). The needle of suspicion was on Osma Bin Laden, a Saudi based in Wazirstan in whom CIA had reared through Pakistan and funded with millions of dollars in Afghanistan, to throw out the Russians from there. The exact figure on the Afghan war is not known, but with weapons and money spent in buying loyalties the figure would have crossed $ 3 billion.

"It is pretty inexpensive" said Steven Kosiak, an expert on military spending form the Centre for Strategic and Budgetary Assessments, noting the Gulf War cost more then 60 billion dollars while the Kosova operation against Serbia which included 78 days of bombing raids stood at around three billion.

One of the biggest outlays in Afghanistan – 634 million dollars was for the deployment of extra ships and some 400 planes, to the region around Afghanistan. The cost of ammunition and bombs, used against Taliban targets and al-Qaida hideouts was around 185 million dollars in October, 2002 alone. The price of bombs varied greatly. A conventional one-ton bomb cost 2,500 dollars, a CBU-89 cluster bomb would cost 50,000 dollars. A Cruise missile fired form ships or planes, can cost anything between one and two million dollars each. Keeping planes in the air is also expensive and variable ranging between 5,000 dollars an hour for an F-18 fighter but 13,700 dollars for the B-2 stealth bomber, which had flown from mainland United States to drop bombs on Afghanistan.

USA feels that Afghanistan operation was modest in many ways than either of those wars, certainly less than the Gulf War. The US warplanes launched some 90,000 sorties against Iraq during the Gulf War, compared to just 2,000 in Afghanistan during the operation's first month. In any conflict, there are a lot of hidden costs, so the above figures may not be taken as authentic to the last cent. USA did succeed in vanquishing and dethroning its erstwhile cronies Talibans, by its own might and with the active assistance of perennial turn coat, called Pakistan. After the withdrawal, USA had left the battered, bruised, distressed and shattered Afghanistan in the hands of the Afghans faithful to it. In the Senate Committee hearing the following observations were made by the Senators and other witnesses on 19th June 2003. "The reconstruction efforts have quite a way to go before the goal of a peaceful Afghanistan is realized. Concerns about persistent insecurity and a slow political and economic reconstruction process are prevalent throughout Afghanistan, Despite the military success in Afghanistan peace remains clusive and a senator would concern that the USA is not adequately focusing on nation building. "AL-Qaeda and Taliban remnants, appear to be reconstituting themselves, mounting a concerted effort to destabilize the government, impede reconstruction, and terrorize the population in the hopes of making Afghanistan ungovernable until the Unites States gets tired and departs."

Another observation was that, democracy will be possible only when warlords realize that their continued relevance, lies not with their armies but with the new emerging democratic system in Afghanistan. Afghanistan's new administration under Hamid Karzai has lost the initiative. The drift in U.S. Afghan policy must first be resolved in Washington. A new reconstruction push to increase security is essential. for blending security and development. The current constitutional drafting process is,secretive and apparently strongly influences by Islamist hardliners; there is little or no public input and there are reports about intimidation of democracy advocates and political reformers.

The U.S. has committed to spend over $2. billion [$2,000 million] in assistance to the people of Afghanistan since 2001. In March 2003, the European Commission announced a Euro 400 million package of reconstruction support for Afghanistan for 2003-04, concentrating on rural development and food security, economic infrastructure, public sector reform, and healthcare.

The United States also with assistance from France and other is trying to train and equip a new Afghan national Army. It is a tall order, as the local War Lords are fiercely independent and barely recognise the Government in Kabul. India has already pledged $100 million aid and gifted aircrafts and buses to that country. The highlights of progress made in specific fields of reconstruction, which barely touch the fringe of the problem are:

Reopening Rabia Balkhi Women's Hospital in Kabul, and Vaccination of 4.3 million children has been done against measles and 700,000 cases of malaria have been treated. The Other urgent requirement of Afghanistan are revitalization of the polio eradication programs surveillance system; Completing the rebuilding of 72 hospitals, clinics and women's healthcare centers; building of repairing 550 health of care centers. In the field or Education 1,000 schools need to be rebuilt repaired, as well as training 30,000 teachers to man them, printing of 15 million textbooks for 2.9 million students, 30 percent of whom are girls.

Since the fall of Talibans, more than 2.2 million Afghan refugees and 600,000 Internally Displaced Persons, have returned home. A lot of funds and a vast infrastructure, are required to rehabilitate them. In fact, a battered and forgotten Afghanistan, with next to nothing in economic and military power, is facing unending internal strife.

It is a strange world where, first one country first goes, attacks another, destroys it and them as a kind of reparation or to salve its consciences, helps in its coming up again. Incidentally the interest in Afghanistan has been overtaken by world's interest in Iraq. The interest of USA, whose defence budget for the year 2003-2004 was $ 369 billion, has shifted from Afghanistan to Iraq, where it reportedly spent $20 billions on war in 2003. A friendly Iraq can be a reliable source of oil, which is needed by the Western world. Moreover, the money realized by the sale of oil, can offset the reconstruction cost and used for giving of contracts to companies back home in USA. It will naturally lead to more job generation and development of American economy. In other words, Iraqis will pay for the reconstruction through the sale of oil.

Regrettably, Afghanistan has no such attraction and has ceased to be relevant to USA, after the break up of the Soviet Union. After sometime, the aid to Afghanistan, pouring in torrents, would become a trickle and then dry up. It would be a repetition of the raids of Ahmed Shah Abadali on India, who invaded it 15 times and only when he needed wealth from India. Modern Abdalis camouflage their designs, in high sounding moral language, to show that what they did by attacking the other countries was a favor and the affected country should be grateful. There is literally no defence against the mighty and the powerful, except what generosity and individual or a country chooses, to show or bestow upon its victim or victims. Whatever rich nations or not so rich, neighbours of Afghanistan may do, ultimately Afghanistan has to rise itself and build it up. It must be united in its resolve behind the slogan. Afghanistan first. The Afghan story is a lesson for us that, it is only by being united and peaceful that we can progress.

USA has been cognisant of the terrorists activities almost from the time they are planned, anywhere in the world. US Department of State in its 1993 edition of Patterns of Global Terrorism said that "Muslim militants from around the world received training in Afghanistan's eastern and northern provinces. Members of Egyptian, Algerian and Kashmiri militant organizations were among those who have received training there.

A rather yet frightening side effect of the Afghan has been the CIA concern over the post-war whereabouts of the 1,000-odd shoulder-fired, highly lethal Stinger surface-to-air missiles that the Americans supplied to the Mujahideen via Pakistan. They were handy, as the Mujahideen had brought down hundreds of Soviet aircraft with them. It is their use, which had changed the course of the war to their advantage. After the Russians had been forced to leave Afghanistan, the Stingers and all other weapons pumped into Afghanistan were there for the picking. Who would need or pick them up but an assortment of terrorists and terrorist nation-states. The CIA in trying to retrieve the Stringers, had to spend in the process $65 million from secret service funds. It is double the amount that it had originally spent on them. In spite of the retrieval efforts, several Stringers have passed into the hands of not only governments but other terrorist organizations in Iran, Qatar, North Korea, Tajikistan and Kashmir. It is apart from Pakistan, which has pocketed quite a few of them, for possible use against India. The Stinger is an infra red, heat-seeking missile. It is capable of locking on to and engaging even high-speed aircraft and can play havoc in the hands of terrorists operating against India.

Robert Oakley, former US ambassador to Pakistan, person in charge of the US proxy war in Afghanistan, admitted that while the Vietnam war was closely supervised and directed by the US, the Mujahideen and Pakistan were left well alone, without any accountability or interference. Chris Smith of the Centre for Defence

Studies, London, says that "The logic of this laissez-faire policy was completely unsuited to the culture and history of the region, notorious for corruption, gun culture and smuggling." Could the US in such a situation absolve itself entirely of blame, for the terrorism faced by India?

The Afghan War has turned Pakistan into a pivot of international terrorism, directed not only at India and West Asia but various other parts of the world including the US, Russia, Europe and even distant Philippines. The Philippine government had already openly accused Pakistani terrorists of plotting to kill President Fidel Ramos and even Late Pope John Paul.

Pakistan has many employed Mujahideen for creating problems for India. Former Prime Minister Benazir Bhutto complained that it was America's sponsorship of terrorism in Afghanistan that brought weapons, drugs and militancy to Karachi. She added, 'The entire West landed over here and helped create holy warriors, whose job was to go into Afghanistan and fight the holy war. When the war ended, the West packed its bags and left countries like Pakistan, Egypt and Algeria to pick up the pieces and deal by themselves with the warriors they trained, who wanted new wars to fight' (The Hindustan Times, 1 February 1994).

Pakistan has been transformed into a massive arms bazaar, with thriving shopping centers at Dara Adamkhel, Landikotal and Miram Shah.. You can ask for any weapon there and if you pay the price, it is yours. A mine stick will cost ten rupees. A grenade or a rocket for a mere two hundred and fifty rupees and a Kalashnokov for eleven thousand rupees is available. A former ISI head told the New Year Times that the ISI had access to three million Kalashnikovs, packed and greased. Add to them the rockets and the mines, the Stingers and the blowpipes, the mortars and the LMGs and a vast mixture of other weapons. So many weapons constitute a formidable arsenal, under the command of the ISI. This has naturally produced a promiscuous gun culture in Pakistan and has affected India. India's Home Minister clearly hit the nail on the head by mentioning about the Pakistan's "Terrorist-Promoting Activities."

10

Not a Verdant Vietnsam

People leave their homes and countries in search of greener pastures elsewhere. Search for Eldorado or hidden treasures, has gone on for generations in all nations. It was Columbus, who sailed in search of India and ended up discovering America. It is the same search, which has made 20 million people of Indian origin, NRIs in 107 countries of the world. Sagas are replete, with stories as to the number of people, cheated and lured with attractive pay packages abroad and abandoned to die either on the high seas or end up in prisons, as happened with 281 Punjabi Youths in 1997 and also this year. There is nothing new or strange about people seeking fortunes abroad. More than the population of UAE and Kuwait, is the number of Indians working number of Indians working it is equally true in many other Middle East Countries. The natives of affluent and well off countries, use the people of Indian origin for the jobs, they are reluctant to do or are not equipped or trained to do, or are unwilling to do. Iraq which has been the scene of a bloody war and has led to the toppling and incarceration of Seddam Hussein, is almost in a state of anarchy. Various Iraqi groups are making their presence felt, by daily car bombing, killing or attack on the foreign soldiers and other foreigners. So far as India is concerned, despite the pressure, it has neither supported American presence in Iraq, nor it has in any way approved of the American action in toppling the former Iraqi regime, headed by Seddam Hussein.

On 21st July, 2004, seven truck drivers, which included three Indians, apart from Egyptian and Kenyan working for a Kuwaiti based company, were kidnapped by a little known group from Iraq, which demand that the company stop aiding and working for Americans and pull out of Iraq. The Iraqi group also asserted that if their demands are not met, they would start beheading the kidnapped persons intermittently. The kin of the kidnapped Indians had demanded, that Government should intervene, to save their lives. It is a legitimate demand, as in a democracy, it is the duty of the country, to intercede on behalf and in the interests of its citizens. Of course, anybody in the private sector, could say that the persons working abroad, go at their own risk and cost and it is none of its business to intercede on their behalf. The fact remains, that whatever may be the public demand or the demands of the relatives of the unfortunate victims or even of the kidnappers, India has little or no leverage in the matter, except to request the Americans, for help as they are the effective rulers of that country. Even the American writ runs, only in a few parts of Iraq. Americans themselves have been proved wrong that Iraq under Seddam Hussein had amassed Weapons of Mass Destruction and was a threat to the world peace. The Chief of the Central Agency of USA had to leave under embarrassment dishonor for having fed inaccurate intelligence to the President of the United States.

The White House itself has acknowledged that the USA President was relying on incomplete and perhaps, inaccurate information from American intelligence agencies when he declared, in his State of the Union speech, that Seddam Hussein had tried to purchase uranium from Africa. This statement undercuts one of the key pieces of evidence that the USA President and his aides had cited to back their claims made prior to launching an attack against Iraq in March, 2003 that Hussein was reconstituting his nuclear weapons programme.

Those claims added urgency to the White House case that military action to depose Hussein needed to be taken quickly and could not await further inspections of the country or additional resolutions at the United Nations. Despite having captured Seddam Hussein, America's No.1 enemy, it is obvious to the meanest intelligence, that the war on Iraq, not only brought privation and sufferings to the millions of Iraqis, has itself cost over $ 229 billion till 2003. One result of America's war with Iraq in 2003 is that the United States President has asked, on 2nd August, 2004 for the creation of a National Intelligence Director, who will be appointed by the President with the advice and consent of the Senate and will hold office at the pleasure of the President. He will serve as the President's Principal Intelligence Advisor and will oversee and co-ordinate the foreign and domestic activities of the intelligence communities. However, CIA will be managed by a separate Director. The American President, in the same message, also asked for creation of a new counter terrorism centre, which will co-ordinate and monitor, counter-terrorism plans and activate of all government agencies and departments, "to ensure effective joint action and that American efforts are unified in priority and purpose". America has spent more on wars than in helping others in alleviating poverty, disease and suffering as the following figures of American expenditure on several wars will show:

War	*Cost ($ billion)*
World War II	4,530
Vietnam War	826
World War I	555
Korean War:	385
Desert Storm	86
(In defence of Kuwait)	
Gulf War (2003-2004)	229 (Total including the staff cost)

The United States has a history of trying to chase red herrings, which quite often have proved to be ineffective and counter productive. In the recent years, it suspected Al Qaida and Osma Bin Laden, for having caused devastation in USA on September 11, 2001. Afghanistan was ravaged and when American found the going tough, they quietly handed over the power to selected Afghani leaders and withdrew. Net result, is chaos and worse than the situation, under Talibans, according to many observers of Afghanistan. Of course, Americans salve their conscience, by throwing a few millions dollars, here and there, like the pea nuts thrown to the monkeys, to make them keep quiet. Not the same story has been repeated in Iraq. I am no supporter of any dictator, least of all of Seddam Hussein, who was ruthless and who had his own territorial ambitions on the neighbouring countries like Kuwait. But it must be mentioned, that he generated a kind of National Pride in most Iraqis, which enabled them to withstand sanctions for any trade or other dealings with the rest of the world, for nearly a decade.

Before the Iraq war, which commenced on 20th March, 2003, US President had said "Iraqi dictator has been fooling the UN inspectors and could join hands with terrorists to attack America and never leave a fingerprint behind...Saddam Hussein has terrorised his own people... He is a danger not only to countries in the region, but... because of Al Qaida connections, his history, he's a danger to the American people... We've got to deal with him before it is too late... The risks of assuming the best from, Saddam Hussein, it's just not a risk worth taking". No war proceeds exactly as the best thought out and best laid plans wish it. No side tells the truth in war. Iraq War which the USA and UK expected to finish quickly, is going on to its 3rd year. It shows no signs of any victorious conclusion which the coalition forced had anticipated. As in 1991, the war started on 20th March also began with the bombing of Baghdad and other targets. The 1991 air action lasted more than 40 days, with just the last two days reserved for action on the ground. In 1991 the Americans had virtually the entire world behind them, as many felt all over the world, that Iraq had unjustifiably attacked Kuwait with a view to annexe it. This time they cannot count on many allies. Most countries, including the UK and USA citizens apart from the Europeans have sniggered at the war. While the Indian Government due to its own compulsions, has not formally criticised American action, the legal luminaries of India have said: "After failing to secure the second UN resolution to justify the use of military force on Iraq, the US and the British government have unilaterally attacked a sovereign country, after disarming and debilitating it with 12 years of comprehensive economic sanctions". Former British Foreign Secretary Robin Cook who resigned from the Government on this issue says: "I have already my fill of this bloody and unjust war... I want our troops home and want them home before more of them are killed."

A vast majority of Muslim population all over the world disapproves of the war. Even in India, Darul Ulooom, Deoband, one of the oldest and most prestigious religious schools of Sunni Muslims around the world, has reissued a Fatwa or a diktat asking Indians in general and Indian Muslims in particular to boycott consumer products of American and British companies in protest against the US led attack on Iraq. Earlier, the same institution had issued a similar Fatwa against US Companies during the American attack on Afghanistan. Pushed to the wall, suicide attack is the latest weapon that Iraqs are using. Iraq on 30th of March 2003, promised more suicide attacks against US and British Forces. This complicated the coalition forces drive towards Baghdad. Iraq was determined to use all means for resisting the attack.

In 1991, a clear war objective was to evict Iraqi forces from Kuwait. The Iraqi territory was bombed, only to humble its military machine and force it to withdraw its army from Kuwait. The war aim of 2003 is a mix of eviction of Saddam Hussein, restoration of democracy in Iraq and to destroy the Weapons of Mass Destruction, which incidentally are still to be discovered. America has already committed a huge ground force of about 2,00,000 personnel. US army has not seen any major action since the infamous Vietnam war. Its special ground forces are still scouting the hills and caves of Afghanistan, in search of Talibans and their chief, Osama bin Laden.

American Army had earned the nickname of a Christmas Pudding Army. During Vietnam war, some Americans had reportedly refused to fight unless Christmas puddings were airdropped. In Afghanistan, they are branded as the mineral water army, as they are suspicious of the local water and carry heavy water loads with them. It is much worse in Iraq, where even ordinarily water is difficult to obtain, what to talk of mineral water. With almost woeful lack of intelligence, the coalition forces have been raining bombs and missile on Iraq. A cruise missile costs between $ 65000 to $70000 or in Indian Rupees, it costs between 38 to 50 lakh. A shower of 1000 missiles a day means Rs. 500 crore burnt in a day. The target was to decapitate Iraqi leadership. The job of American President is threatened by his own countrymen, who all over the United States, whether it is Chicago or New York, are opposing the war in no uncertain terms. Every body worships a hero and American President, might have started the war for good reasons to end terrorism, is no more considered a sage leader. There is a huge credibility gap between American protestations and deeds on the ground. A prolonged war is only adding to his unpopularity. With more and more coffins of dead Americans arriving from Iraq, the hue and cry against the war would reach a new crescendo. This number may increase with the reported 4000 Arabs joining the fray as suicide commandos on behalf of Iraq.

With the hit and run tactics, US bombs would be chasing an elusive enemy. Iraq war has led to the booming of terrorists or Jihadi factories in our neighbourhood Pakistan. According to the experts, their number stands at over 2 lakh, leading to a swelling in their ranks due to Iraqi war. Muslims all over the world, have called the war with Americans as Jihadi. More than 40 Jihadi publications have come up in Pakistan including a Magazine called 'Allah's Army'. A Jihadi newspaper called 'Islam' in Pakistan, is reportedly the second largest selling newspaper. The main target of the Jihadis would be India and more specifically to accelerate proxy war in Kashmir.

Incidentally, neither Iraq, nor Saddam Hussein, for which many Indians are shedding tears or beating their breasts, had ever said a word against terrorism or proxy was launched by Pakistan trained and sponsored Jihadis against India. It is more important to us, as to what happens to us, than what happens in Timbuktu or in some other country of a dictator. Seddam Hussein was or is no angel or protector of Indian interests. Though we do not like wars anywhere in the world, there is nothing we can do about what happens in Iraq. We are member of NAM.

Iraq war, which the USA and UK expected to finish in a few days took twenty days to end. Baghdad airport fell to the American Forces and later capture of Baghdad was too easy, with hardly any sign of much touted Republican Guards. Some people rejoiced the fall of Saddam Hussein by pulling down his statues and later looting his palaces, the houses of his close aides and Government offices. The victory, the coalition thought probable, came sooner than expected. The war had ended in less than four weeks. Like in 1991, the enemy was Seddam Hussein.

Pushed to the wall, a few suicide attacks were resorted to by some members of the Iraqi forces, with a promise of more suicide attacks against US and British Forces. Iraqis determination to fight or resist the invaders with all their might, daily proclaimed to the world, ended as a verbal blast.

Incidentally, Seddam Hussein had been alternating to USA both as its tactical ally, an evil or a tyrant, depending upon how he served US interests. In 1980s, when Iran's spiritual leader, Ayatollah Khomeini was America's enemy, it suited USA to finance Seddam Hussein to foil Iranian expansionism. The American explanation is that you have to adapt your policies to the nature of the threat. In many cases like that of Osama Bin Laden, the American policies have demonised its erstwhile friends and allies. Until 1990, before Iraq invaded Kuwait, hefty US Agricultural loan guarantees and trade credits flowed to Iraq, despite the evidence of severe human rights abuses. The President Bush senior had signed a waiver on grounds of National Interests in January, 1990 to override a Congressional Block, on trade credits to Iraq, that lawmakers imposed after Seddam used poison gas against Iraqi Kurds. Causality wise, fire power wise and military might wise, it was an unequal battle.

After Seddam was toppled, reconstruction work started in Iraq. The US House of Representatives passed a resolution on 4th April, 2003 excluding France, Germany, Russia, and Syria, from any post war reconstruction contracts, as they had opposed the war. This measure even barred the access by four countries to information on the reconstruction bids. The US Senate voted $ 78.7 billion for the Iraq war and related needs. The French Prime Minister Jean Pierre Raffarin said on 3rd April, 2003: "The Americans made a triple mistake; first of all a moral mistake and I think, we have to say this; there was an alternative to war. We could have disarmed Iraq differently...Also they made a political mistake, because we know very well the difficulties of this region... It is a serious political error to start trouble in this region. And then, there is a strategic mistake that, today one country can lead the world". The US, where possible, has been purchasing cooperation. Pakistan was rewarded with a waiver of $1 billion debt and rescheduling of remaining $ 2.3 billion to be paid in easy instalments in the next 38 years, by an agreement signed on 5th of April, 2003. This was a fulfilment of a promise for a financial reward to Pakistan for giving its bases and logistic support for fighting the Talibans in 2002.

Nevertheless, the American President and British Prime Minister have sought to calm the Iraqi and Arab fears that coalition forces would not become occupying forces and they would help in building a peaceful and a representative government that protects the rights of all citizens. It was also claimed by the British Prime Minister that "Our forces are friends and liberators of Iraqi people, not your conquerors". This is a claim which needs to be accepted with a pinch of salt. Experience has shown that wherever Americans have gone, whether it is Pakistan or Kuwait, Qatar, Philippines, Afghanistan any country in South America, they have stayed put there, ostensibly in the name of serving the democratic values, but actually to maintain their hegemony. Let us hope that Americans do not reduce Iraq to their colony for the oily interest.

11
Mother of Corruption

The poor financial management of the States can be gauged from the fact, that more than half a dozen State Governments were forced, to stop all payments, except the salary of the employees and the pension of the pensioners. Most States are passing through financial crisis, almost on regular basis. But this has not prevented some of them from indulging in gimmick and populist measures. Normally, there should be some kind of a goal before the Government. All efforts should be directed towards achieving it. But what happens in actual practice is that the game of please all, jealousy and intense rivalry between those in power and those who might make it next time has the upper hand. It leads to the ruin of administration in numerous ways.

Money is required for everything worthwhile and desirable in life. The lack of transparency and the dubious means for its collection, by those who should be models in our country, affects the quality of the polity. An election to a single Parliament seat may cost over Rs. one crore to twenty five crore. In some cases, candidates have reportedly spent over Rs. 32 crore on their election and lost it. A stage had reached during the elections to the 13th Lok Sabha, that in some constituencies, money had ceased to be a factor. The person commanding five to ten votes could ask for a Maruti car, fridge or television and it would be delivered to him by the evening. The other expenses are on the supporters, vehicles, food and other infrastructure created for contesting elections and for purchase of votes, wherever possible. Nobody will admit that he has purchased the votes. A few candidates of the main parties end up collecting more money than they spent. All the money collected, is number two or black money. It suits both the receivers and the givers. However, if the elections are held every year or more frequently, such contributions are likely to come down.

In United States, the Republican Presidential hopeful candidate collected over 36 million Dollar, in the six months period prior to the election. As compared to him, the Democratic hopeful residential candidate collected $18.5 million. The ones with the money only can go for expensive contests. One of the Publishing house giant, spent on its boss 37 million $ in 1996, for unsuccessfully contesting the elections. In our country, for elections to Rajya Sabha or the Upper House of the Parliament, cross votings show the forces at play, including the money power.

Despite the massive adulteration of the mustard oil and the death of over 100 persons and more than 2500, afflicted by the dropsy in 2002, the Government apart from making noises in the media, showed total inaction in tackling the problem. On an average, an Inspector took only 16 samples per month for checking adulteration, as pointed out by the Comptroller and Auditor General of India. Even after occurrence of serious incidents, adulteration goes on, in the maze of inactive and self-justifying bureaucracy. In its report for October, 1999, Transparency International, a global anti-corruption organisation, assessed the prevalence of the malady in 99 countries, as against 85 countries in 1998. Out of 99 countries, with ranking done from the top for the most honest to the most corrupt, India was positioned 73, with a score of 2.9 in the scale of 10-1. From the bottom, it was the 26th, most corrupt country, with Pakistan occupying 88 position or the 11th most corrupt country in the world, with a score of 2.2 in the corruption perception index. Denmark scored ten out of ten, Finland, 9.8, New Zealand 9.4, U.K. (13th position from the top), with 8.6, USA (18th from the top honesty wise) with 7.5 and China (58th position from the top or 41st most corrupt country) with a score of 3.4. Transparency International has also assessed Nations on Bribe Payers Index. No exporting country has been found to be totally honest on this score. It says in its report: "The data provides a disturbing picture of the degree to which the leading exporting countries are perceived to be using corrupt practices". On a scale of 0 -10, 10 represents a corruption free exporting country. Sweden scored 8.3, Australia and Canada scored 8.1, U.K. 7.2 and US 6.2. China including Hongkong showed the greatest willingness to offer bribes.

It is a sad reflection on the probity in the public life that a country, which claims ancient value, is considered the 26th from the bottom from the integrity point of view. It is true that reforms, which affect the public, cannot be implemented without the people's support. No person wants to bribe. Should the Government launch a meaningful and focussed drive, it would be overwhelmed, by the public support. People would break caste and communal barriers to assist in the onslaught against corruption. At present, all the legal authority for dealing with the dishonest and corrupt, vests with the Government. There is no Right of Private Defence against corruption, as it is there, against a physical assault, rape or dacoity, robbery or hurt. There is no militant trade union against corruption, protesting against the violation of human rights or breach of fundamental right.

The transformation of the society is possible only if the fight against corruption is also privatised. One way is to introduce transparency in the functioning of the Government. The second is that outmoded restrictions and laws, which have outlived their utility, should be scrapped. The third is to increase the supply of goods and services. This will eventually take care of the problem. In the 1950s and 1960, the only cars in the Indian Market were Fiat, Ambassador and Standard Herald. Bribes in the name of premium had to be paid, if you wanted any of those cars early. It was said, that if you wanted to give a Fiat car, as a dowry to your daughter, you had to book it, as soon as she was born. The same was true of the scooters. As a measure of patronage, the Government had a discretionary quota to allot cars to its officials, Legislators, or other influential people. The quality of the cars was such that almost from the showrooms, some of them had to be taken to the repair garage. In the absence of any remedy, the substandard vehicles ruled roost. With the onset of liberalisation, the demand of the favourites of first 4 decades of the Independent India, has nose dived to zero. The survival of the fittest has pushed down the demand of fuel guzzlers and first day repair needing cars, in favour of better models.

The Hong Kong based Political and Economic Risk Consultancy, which had compiled the corruption rankings in 2003 on the basis of a survey of over 1,000 executive in Asia, says: "Corruption is perceived to have worsened as a problem" in eight of the 12 Asian countries covered. Indonesia is most corrupt, according to the survey, with India as a runner-up. The others, in order are, China, Taiwan, Hong Kong, Malaysia, Japan and Vietnam. Singapore, is reported to have very low level of corruption. There are no common causes of corruption, as regimes and types of Government vary from country to country. China and Vietnam have almost dictatorship or at the best semi-authoritarian set up. All the power there emanates from the ruling party. Still corruption is increasing there. Indonesia has seen a steady breakdown of law and order and increase in terrorism in recent years, apart from high level of corruption. The report says: "It is a cruel injustice, when the economy is continually raped by corrupt officials and politicians, by drug mafias, and loan defaulters by those who misappropriate state patronage... They are creating news, unethical norms which destroy the very fabric of a society". This had led to the absence of good governance.

On the subject of "combating bribery", OECD had made following recommendations:

1. Enterprises should not offer, nor give into demands, to pay public officials or the employees of business partners, any portion of a contract payment. They should not use subcontracts, purchase orders or consulting agreements, as means of channelling payments to public officials, to employees of business partners or to their relatives or business associates.

2. Enterprises should enhance the transparency of their activities, in the fight against bribery and extortion. Measures could include making public commitments against bribery and extortion and disclosing the management systems, the company has adopted in order to honour these commitments, against bribery and extortion and disclosing the management systems. The enterprise should also foster openness and dialogue with the public so as to promote its awareness of and co-operation, with the fight against bribery and extortion.

3. Enterprises should not make, illegal contributions to candidates for public office, or to political parties or to other political organisations. Contributions should fully comply with public disclosure requirements and should be reported to senior management.

Ultimately, the responsibility for good governance falls on the politicians, who like everywhere, as in India, need tonnes of money. It will be futile to say, that money should play no part in elections. It is a fact, that if you want to get a ticket for contesting any election of any major political party in India, you have to shell out a lot of money in the form of a donation to the party, though quite often such money does not land in the party coffers.

According to a political observer in Assembly elections, the price of a ticket varies from Rs. 25 lakh to a maximum of Rs. 1.25 crore to candidate of major political parties. The figures may appear wild and beyond imagination to a layman. But sometimes, reality and truth beat even the wildest imagination. In a small home town called Jalalabad, in one Municipal Elections, some candidates paid as much as Rs. 30000 per vote. It was confirmed to me by some voters themselves. This town has a small population of 25000, but has a lot of millionaires, who spent a total of Rs. 7 crore in contesting 20 odd Municipal seats. When I suggested to them, that if they had contributed this amount to the local college, which is getting no Government grant, we would have been able to impart first rate education. One of them jocularly said that they would gladly spend a similar or a large amount on another election, but education or clean elections were not on their priority list.

Frequent elections, in one State after another, have again been responsible for declining standards in administration. Elections all over the world, cost plenty of money. In our country, the votes in many cases, are for sale for cash. Some voters prefer to receive their payment in kind, in the form of a job for themselves or their near ones. The Vice President of India, who a seasoned politician and has been the Chief Minister for a decade, observed that the Constitution of India, envisaged that the Lok Sabha and State Assemblies elections be held simultaneously every five year. He added. "But since 1977, the spirit of the Constitution has been given the go-by. Today a stage has come, when people have started calling our democracy as a democracy of frequent elections, nay elections almost every year. Every year, everything goes in an election mode. This is having adverse impact on governance. Compulsions of elective politics, overtake genuine public welfare and national interests and short-term gains triumph over vision of growth. The adverse effects of frequent elections are a big luxury for our country to afford"... He has suggested "generating a wide public debate... and the pressure of public opinion will lead building up of political consensus on feasible solutions."

The Law Commission of India had suggested in its 170th report that India could follow Germany. The German Constitution in Article 67 of the Basic Law for the Federal Republic of Germany, says: "(1) The Bundestag may express its lack of confidence in the Federal Chancellor only by electing a successor, with the majority of its members and requesting the Federal President to dismiss the incumbent. The Federal President must comply, with the request and appoint the person elected". The Law Commission had said this could be done "in this respect merely by amending the Rules of Procedure of the Lok Sabha". If the suggestion were to be accepted, it would mean, that a motion of no-confidence could be moved only, if accompanied by a motion expressing confidence in another individual by name. In other words, a motion expressing confidence, in the named individual shall be put to vote. Also, once a motion of no confidence is moved, no fresh motion can be moved for a period of two years.

The Suggestion to have uniform elections is eminently sensible, though there would be daunting obstacles, in having a fixed term for the Lok Sabha, as well as to the legislative assemblies of the states. It might mean cutting down the tenure of some and extending that of the others. Simply because a proposal is right, correct, reasonable and sensible, offers no guarantee that it would be accepted with open arms by the law makers, who might have won their seats after a lot of expenses, labours, arms twisting or even by use of extra constitutional means. Unless the self interest coincides with the public and National Interest, rarely the latter prevail. It is a simple question whether the political parties are willing to give up the politics of loaves and fishes of office, at any and every cost.

We have about 543 parties registered with the Election Commission and there is no warranty or assurance that there would not be a further proliferation of political parties in our multi party system. As the matters stand, only a coalition of parties alone, can form a government. It is utopian to accept as true that, opposition parties will accept a single leader to form the government merely to topple any existing government. In fact, every Member of the Lok Sabha considers himself fit to lead the country and with everybody trying to lead, it is doubtful to expect any change in the present set up. Moreover, the Supreme Court has said that the basic structure of the Constitution, cannot be changed. It is doubtful whether first of all such a proposal to have elections at the same time, would be acceptable to all, as some of them might have to face elections sooner than they had bargained for and secondly, whether such a proposal would be legally sustainable without amending the Constitution, notwithstanding the fact that, it offers light at the end of existing darkness and would prevent Aya Rams and Gaya Rams ruling the roost.

The Samajwadi Party in U.P. released a video recording of Ms Mayawati on 3rd March, 2003 asking her party MPs and MLAs to divert some money from their constituency development funds to the BSP party coffers. This tape was made of the alleged speech on 11th February, 2001 when Mayawati was not the Chief Minister. What she is supposed to have allegedly said is :

"Every MLA gets 75 lakh as his constituency fund. For MPs the figure is two crore. Whatever work is carried out from this development fund and how it is done, depends on the MLA. So if you make five lakh out of this development fund, do not keep everything for yourself. Use four lakhs for your constituency and give at least a lakh to the party...The same stands for MPs also. After all the BSP has made you an MLA or an MP. You should give something back to the party. Am I saying anything wrong?"

The entire Opposition in Uttar Pradesh, led by the Samajwadi Party, served a notice of no confidence on 4th of March against the Mayawati government. The no confidence motion was defeated on the floor of Assembly on 5th March, by a voice vote, without any debate. However, the levels of mud-slinging reached the lowest ebb in the war of words. There were reverberations of the incidents in the Lok Sabha, where it was charged that Ms Mayawati was "encouraging corruption" as well as demanded Ms Mayawati's resignation. There was also a demand for a CBI inquiry into the allegations of corruption. CBI cannot take up the case, for inquiry on its own. It has to be referred to it by the State Government and it is doubtful, if Mayawati, would order inquiry against herself by the CBI. Ms Mayawati has accused the Samajwadi Party of tampering with the video recording and using edited portions saying: "It has been edited out of context which alters the entire meaning of my speech". The UP Chief minister also ordered an inquiry into the money disbursed from the chief minister's discretionary fund during Mr Mulayam Singh Yadav's tenure from 1993-1995. On the other hand, one Samajwadi MP said that no other political leader in the world has been shown taking classes in corruption like Mayawati," He also called on Ms. Mayawati, saying that, if she has any morals left, she should immediately step down... She is the fountainhead of corruption, as has been proved in the video cassette."

One MP said: "She has insulted all MPs by saying all dips into the MPLADS funds and this includes the PM because he is an MP from her state. And if there could be a judicial inquiry into Tehelka, in which George Fernandes was asked to quit despite no direct link to the case, our tape is far more serious, as it shows Mayawati clearly asking for a cut from Government funds". Another CD was released by the Samajwadi Party, in the second week of April, 2003 showing the Chief Minister of UP abusing Hindu Gods. Abusing or praising downgrading or upgrading Gods is done by the politicians suiting their convenience and if somely does not abuse any God or Goddess, it does not mean that he or she has respect for it. But God or Gods or Goddesses are too big to survive or fall at the mercy of mere mortals.

Whatever politicians may say against each other, the public perception about almost all politicians in the public mind is that, a vast majority of them cutting across the party lines are corrupt. It is also the view of The Transparency International, a German based Non-Governmental Organisation, which has classified India amongst the 30 most corrupt countries in the world in its "Corruption Perception Index (CPI) 2002", after carrying out an extensive survey in 102 nations.

According to the Report, politicians, multinational and kickbacks are trapping whole nation in poverty and hampering sustainable development....Corrupt political leaders and unscrupulous investors are killing sustainable growth in its tracks. Political elites and their cronies continue to take kickbacks at every opportunity. Hand in glove with the corrupt business people, they are trapping whole nation in poverty. Politicians increasingly pay lip service to fight against corruption, but they fail to act. They must clamp down on corruption to break the vicious circle of poverty and graft.

Politicians have taken the nation to its lowest ebb. Year after year, they make false promises of fighting corruption, especially when they are out of power. The tentacles of corruption have started gripping even the institutions created for the protection of the Republic. Unless those tentacles are intercepted... through strong legislative, executive as well as judicial exercises, the corrupt public servants would even paralyse the functioning of such institutions.

In a conference on "Women in Urban Local Governance", organised by the Institute of Social Sciences and Centre for Sciences of Humanities, it has been revealed, that women in politics are not much different from men. The women who replaced their husband or male relatives are more prone to corruption as they have to maintain the same relations of "give and take" with the contractors.

Sher Shah, a great ruler said, "Whoever has wealth, whether loyal or disloyal, can get his business settled as he likes by paying for it. But if a man has no money, although he may have displayed his loyalty on a hundred occasions or if he be a veteran soldier, he will never gain his end". This fact that has not changed very much. Edward Gibbon said that corruption is the most infallible symptom of constitutional liberty. Our politicians have bent and twisted the institutions of democracy to suit their particular genius for deviousness. It is more so in the era of coalitions where, survival in power is considered more important, than any doing for the right thing.

The Governments always go on complaining about shortage of funds. Corruption is a kind of random, unpredictable and arbitrary tax, that has to be paid, to get a sanction or get some other favour from the Government. Primary source of bribery is black/unaccounted money and wealth acquired through illegal means. Corruption and black economy have derailed the normal development activity of the country. The flow of revenue to different layers of the government especially in the proventials, has lagged much behind the expenditure. Consequently governments have gone bankrupt.

12

Collective Corruption

Sting Operations are generally done to catch the corrupt, drug gangs, and spies. They are also undertaken to prove adultery in marriage. Other uses of sting operations, have been staged to arrest terrorists and anti national elements. The gadgets generally used are camera, recording gadgets, audio and video equipment. Generally media has used it to expose shocking acts of politicians, officials and others, who are alleged to be guilty of subverting the rule of the law. In the last week of January, 2004, in a sting operation for alleged sale of justice warrants, a TV channel recorded shady proceedings involving a Court of Justice. Supreme Court of India and High Court of Gujarat acted promptly by suspending with immediate effect, the presiding Magistrate of the concerned Court in Gujrat and ordering a CBI inquiry for his conduct, unbecoming of a judicial officer. The CBI immediately registered an FIR against three Ahmedabad based lawyers who allegedly struck a deal with the Magistrate to secure the warrants for Rs. 40,000. The case was filed under section 120-B (criminal conspiracy) of the Indian Penal Code and section 8 of Prevention of Corruption Act. Chief Justice of India remarked: Look at what is happening. You can get an arrest warrant for Rs. 40,000. The time has come to take a strict action, otherwise nothing would remain."

The Supreme Court ordered that all the records summoned from the High Court and the videotapes and other documents submitted by TV journalist be handed over to the CBI. The TV journalist claimed to have conducted a sting operation to expose corruption in subordinate judiciary in Gujarat. The Ahmedabad lawyers, involved in the case had assured the journalist that once Rs 40,000 was paid, "he should not bother about anything". They had also assured him that the substance of complaint, the complainant and witnesses would be their "bother". On the court's request, Attorney-General of India agreed to put forth suggestions to improve the judicial system. Earlier, TV journalist's counsel had pointed out that a similar incident occurred in 1999, when a court at Dakor, in Gujarat's Kheda district, had issued a non-bailable warrant against the then Chief Justice of

India. There is no doubt that a few black sheep have tarnished the fair name of the judiciary. In May, 2003, a judge was arrested in Chandigarh by the CBI in a corruption case. Along with him a Jullundur District and Sessions Judge, on whose behalf a judicial magistrate had allegedly demanded a sum of Rs.11 lakh from a litigant, was also arrested. Indian scene is currently at its lowest ebb.

Around the same period a former Delhi High Court Judge, who resigned following the DDA scam, was arrested and booked under the Prevention of Corruption Act.

A household survey conducted by Transparency International (TI) in December, 2002, reported high levels of corruption, in public institutions across South Asia. Of the seven major public institutions, the police emerged as the most corrupt in all five countries surveyed. The judiciary was identified as the second most corrupt area in all countries except Pakistan, where land administration and the tax authorities were identified as the second and third most corrupt areas respectively.

Land administration figures prominently in the list of the most corrupt sectors in four out of the five countries. The latest report by TI, entitled 'Corruption in South Asia - Insights and Benchmarks from Citizen Feedback Surveys in Five Countries', identifies high levels of corruption encountered by citizens attempting to access seven basic public services. "The survey results show that even when public services are meant to be freely available, bribes and delays keep many from receiving them, and it is most often the poorest in society that suffer most."

A former Chief Justice of India, S.P. Bharucha, publicly expressed remorsefully that "eighty per cent of the judges in the country were honest and incorruptible and the smaller percentage was bringing the entire judiciary into disrepute". Over the years, some judges of different high courts have been hauled up or advised suitably by the Supreme Court, for alleged misconduct and impropriety affecting the discharge of their judicial functions. Some of them resigned or have been transferred. It is a matter of great satisfaction, that whenever any misdemeanour has been brought to the notice of the superior Courts, they have lost no time in stemming the rot. Superior Courts have been prompt in disciplining judges guilty of any misconduct.

However, as the matters stand, the procedure for disciplining errant deviants is not only too unwieldy, but too cumbersome also, especially when it comes to impeachment in the Parliament. How can Parliament, which has some gentleman facing criminals cases of scam judge the judges? Politics in our country, which is the largest democracy, is at present at its lowest ebb. The infamous Cash on Camera scam involving a former Central minister, followed by the Cash for MLA scandal, involving the outgoing Chief minister of Chattisgarh, who was caught on audio tape, striking an odious deal, with senior members of the winning Bharatiya Janta Party to effect a split. The Union Law Minister had organised audio part of the sting operations, with the approval of the Deputy Prime Minister of India.

There is no law, at present in our country, to regulate or legitimise the sting operations. Police do it for prostitution cases, corruption cases, as well as catching the drugsters and spies. Decoys are used to trap offenders in such cases. Sting operations are done all over the worlds, sometimes in National interests or sometimes in personal interests, like to prove marital infidelity. Many would question the legitimacy of the sting operations, on the ground that it is unethical or not approved by law or broadly speaking, it is illegal or the sting operations do not change anything or there is no dividing line between sting journalism and yellow journalism. A Chinese proverb aptly says: "Going to the law is losing a cow for the sake of a cat". About laws, it is said that they are like cobwebs, which may catch small flies, but let hornets and wasps break through. However, sting operations keep the guilty on tenterhook, as well as keep the Government of the day alert. The fact remains, that there is a tremendous deterioration in public morality. Regrettably, the systems do not seem to be working, as the common man would like them to work. Public is already aware, of the wrong goings on in the country in different areas of life. For instance, the Right to Information Act passed is hedged by many ifs and buts. Anything which promotes maximum good of the maximum numbers should be welcome. The right to sting operations should be guaranteed legally, not only to the press, but to any private individual. Sting operations should be legitimised only where public interest or public money or public figures are involved. We must remember, that the straight line is shortest both in morals as well as in geometry. It must also be remembered, that sting operations can catch some of the offenders, but they do not necessarily induce honesty. Moreover, with the arrival of new technology, it is unfair not to use the same for effective enforcement and to ensure the highest standards in public life, in the overall public interest. The law can make some people quit smoking or drinking, but it cannot make them the kind, that makes them, quit smoking or drinking, because a law is there. However, some sting law is better than nothing at all.

There was a time when corruption was hidden behind the doors and curtains. To be considered even having a stain on the reputation was a mental torture. You could count on your finger tips, the persons of doubtful integrity. Now all the fingers and toes tips would be insufficient for this exercise. Lord Krishna says in Gita that people follow the leader no matter where he leads them. It was for this reason that the scriptures had prescribed a very high standard for those charged with ruling. The ancient Kings and Emperors have been replaced in democracy by the Prime Minister, Chief Ministers, Ministers and others occupying public offices. Kautilya said in Arthsastra: "In the happiness of subjects lies the King's happiness, in their welfare, his welfare; what pleases himself the King shall not consider as good, but whatever pleases his subjects, the King shall consider good". The duties of King were prescribed as "To punish the wicked, to honour (protect) the good, to enrich the treasury (exchequer) by just methods, to be impartial towards the litigants and to defend the kingdom."

What Kautilya prescribed was the ideal, which probably could not have been achieved in his time. In the vast polity which India is, all the political leaders irrespective of the party or parties had to compromise from the beginning. With a few exceptions, no Minister has fitted all the qualifications prescribed as under by Kautilya. "A native (citizen), having good family background, pure in character, endowed with excellent conduct, influential, well trained in the arts, possessed of foresight, wise, of strong memory, bold, eloquent, skilful, intelligent, full of devotion, endowed with strength, health and bravery, free from procrastination and fickle mindedness, unexcited, affectionate and free from hatred and enmity is, qualified to be appointed as Amatya (Minister)."

For more than fifty years, we as a nation have been fighting with scandals. Right from the time of Nehru, who was both an idealist and a missionary, the country has been facing one scandal or the other. We, as independent Nation opened our account with LIC Scandal involving Mundhras, then graduated to the jeep Scandal during Nehru's time. We also had Das Commission at that time looking into the conduct of late Sardar Partap Singh Kairon. In all fairness, it must be said that neither Nehru nor Kairon was personally involved. The fault of Kairon was non exercise of the control on the members of the family, which Commission felt should have been done. After Nehru's death, there has been a progressive increase in deterioration in public probity. To recall briefly, we had the rags import scandal in 1970's in which almost new clothes were imported in the name of converting them to shoddy yarn for hosiery industry. It was followed by Sugar Import Scandal involving the State Trading Corporation, Beef Tallow import scandal. Later years surpassed the immediate three decades of post independence, with HDW Submarine, Befors Air Bus Industries scandals, Housing Allotment Scandals, Gas Agencies and Petroleum Allotment scandal and the famous telecommunication scandal to recount only a few. States also did not lag behind with Bihar topping with fodder scam, Bitumen scams and medical scams.

In this climate those who could help themselves, even in private sector did not lag behind Harshad Mehta leading with a rough tally of Rs.8200 crore, followed closely by CRB scandal of Rs.1032 crores. Their plunder was possible due to connivance, indifference or contributory negligence of those charged with the duty to prevent the public being taken for rides. It was for the first time that an allegation had been made by a private individual of having paid Rupees in crores to the Prime Minister, call it a contact building or good will amount. We have moved far away from the prescription given by Kautilya. No single individual can be faulted for this and no single cause can be held responsible for this.

It is the general climate of tolerating of whatever is going on by everybody. When I Joined service in 1961, it was taken for granted that honesty was not only the one thing in the services, but the only thing. The elected representatives would once in a while make some recommendations. It was open to the officials to reject the same without inviting the wrath of the day. I recall only one instance of the then Chief Minister of Karnataka getting annoyed with an All India Services officer. He told his Secretary to have that particular officer dismissed from service immediately. The Secretary told him, "Sir it cannot be done". The Chief Minister said: "You are saying so because you are one of them and you want to help. I will tell the Chief Secretary myself, if you are that helpless". The Chief Secretary told him; "Sir, under the All India Services Rules, first charges will have to be framed against the officer. Only after a properly conducted inquiry, the matter will have to be referred to the Home Ministry. They will take a view and then refer the matter to the Union Public Service Commission. Only after the advice of Commission is received, then some Presidential Order will be passed. The officer is upright. How can I frame charges against him on the ground that Chief Minister is annoyed? Then you would be cited as a witness and the officer will have every right to cross examine you. I will have to give specific grounds for taking action". The CM left the matter there and the concerned officer retired as a Governor of a State.

Now transfer has become a paying industry. In one State, the Chief Minister transferred as many as 144 IPS officers and 102 officers, within 15 days of his assumption of office. Of course, the Chief Minister did not known even twenty percent of them personally. It was the annoyance of the local satraps who were supporting his precariousness which swelled the transfers. Many local leaders with clout not only threaten transfers, but levy a fee for allowing officials to stay put. Many compromise either for enriching themselves or in the interest of education of their children. Those who can move out of the States to Centre, the transfers are done there generally as per the norms. Only the most inconvenient ones are shunted out before the completion of their tenure.

The problem of corruption control is not impossible to solve, if there is a will and the political compulsions are kept under a reasonable check. More than that we need to pay our rulers including the Ministers and M.Ps well so that they do not resort to selling their telephone or gas coupons to make some extra buck. At present, the Central Minister and State Ministers get less salary than that of a Deputy Secretary to the Government. But the hidden perks like the free car, gardeners and spacious bungalows cost lakhs along with a lavish entertainment allowance. Let a Minister be paid two lakh a month and the MP about a lakh per month. This should be the total sum and no more. The Government should not foot any bill of either of the telephone or electricity. As most of our politicians are full time leaders not having any independent source of income, it is worthwhile to pay them more, so that there is no justification whatsoever for them to barter away their influence for a few pieces of silver.

It should not so happen that the elected representative get both higher salaries and perk from the Corporates under their control. It is generally seen that apart from the official vehicle earmarked for a Minister or a Secretary, half a dozen extra vehicles are requisitioned from either the attached or subordinate offices. It is because, the officials heading those organisations, want no problem. The Government system is such that there is no accountability in the higher echelons. The boss does not have to give any reasons or justify his inefficiency. It appears that the rules and laws are made for field organisations and not for those who make them.

Corruption has been pushed under the carpet in our country by those, whose duty is to ensure good governance. Good governance, perse implies a corruption free running of the administration. When a former Chairman of the Punjab Public Service Commission was caught with crores, it did not ruffle many feathers. Cash for jobs has become the norm, because the law of supply and demands equally applies in all fields of life. It is a simple truth, where the supply exceeds the demands, the corruption disappears. At one time, only bribery or recommendations worked for getting a telephone connection. It was so when the Government had the monopoly in telephone sector. With the opening of the communication to the private sector, telephones are going abegging. In fact, the telephone companies are coming out with newer and better schemes to lure customers to use their particular brand. Business, whether of the Government, or of the private sector, needs to be run professionally as business and not as a kind of a charity, where both the best and mediocre get the same rewards or commendations. However the problem in the Government arises, when the office is converted into a gold mine for self aggrandisement.

The culture in the Government is not of public service, but one of treating the public, for whom the Government employees are supposedly existing, as a cow to be milked. The former Chairman of Punjab Public Service Commission, according to confession made by his co-accused, had personally approached him, late in 1997, to get candidates, who could pay money to get selected in the PCS (Executive). He added that following this, he formed a team of sub agents, which spotted candidates who could pay Rs. 50 lakh to 65 lakh for selection in the State Civil Service, PCS (Judicial), Deputy Superintendents of Police, Block and Panchayat Development Officers (BDPOs). Incompetent political governance is one factor, which dooms our country, notwithstanding any claims made to the contrary, by several political parties. It is amazing, as to how, the hangers on of the politicians and Ministers have made millions.

The lack of political will is intertwined with a deeply entrenched culture of corruption. The large number of public officials, stained with criminal acts, get away for one reason or the other, the chief being that no body wants to bell the cat. I asked a senior official as to why such people, against whom prima facie sufficient evidence is available could not be dismissed under Article 311, of the Constitution, which gives ample power to the Government. He replied, that the bureaucracy did not support such a proposal as the affected person was bound to approach the Court. I told him that it was the Constitutional Right of every aggrieved person, to approach the Court and what was the guarantee, that if a person is dismissed, after long and protracted departmental inquiry, he would not approach the Court. When pressed further, he let the cat out of the bag, by saying that most politicians used obliging and unscrupulous civil servants as their conduits to make fortunes. They would not be happy or willing to strike against such elements. He said that an old saying said that 'Caesar's wife must be above suspicion'. But what could Caesar's wife do, when Caesar himself was drenched in suspicion, of being a party to whatever was going on in the country. It is not merely a matter of cynicism to doubt their motives. It is clear that bureaucrats and politicians, are reluctant to give up their control over public assets that can be used as personal cash cows, or as tools of political patronage.

Let us recall the cancellation of thousands of lucrative petrol pump licenses by the Prime Minister in 2002. The recipients of petrol pumps had political connections, both with the ruling and opposition parties. The decision was contested and the Court has stayed it. But the question arises, as to why in the first instance, an opaque or slanted method was adopted. It is a different kind of criminalisation of India's politics and one gets the impression, that most decisions or indecision, are both motivated and tainted.

One good thing about the 2004 elections was that every one was talking about development. But development and corruption do not go together. In the Human Development Report 2003, India ranks 124th in the human development index. Transparency International has also reported that Indians pay a whopping Rs. 26,780 crore in bribes annually. This figure, of course, cannot be taken as absolutely correct, as the transactions of bribe are strictly between the giver and the receiver. But it indicates the dimension of the problem. This unfortunately makes people cynical about the talk of corruption and they feel that you cannot even live without bribing.

Corrupt are boldly overconfident, daring and audacious, in the belief that they can get away with it, without any fear of nemesis. It applies, in all aspects of life, whether it is copying in examinations or selling questions papers or selling fakes and spurious. There are over 19 million people drawing salaries from the State and Central governments. 20,000-odd Central services officers control the collection and disbursement of over Rs.5,25,000 crore every year. There are 400 Secretaries and Additional Secretaries or equivalent, 25 Chief secretaries, about 500 District Magistrates, 700 Income Tax and Customs and Excise Officials belonging to the Indian Revenue Service, who control the nation's affairs in economic sphere. Apart from this there are about 3000 Indian Police Service Officers, who deal with law and order, terrorism and internal security. This is independent of nearly 5,300 Members of the State Legislatures and Central Parliament. In a Nation of over 1000 million, what we need is only a couple of thousands of effective and sincere well meaning people, who can rewrite the corruption free, economic development route.

Successive Prime Ministers have lectured and expressed their strong determination to tackle this age old problem. Nobody has gone beyond making bold statement. Some of them earmarked special cells to deal with corruption and for weeding out the corrupt officials. Experience so far has shown, that quite often, tainted officials, end up getting, what are traditionally called "wet posts" or even post retirement jobs. In the present scenario, the chances are that those very low on the honesty matrix, will grab the key jobs, as they are considered not only more "dependable", but also extremely pliable, who will do any biddings. Late Prime Minister Indira Gandhi, talked of a 'committed bureaucraey. It appears, that is what all the political masters really want. Said Falconer: "Do not talk about disgrace from a thing being known, when the disgrace is, that the thing should exist."

In the play, Hamlet, William Shakespeare says about the Prince of Denmark that there is something rotten and wrong in the realm of Denmark. During the first two decades after independence, we in India, used to blame, for every thing wrong, or all ills and evils, the British rule. After over five decades of independence, this excuse has rather worn thin and nobody even talks about it. These days, hardly any section of our public life, is corruption free. Unprincipled businessmen also stand to benefit, from this state of affairs. There is Hindi saying that Bhaiti Ganga Mein Hatth Dho Lo (wash your hands in the running Ganga). The criminals indulging in extortion and looting, have got joined their kindred in bureaucracy and politics. Charge sheetel murderers, dacoits, rapists and hit men of various hues have made it to the Parliament and State Legislatures. Lack of transparency, coupled with red tape and time consuming obsolete rules and procedures, encourage speed money. More than that, cushions of legal safety, in the form of appeals after appeals and the principle, that everybody is innocent till proved guilty, leads to the guilty escaping for one reason or the other. Such persons hire the best legal brains, who are able to get them out of trouble, by legal quibbling. Says Shakespeare in his play: Measure for Measure "that laws are like scarecrows". They are initially installed to scare the birds. Once the birds know that they are scarecrows, they do not even give them a second glance.

In the second week of April, 2004, the Delhi Police cracked the case of leakage of CBSE paper. It is reported that the paper was leaked to a coaching institute for an astronomical sum of Rupees fifty lakh. Even small functionaries, whose total salary for a number of years, would be a petty sum, made lakhs of Rupees. The lure of money was too much for the investigating officer, who demanded a cut, to spare some people. He was trapped by the CBI on 30th of April, 2004 along with his other police associates for demanding Rupees eight lakh.

Corruption to some degree, exists in every society. But in our country, public servants routinely accepting, demanding or extorting money for the work, for which they are paid, has become an all pervasive phenomenon. Public service has been substituted by an unabashed greed for private gains. Campaign or warfare against corruption is not an end in itself. This crusade is not only on moral grounds. The struggle against malaise is necessary to have an effective, fair and efficient government, which at least, is the professed aim of all political parties. It is true that corruption cannot be totally eliminated. It should not be forgotten that it has a negative role on all our development schemes.

There is only model for dealing with the corruption, that is, it is the Government's responsibility to deal with it. In fact, maintenance of law and order is also the function of the State. But this function has been privatised to some extent. Finding that the State is not able to look after the individual of even collective needs both the individuals, associations and even private industries have hired out the security functions to the private agencies. Due to the shortage of policemen it has been reported that some police stations have hired security guards to do the police functions. Where Government cannot provide protection, the security agencies slip in to do their job. Some of them do a commendable job. The village Chaukidari system, is nothing but policing, but without the power to prosecute offenders. I was in USA when in service to lead an Indian delegation. I was surprised that the security and guarding job in the State Department as well as in Central Intelligence Agency was performed by the private agencies. Even under the existing Indian Laws, every individual is given some police powers for defending himself, his property and life of others. Causing a death of others, is also permissible, under the self policing or right of private defence, if no other course is available, except the death of the defender himself.

Corruption, in no form is acceptable to any civilised society and it is totally unacceptable in those, which are charged to protect life and liberty of others. The police inefficiency and corruption directly affects a common man's right to life, and liberty. Like the disinvestment policy started by the Government for its public sector undertakings, it is time to start seriously thinking of disinvestment in policing side also. For corruption to stop, the supply side needs to be checked, as has been done in communication and petroleum sector. Monopolies play hell and police monopoly has played havoc with the country. It is this monopoly, which has resulted in only a mere six percent conviction rate in corruption cases. It exacerbates the situation. In other words, any'body without money or the contacts, faces both a difficult and sometimes, an impossible situation.

The alleged involvement of senior police officers in crimes like murder, land grabbing, extortion and other similar crimes is symptomatic of an unfortunate trend of the increasing criminalisation of the police force. Their delinquency is not confined to mere violations of the conduct or discipline but embraces major offences.

On January 1, 1998, the UP government identified 850 policemen, who had an alleged nexus with criminals. The list of policemen, included two officers of the rank of additional director general of police, one of whom later became director general of police. In Kolkata, a police commissioner had maintained close links with the underworld. In Haryana, an officer of the rank of director general of police was caught accepting a bribe and another director general was involved in getting a person in custody killed. A third one was accused of molesting a teenaged girl, who subsequently committed suicide. Another officer of the rank of IGP was allegedly involved in smuggling operation. He was caught by the Customs Department. One IGP of the same State is facing murder charges. In Karnataka, senior officers were chargesheeted in court of law with murder charges. In Assam, two senior officers were involved in cases of rape. Officer of the rank of DIG in Rajasthan was allegedly accused of raping his orderly's wife. In Delhi, a senior UT cadre officer of the rank of DGP had grabbed land illegally. Some time ago in Bihar, an officer of the rank of SP was reportedly making a fast buck dealing in stolen cars. It may be argued, as why to single out the police only for such instances, when the standards of public morality have plummeted in the political masters, as well as in other departments of the government and administration. A policeman committing a crime, violates the trust of the community placed in him. It is fact that there is a co-relationship, between the crimes committed by police and the growing criminalisation of politics. The nexus between the criminal policemen and criminal politicians subverts and undermines the authority of the police leadership, as well as the discipline of the force.

If the number of complaints received by the National Human Rights Commission is any forewarning, the police in the Capital of the Nation has a lot to explain. In one year, the NHRC has been generally receiving between 425 to 627 such complaints against police. This is only a tip of the iceberg. The conditions in other places are much worse, as the involvement of top brass of the police in various scams like the Telgi stamp scam shows. It is time to think of a new approach to policing, rather than sticking to the old outmoded methods and concept. It is not to plead that the Police Department should be closed. It is only to emphasise that the Police should be utilised for policing and not for acting as a social policeman of the society. Surely, there is a lot of scope for the private sector to take up duties like traffic management, normal watch and ward functions, illegal distillation, patrolling in the night, and simple cases of cheating or cheque bouncing or even property disputes or service of summons and warrants. One reason for the corruption and malpractices in the administration is the resistance to change and discard what has outlived its utility. The British have discarded their old administrative system in favour of a more responsive one. But India is fanatically sticking to the model given by them. British had made different rules for occupied countries with excessive powers to the executive.

Government of India, had announced plans to regularise illegal colonies in 1993. A Public Interest Litigation was filed against it on the ground that it was condoning illegalities and encroachments committed by some people. Since the filing of the petition against 1,000 such areas,. the number has increased by more than twice. It was thought that filing of petition would lead to Government waking up. On the contrary, the game of overlooking further formation of illegal colonies in Delhi and elsewhere continued. The functionaries, charged with the responsibility of preventing their formation, ignored it for a price.

The country's problems are a compound of lack of accountability of the government, and pervasiveness of all forms of fraudulent and deceitful activities. Today, there is hardly any area in which a citizen of this country does not feel harassed for seeking a service, which he is rightfully entitled to receive. This crisis extends to all levels. Hence, bribes became widespread and rampant. Extensive corruption is upsetting public administration. There is a nexus between lower, middle and higher bureaucracy with regard to corrupt practices. The numerous scams only prove that India suffers from a leadership crisis. Our country's population is growing by two crores every year. This means that we need further infrastructure for two crore people every year, which is more than the population of Australia.

It is the scarcity of goods and services, which is one reason for corruption. In the highly developed countries, bribes are non existing or at the lowest level. Despite the extra trains being run during holidays, tickets are not available, as touts buy up all tickets and sell the same in black. Once the capacity of trains is increased or more trains are run, the corruption will disappear in that sector also. Corruption has been born out of scarcity created by the public sector and the controlled economy from the Second Five Year Plan in 1956 as well as dishonesty and inefficiency of the bloated bureaucracy. Monopoly of services, and goods can be appalling. In 1960, in Mumbai and a till a decade later in Delhi, you needed a Minister's or an official's recommendation to get a permit for purchasing a bottle or two of milk from the Government monopoly of Aarey Milk in Bombay and Delhi Milk Scheme in Delhi. Getting a milk token for two bottles of milk at that time, was nothing less winning a battle. Even for these two bottles, you had to stand in queue at 4 AM and if you were late, you would miss getting your rationed milk. Now with a number of cooperatives or suppliers around, you do not have to bribe any body to get any quantity of milk.

Poor and corrupt administration has a direct impact on the quality of life of citizens. A 2003 World Water Development report of the United Nations has categorised India among the worst countries for poor quality of water as well as its ability and commitment to improve the situation. It says that Asian rivers are the most polluted in the world, with three times as many bacteria from human waste as the global average. These rivers also have 20 times more lead than those of the industrialised countries, says the Report.

Doing away with the Inspector Raj will mean giving up the power to twist the arms of others in industry, commerce or business over which the Inspectors have almost life and death power. Despite the lip service, nobody wants to give it away. Survey after survey has revealed that corruption is the undoing of our country. Wrong priorities of political parties, which are slanted towards as to which slogan will get them more votes have pushed the issue to the background. The annual survey conducted and released by Hong Kong based Political and Economic Risk Consultancy Limited (PERC) on 10th March, 2003, has said that corruption in India, affects people's daily lives in such basic ways, including paying for admission to better schools and to get electricity installed.

In one corruption case, the Supreme Court of India observed: "Corruption by public servants has now reached a monstrous dimension in India" and "its tentacles have started grappling even the institutions created for the protection of the republic". The Bench added: "Unless those tentacles are intercepted and impeded from gripping the normal and orderly functioning of the public offices, through strong legislative, executive as well as judicial exercises, the corrupt public servants could even paralyse the functioning of such institutions and thereby hinder the democratic polity."

Noticing that sometimes corrupt take advantage of the legal cushions and get stay from the High Courts on frivolous grounds, the Apex Court observed: "If honest public servants are compelled to take orders from proclaimed corrupt officers on account of the suspension of the conviction, the fallout would be one of shaking the system itself" the Bench noted. "Hence, it is necessary, that the court should not aid the public servant, who stands convicted for corruption charges, to hold public office, until he is exonerated after conducting a judicial adjudication at the appellate or revisional level."

37 per cent people in India who are below the poverty line, cannot offer bribes because they have nothing to offer. Nor can they

lay hands on any bribes, because they have no power or authority to oblige. The very rich do not want corruption to go or do not care for it, because they can get their jobs done by tossing a few notes of their black money. They are the happier for it, because their money can buy them any immunity. That leaves the middle class in the field, to suffer. They are the sufferers, who raise their voices against it. Many a time, doubts arise whether this minority can force the radical reforms for bringing about a clean and responsive governance and whether they have the will or means to launch a sustained war against corruption?

According to a regional survey, corruption and political interference are rife throughout police and justice systems in Asia. According to the survey, India's legal system has been seriously hurt by corruption, brought on by low levels of pay for the judiciary and police. Global Competitiveness Report says, that effective anti corruption measures could dramatically improve prospectus of growth in India. The report ranks public institutions in India, decided on the basis of contracts and law and corruption sub indices at 49. As per the same report, India ranks as 33rd so far as the contracts and law sub index is concerned. In corruption it occupies the 66th position. In the 85th report of the Standing Committee on Home Affairs, the High Courts are mentioned as the slowest layer in the judicial with 35.4 lakh cases pending in the 18 High Courts in our country.

The fault truly does not lie with the judiciary, but with the Government. It is for the Government to ensure that there are adequate number of judges to dispose of the heavy work load. According to a report of the Law Commission submitted in 1988, there was a requirement of at least 50 Judges per million population, where as we have less than 12 judges per million population.

Many people rightly or wrongly believe that most Indians have not only become cynical about corruption, but they accept the same. Many leaders including late Indira Gandhi rationalised the corruption on the ground it has existed since time immemorial and is also a global phenomenon. It is also true that there are no absolute standards of morality in real life. Conversely, it is easy to point out, when somebody is dishonest or does not follow the path of rectitude. Those who believe that corruption in public life does not matter or is not an issue, are often themselves extremely cynical. Corruption matters a lot to the man on the street. It is not a problem, which can be discussed on a cocktail party circuit and disposed of, by saying (to use oft-quoted phrase) voters would continue to elect corrupt politicians to power. The proponents of this viewpoint contend that since all rulers would tend to be corrupt, what is more relevant is whether corrupt rulers are efficient or not. The correct view is that we should strive for honest and efficient rulers, who can take the country out of the morass.

Our Country has taken up or wants to take up mega projects, some of which are as under:

Interlinking of Rivers project visualises the connecting of major rivers in India so that the water could be distributed evenly all over the country and the water diverted from surplus states to scarcity states. It is hopefully expected to solve the problem of both floods and droughts at an estimated cost of Rs. 5,60,000 crore. Its likely date of completion is 2016. The project envisages a financial outlay of almost a plan period. Water being a State subject, the project will not have a clear and smooth acceptance from States. Difficulties would arise, if the Centre expects the States to fund the project even partly. The country has not been able to solve even simple water problems between Punjab and Haryana and Tamilnadu and Karnataka, mainly on the grounds that some rivers do not have water all around the year. Every State from where the rivers emanate wants to hold on to the water, partly because of its needs and partly because it is more vote catching to be chauvinistic than generous or patriotic.

Another mega project is the formation of a National Power Grid, at an estimated cost of Rs. 80,000 crore and is expected to be completed by 2012. The idea of forming this grid is like the interlinking of the river, that is, shifting power from surplus to deficit States. But the trouble is that no State wants to carry out the power reforms. If anything, some of them have vied in distributing powers as goodies. The arrears of the over Rs. 26,000 crore from the State Electricity Boards had to be written off by the Centre, because of poor governance and lack of will on the part of the States to realise the same from some consumers. In Delhi, the power distribution had to be privatised as the State Distributors had failed to perform its duty due to mammoth corruption, where loss and transmission exceeded over 50per cent. The Governments have become poor and poorer but not the civil servants or bureaucrats or some politicians charged with the full time duty of public service. Mega projects give a mega chance of corruption. Ganga Action Plan, planned a decade back, conceived of the cleaning of river Ganges, which was full of pollution at places.

The river remains as filthy as it was. But over 500 crore have gone in the water of Ganges to line up the pockets of bureaucrats and politicians. Another similar project was undertaken in 1997, at a cost of Rs. 500 crore, to 'Save Dal Lake' in Srinagar. The State Government ordered a vigilance probe. Despite a lot of money having been spent, the lake continues to be murky and perishing. It appears that Kashmir Lakes and Water Ways Development Authority, had manipulated the records and fudged the bills We seem to be learning nothing and committing same mistakes again and again. While lakhs of crores are planned and earmarked for development, nothing is earmarked for strengthening vigilance machinery in the same projects. It needs to be built in any project costing over 1,000 crore, that at least 2 per cent of it shall be earmarked for strengthening vigilance and security arrangements. I was shocked to learn that Maruti, as a Government company in the past was losing 140 plus finished cars from its factory premises, till one of the enterprising bosses decided to privatise security and keep a strict watch on its inventory. This is strange that fully assembled cars should disappear from the godowns of the company. The rationale behind tolerating the losses, by the then CEO was that it was less than half a per cent of the turn over of the company and hence an acceptable loss. But nobody calculated the loss in terms of moral principles and ethics and an encouragement to corruption, mismanagement and negligence. What is the point of locking the stables after the horses have fled? Scams after scams reveal the same story and the only thing different in each story is the names, places and dates. A State to prosper, must be built on the foundations of a moral character. This character is the principal element of its strength, permanence and prosperity.

13
Stakeholders of Loot

A late lady dacoit MP, who was shot dead in July 2001, only represented the larger issue of criminalisation facing the Indian polity. Many criminals like her, have joined politics and one MLA from Gujrat was sentenced to life imprisonment for murder in August, 2004. Such elements have been encouraged by political parties, who want strong candidates to win by hook or crook. The position has become so bad that, some chargesheeted individuals have found berths both in State and Central Governments. Another question, which political class has never asked itself is, as to how someone born in poverty, including former Chief Ministers or Central Ministers have accumulated worth tens of crores (at official valuations) in a short political career. Whatever may be said about the bureaucracy, it is a glaring truth that both the criminalization of politics and the politicization of the people have become much worse in the past few decades. From a dribble of complaints about a few criminals entering the legislature in each state, according to an Election Commission study in 1997; 40 sitting members of the Lok Sabha and around 700 of the 4,072 members in the various state assemblies, had a criminal record. Even in 14th Lok Sabha, more than 100 MP's are involved in one or the other criminal case. Officially the cost of the election to the 14th Lok Sabha was estimated around Rupees 1200 crores, apart from what candidates and political parties. Good governance is India's need of the hour. Roughly, India spends about Rupees 1800 crore daily. The fundamental problem facing us is, not any of lack of resources, but of the proper utilisation of resources, our country already possesses, Good governance is the key to improve the lot of 37% or 370 million Indians who live below proverty line. The pillars on which the good governance can be based, is transparency, an efficient criminal justice system and a good delivery system of the Government plans and schemes. Last but not the least, is an exemplary and a totally untainted leadership.

Good governance is not important only for India, but for all countries, irrespective of the stages of their development. Responsibility for good governance rests with the Government of the day. International Financial Institutions, all over the world including the IMF, before opening their purse strings, lay the conditions of good governance, transparency and avoiding the corrupt practices.

Transparency restrains corruption as well as encourages good governance. Enhanced transparency of government in collection of its revenue as well as in expenditure, coupled with strengthened enforcement efforts against bribery and corruption, will contribute to attaining these goals and in improving integrity in government decision-making. Despite the Right to the Information Act, having been passed, the working of the Government still by and large remains shrouded in mystery. Implementation of the Citizen's Charters, proclaimed with a lot of funfare, still remains a dream. Accountability, responsibility and transparency need to go together along with the enhanced supply of goods and services.

A human development report of a United Nation Agency says: "Who wants to invest in a country, where a business partner may turn to be a gangster, who settles arguments with a gun? Who in the international community, will want to be seen, supporting a government, mired in the corruption, to which unchecked criminal activity so often leads"? The impact of the crime syndicate is not only confined to the private sector. The State enterprises are equally affected. Crime syndicates effectively operate with impunity, in mis-utilisation of allocated resources in many areas. In some cases, the amounts allocated to the social sector especially for the poor sections of the society, have been misappropriated. It is an established fact that powerful crime syndicates are functioning in the country. Nexus between mafia dons, police, bureaucracy, and some politicians, is a reality. The political morality is in a bad shape. Criminals and politicians are two-in-one in a number of cases. The effective functioning of the crime syndicates like impositions of criminal patronage/protection tax (rangdari tax) and ransom (firauti tax) in addition to the greasing speed money have emerged as strong limiting factors in the way to smooth functioning and progress of the country. Consequently, development is both a causality and ultimate victim.

According to 57th National Sample Survey, a Government of India Organisation, pertaining from June 2001 to June 2002, one in every 200 rural households and one in every 1,000 urban households, goes "chronically hungry". In simple words, they don't ever get enough to eat. Sixteen of every 1,000 rural households are "seasonally hungry"; they starve for a substantial part of the year. The corresponding figure for urban households is three out of every 1,000. With 200 million households in the country with five or more members, these figures translate into millions of starving Indians. Incidentally, just 52 per cent of the rural population has access to electricity. In urban India, eight per cent live without power.

Good Governance and corruption cannot co exit and are not compatible with each other. Despite various Prime Ministers proclaiming from the ramparts of the Red Fort, their intolerance to corruption, the problem has rather aggravated. Regrettably, India still has to celebrate its fearlessness from the nagging and persisting poverty, social injustice and corrupt practices. It still has to celebrate its fearlessness, from the criminals masquerading as political leaders, who mislead people with false slogans and insincere promises. The truth is that, our independence has been hijacked by the corrupt, who enjoy social respectability. There is no disgrace involved in embracing the corrupt, as long as they can win elections or control caste vote banks.

Rampant corruption is eating into the vitals of our nation. We have the questionable distinction of being classified as one of the most corrupt countries in the world. Only the highest possible degree of transparency in all aspects of government, can promote integrity. These need to be combined with the procedures that reduce opportunities for corruption and create incentives for public integrity. According to a survey conducted by an NGO and Transparency International India Chapter, Indians pay Rs 267 billion or Rs. 26780 crore in bribe in exchange for the services they get. The survey found the following sectors most corrupt in this descending order: Health, Power, Education, Land, Judiciary, Police, Taxation, Public distribution system, Telecom and Railways.

The key actors in corruption in each of the above sector were found to have directly demanded money from those wanted their services. Lack of accountability was identified as the main reason responsible for corruption. During his visit to India, US Treasury Secretary Paul H O'Neill described India as one of the most restrictive economies in the world riddled with corruption and bribery, frightening away businessmen and investors. Good governance means ruling justly enforcing laws and contracts fairly, respecting human rights and property rights and fighting corruption, he added.

Most of the Government offices, in almost all cities, are sprinkled with "middlemen". In some places, they operate rather openly and in some cases, some offices have made the requirement of a middleman desirable, to get any job done or get the request considered favourably. In such places, middlemen operate openly in front of such offices, as if they are a part of the office itself. Corruption has become rather unavoidable to get any job done. Government needs to address this problem exactly in the same way as it did away with corruption in railway bookings by computerization. Unfortunately no Government has ever conducted any survey as to how far its delivery system or service sector has been successful in rendering the service for which it is created. On the contrary, all Governments have patted themselves on their back for having done well. Emerson said: "The less Government we have, the better the fewer laws and less confided power. The antidote to this abuse of formal Government is the influence of private character, the growth of the individual". The aggregate happiness of society, which is best promoted by the practice of a virtuous policy is, or ought to be, the end of all Governance and Government.

Preamble to the Constitution of India has defined the direction Indian polity should take in the following words.

"WE, THE PEOPLE OF INDIA, having solemnly resolved to constitute India into a SOVEREIGN SOCIALIST SECULAR DEMOCRATIC REPUBLIC and to secure to all its citizens: JUSTICE, social, economic and political; LIBERTY of thought, expression, belief, faith and worship; EQUALITY of status and opportunity; FRATERNITY assuring the dignity of the individual and the unity and integrity of the nation."

The Preamble emphasizes Justice, Liberty, Equality and Fraternity. Our Constitution has established a federal government, of three branches, Legislative, Executive and Judicial. One fundamental principle, guiding and motivating the Constitution makers was that concentrations of political power in one institution could prove fatal to ideals enshrined in it. They rightly felt that the concentration of the legislative, executive, and judicial functions, in one branch would lead to an oppressive governmental system. To a limited degree, all these powers are merged, where a regulatory agency has been assigned a specific role for performing a specific task, whether it is in the Income tax or Customs or Revenue Department. The Supreme Court has also laid down that it is beyond the scope and powers of the Government and Legislature, to change the fundamental basis or structure of the Constitution.

According to a report of the USA Senate Internal Security Subcommittee, Mao used gun power to eliminate nearly 64 million of his own people to bring about and then sustain the change in the regime there. George Washington, also had similarly observed: "Government is not reason; it is not eloquence; it is force". But Washington, made sure to bind that force, with the powerful chains of the Constitution, defending the right of free men to live, produce and prosper in a free economy.

All the same, much as we may condemn the Government, as being inefficient or corrupt, the fact remains that no country can do, without the apparatus or organization of Governments, at Federal, State and Municipal levels. Consequently, for it becomes essential to create government institutions as the Basic, Key and Fundamental functions of governance, cannot be privatized in toto. So the only choice available is, to increase the efficiency of State machinery, to meet the aspiration, hopes and expectations of its people.

The indispensable areas of the new prototype of governance, should be patterned, on efficiency, effectiveness, productivity, optimum utilization of resources including human talent, and creation of wealth and economic opportunities. It is disappointing that, the Governments and Government institutions in India (we can call them jointly as Indian State, have become large, gigantic configurations, with outrageously and ludicrously low levels of inefficiency, mixed with corruption and occasional malafides. Indian State has become the biggest scrounger, as the sale of the Public Sector Undertakings shows. The result is that, in the quest of giving jobs to the unemployed, the productivity is being sacrificed. This is the direct result of resorting to the vote bank politics. Such approach naturally affects the efficiency of its apparatus, which is the Executive. Ministers and bureaucrats swing from one extreme to another in tackling any problem, be it a question of giving a political largesse like the free power, free loans or reservations. Even the desire to act as a medium for social justice, is not independent of social dynamics and ground realities.

Kalidasa, the ancient Indian poet laureate (5th Century A.D) mentioned in one of his epics that the king collects taxes for the good of his subjects just as sun draws moisture from the earth to give it back a thousand fold, Kalidasa: Raghuvainsa (Canto 1, Verse 18). Emotional outbursts and calculations of political mileage have replaced every sense of responsibility that such an exercise should have involved.

Some aimless exercises are indulged in, like setting up of a body to Review the Constitution. An amendment of the Constitution, is possible only, if more than two thirds of the Members of each house of Parliament support it. For major changes, ratification is needed by one-half of the legislatures of the states. Given the numbers in the 13th and 14th Lok Sabhas and in Legislative bodies of states, there is absolutely no such possibility, for the ruling alliance to get any Constitution Amendment bill cleared. Getting approval for major changes is an unattainable dream. The ruling alliances of the past and even the present one, as well as the opposition, are fully aware of it. The report of such a commission, having no legal sanctity, in all probability, gathers dust. Political parties are generally supposed to provide meaningful leadership by floating new ideas, in the public interest and think ahead of their time. One of former the President Of India, when in office said that it is not the Constitution that has failed, but it is the people of India who have failed the Constitution. While conceding failure of the system, he did not shed any light on the way he planned to change the people or get a better set of people.

Notwithstanding the laws on corruption or the infamy, which goes with corruption or corrupt practices, there is a steep increase in the volume and the level of people involved in this phenomenon. A Hindi newspaper, published from Ranchi said: It had an audio CD to prove that a Minister of Jharkhand Government had allegedly accepted a bribe of Rs. 50 Lakhs, for propping up a candidate in the Rajya Sabha polls held in June, 2004. However, the Minister concerned, who was dismissed, had denied the allegations saying that it was a conspiracy to spoil his career. This is the same standard excuse, trotted by all those who are caught with their pants down. We also have a case of an outgoing Chief Minister of Chattisgarh, attempting to purchase MLAs, (like one purchases vegetables) to stay in power. The head of a political party was caught on camera, accepting Rupees one Lakh. Of course, he lost his job.

Unfortunately, rhetoric has replaced the action. More than one Prime Minister has expressed zero tolerance for corruption. But when it comes to action, where even public servants have been caught with crores are hidden in their flats or even mattresses, no Government has used its power to rid the country of such scourges, by resorting to Article 311. Nothing happens even to the Constitutional functionaries like the Chairman of the State Public Service Commissions, who sell jobs for lakhs to stash crores. Politicians accused of collecting crores, lionised on the Indian scene. There are no pariahs, as long as they can swing votes. There is no shame in being accused of being corrupt. Prime Minister of India while addressing a meeting of the Chief Justices and chief Ministers on 18th September, 2004 said: "More than one retired Chief Justice has drawn attention to the growing incidence of corruption, among certain sections of the judiciary. The confidence of the public, can be sustained only, if apart from efficient and effective justice, there is a firm belief that judgement will be rendered without any extraneous consideration". The Chief Justice of India, said in the same conference that the financial crunch becomes acute as the Central grant, was being made conditional to the effect that it would match the money given by the state governments. He did some plain speaking by clarifying that there was no money to make additional appointment of judges and to provide them with modern infrastructure... "We have diagnosed the ailment. The medicine is known, but we have yet, to make provision for purchasing the medicine and administering it. We cannot leave the patient alone, to cure his illness all by himself," the Chief Justice concluded.

Incidentally, the Government is the biggest litigant in the Courts and quite often, litigation goes on between the Government and Public Sector Organisations and some times between the Government Organisations. The Prime Minister, during the same conference admitted the need, to reduce the number of Government cases, in courts. He said: "A sample survey conducted by Karnataka found that in 65% of civil cases, the Government was a litigant, sometimes on both sides. Government litigation crowds out the private citizen from the court system. Much of the Government litigation is, in the form of appeals and this survey again found that 95 per cent of these fail. In a way, they are appeals that shouldn't have been made in the first place."

The Prime Minister's statement that in 65% cases Government is the litigant and sometimes on both sides and 95 per cent appeals which clutter the Courts and which finally fail, is a damning criticism of the way Government functions. It is for the Prime Minister to put an end to Government Departments rushing to the Courts for appeal, just to justify themselves or their stand. If the Prime Minister of India, cannot rectify the situation, then nobody else can. I can say with confidence that Government cases are not only improperly prepared, but sometimes have no basis and also quite improperly presented in the Court. In fact the Executive machinery of the Government which is chosen from the party, commanding majority in the Legislatures, badly needs to put its own house in order before it can become a role model for citizens to emulate. Colton said: "In life, we shall find many men, that are great and some men that are good but very few men that are both great and good."

An NGO called Common Cause had in his complaint on January 31, 1996, alleged that officials of the Ministry of Petroleum, had shown favours to different allottees for allotment of petrol pump and gas agencies. Thus, they had abused their official position as public servants. Based on the above complaint, the CBI in September 1997, had registered 15 cases against the then Petroleum Minister Satish Sharma and the allottees under Section 120 B (criminal conspiracy), Section 409 (criminal breach of trust by public servant) of IPC and relevant sections of Prevention of Corruption Act. Sharma was Minister of State for Petroleum and Natural Gas from January 19, 1993 to May 15, 1996. The Supreme Court, too, had ordered a CBI probe into the allotments after finding Mr Sharma's conduct "unjustified" in a 1996 judgment. It had directed Mr Sharma to pay, Rs 50 lakh as exemplary damages, for irregularities in allotment. But, three years later, the Apex Court accepted a review petition from Mr Sharma to waive off the penalty imposed on him.

In almost a similar case in 2004 itself, the CBI was also not allowed to file an appeal, in the Delhi High Court, against a lower court verdict acquitting JMM chief Shibu Soren in a disproportionate assets case, arising out of the JMM bribery case. Ultimately the long rope ended justice has prevailed upon evils.

The CBI said it had received a Union Home Ministry letter, dated September 27, 2004, refusing sanction for Mr Sharma's prosecution. The letter of the Home Ministry said: "The matter has been considered carefully in this Ministry in all aspects, in consultation with the Law Ministry. After considering all the factors in totality including Supreme Court's review judgment dated August 3, 1999, it has been decided, with the approval of the Home Minister, not to grant sanction for prosecution of Satish Sharma". Scams in Petroleum Sector are nothing new. Where there is money, people will flock to it like bees flocking to a beehive. Public memory is proverbially short. No body learns from the past and continues doing the same things, with the hope that, he or she would not be exposed. Hardly ink had dried on the Satish Sharma's cases regarding petroleum sector, which went up to Supreme Court, the country was faced with another scam in petrol pump allotments, in 2002.

The Congress when in opposition, mounted a scathing attack on the Government in the wake of a newspaper's investigation report, in July, August, 2002, on the allotment of petrol pumps and LPG agencies to the kins of BJP leaders and allies. Parliament had to be adjourned a number of times. The opposition, led by the Congress, kept chanting "BJP is PPP, petrol pump party" and "a party of looters". The political storm caused by the petrol pump allotment scandal continued to rage in August, 2002. The NDA Prime Minister, later on ordered the cancellation of all allotments since January 2000 to prevent parties from getting interim injunctions in courts. The thinking in the ruling party at that time was that, the Congress had "enjoyed this perquisite" for about 20 years and if the allotments to BJP workers' relatives were to be cancelled, all the allotments for the last 20 years must also be cancelled. It was to adopt the policy that if we lose, let opposition also lose. According to one estimate, the beneficiaries either belonging or sympathising with the then party in power benefited anywhere between Rs. 2,500 crore and Rs. 3,000 crore. Loot share if missed when in opposition, must be recouped when in power.

However, the Petroleum Minister, claimed that there was nothing irregular about the allotments cancelled by the Prime Minister. But, the NDA Government of the day, choose not to order any investigation, into irregular allotments, for reasons best known to it. Here in the case of the former Petroleum Minister, Sharma, the Government has broken a new path and blazed a new trail in which, the people belonging to the party in power, can be forgiven or even old pending cases withdrawn or dropped against them. There is nothing to prevent other politicians involved in scams, but now facing trial to demand a price for their support, that similar treatment be extended to them, by their party in the power. It is only a thin end of the wedge, where even the accused involved in infamous Tandoor case, wherein he allegedly murdered his wife, cut her to pieces and then tried to dispose off her body, as if he was frying a chicken chop can demand similar treatment, because his party is in power. Or for that matter, the Deputy Chief Minister of Punjab, facing trial in a corruption case, will be well within her rights, to ask for the same indulgence, as has been shown to a former Petroleum Minister, as both belong to the same political party. It is encouraging criminalization in another way. Whatever defence may be there for scams in petroleum sector, it is nothing short of an organized, institutionalized loot, without any norms.

Dubious allotments by one party in power, against done by the other party or parties in power, does not either cancel each or justify the action of both. This approach is nothing short of defending the indefensible. Ideal arrangements would be to let the investigation and trials go unhindered. This ideal unfortunately, is unattainable. The Supreme Court in its judgment dated 17th December, 1997 had struck down the orders, which required CBI to take the Government permission, before starting a case against any officer of the Joint Secretary and above. The Apex Court had held such an order as ultra virus of the Constitution, as it militated against the right to equality. It also felt that indulging in corrupt practices cannot be treated as a part of the duties of the public servant. Apart from the bureaucrats, even MPs and MLAs are considered public servants. But instead of complying with the law, the Government again imposed the same restriction on CBI, while passing CVC Bill. Incidentally, the creation of CVC has not meant any more independence for CBI than it already enjoy instead, it has been saddled with another layer for so called supervision, by retired bureaucrats. It is hoping against hope that any government of the day would ever be willing to relinquish its control and the power to interfere or direct investigation into cases against high and mighty. The present position is that, CBI is far from an independent agency. Where any State Government had found the functioning of the CBI inconvenient, it had withdrawn its consent to function there and asked it to pack its bags. The basic law has remained unchanged from the British times. Unlike the Federal Bureau of Investigation, which has jurisdiction on the entire country of United States of America, the CBI functions at the sweet will of State Government. No action can be taken against the Central Government employees posted in the States where no consent has been given to operate.

Even if consent has been accorded for functioning of the CBI in any particular State, no action can be taken against a State employee, without the approval of the State Government. The Income Tax, Central Customs and Excise and Railways officials are there in every State. Even if they defalcate or play hell with the Central revenues, a State can withdraw its consent to operate and nullify the probe. Whenever there has been a clash, the States have withdrawn consent for the functioning of the Special Police Establishment in their area. States like Karnataka, Haryana, Hyderabad had at one stage or the other had withdrawn their consent and the CBI had to close its shops there. Some States give consent on case to case basis. The latest State asking CBI to pack off, is Goa the next corrupt state.

It is essential that Central Government should have vigilance jurisdiction over its employees no matter where they are posted. While 14 States have given a general consent to the CBI to proceed, in all types of cases, 10 States have accorded consent in respect of only a few Acts or against a specific class of persons. The States which have given the general consent to the CB1 are: Gujarat, Kerala, Mizoram, Maharashtra, Meghalaya, Nagaland, Orissa, Rajasthan, Sikkim, Goa, Tripura, Manipur, Arunachal Pradesh and Chattisgarh. The States which have given consent in respect of a specific class of persons or few Acts are: Jammu and Kashmir, Punjab, Assam, Haryana, Uttar Pradesh, Madhya Pradesh, Tamil Nadu, Himachal Pradesh, West Bengal, and Andhra Pradesh.

It is time to remind all our political leaders, that in the late fifties, when LIC had made some investments in dubious firms owned by industrialist Mundhra, the then Finance Minister, T.T. Krishnamachari, had to resign. This happened inspite of lack of any allegations that T.T.K. had benefited personally from the transaction. Many right thinking persons feel that, in the case of a former Prime Minister and Jain Hawala case, the common refrain of the Government of the day and the politicians was: let the law take its course. Forget about the ideal, even the normal functioning of the investigation agencies is hamstrung. Is it hoping against hope, that things must get worst, before they can improve? The question is simply how much they should get worse?

14
Committed Bureaucracy

Every Government wants to change the administration for the better. It is a noble ambition but most of them flounder as the initial enthusiasm gets overtaken by the day's pressing problems. It is more so as the compulsion of coalition and the desire to keep the partners happy, oversteps every other necessity, however pressing it may be. Dr. Manmohan Singh's Government is contemplating a number of initiatives aimed at almost re-inventing the administrative system in the country. The latest is to begin the process of civil service recruitment right after a student passes her/his Class XII examination, on the pattern of National Defence Academy Examination.

The idea is that successful candidates would join a "National Academy" for a five-year course. Two Committees, under the chairmanship of the Cabinet Secretary, will study the recommendations of two earlier committees - the Surendranath Committee and the P.C. Hota Committee - to suggest systematic changes in the administration as well as consider, how to improve probity, efficiency and transparency in the Central and State Governments. Can one really believe that the present Government does not know, as to why the administration has deteriorated and why corruption, dishonesty and inefficiency are dogging the country at every step and why the delivery system has failed?

The rot started when a late Prime Minister of the country said that what the country needed was a committed bureaucracy. Bureaucracy took it as a call for personal commitment to a leader. Almost all bureaucrats are naturally bothered about their advancement and every thing else becomes secondary. 1970's onwards, they vied with each other for being more loyal than the king. Those who showed any resistance, or did not fall in line, were left to sulk in insignificant postings. The politician, once having tasted blood, cried for more and more. A Commission set up by a former Government observed that when bureaucrats were asked to bend, they crawled.

The bureaucracy is a tool to implement the policies of the Government. It is not the master. It is just like a horse, which is to be directed by the rider. Here the political masters are the horse riders. The horse will go in the direction, indicated by the rider. It has no choice. Service have rules bureaucracy from criticizing the Government. It has been specifically debarred from approaching the press. All the doings or misdoings of the political masters, must remain buried in the top secret Government files. In his first letter to all chief ministers, the UPA Prime Minister, in July 2004 has minced no words in his letter. He has pointed out that the failure of the government to tackle the menace of "transfer and posting industry will have a debilitating impact not only on their performance and morale but also on the whole process of governance". This is a right stand but contrary to the most famous speech of the then President of the All India Congress Committee, Jagjivan Ram, in 1969, in which he argued that 'the so-called neutral administrative machinery is a hindrance, not a help' and that the philosophy of a neutral administration was 'hardly relevant to Indian conditions'. His remarks were swiftly replicated by other senior Congress leaders of that time, including the then Prime Minister, Indira Gandhi.

If one goes by the reports in the media, the Chief minister of Uttar Pradesh, Mulayam Singh Yadav, within 40 days of his taking charge, ordered the transfer of over 650 administrative and police officers, much less than the 1,000 mark in transfers established by his immediate predecessor in office, Mayawati. But it will be unfair to single out Mayawati or Mulayam Singh. Similar zeal has been displayed by their predecessors in UP as well as in the rest of the States in the country. Mass transfers take place with such regularity, all over the country. They have ceased to cause any raised eyebrows. Mass transfers have reduced administration and good governance, to an exercise of locating favourites and cronies, in strategic position, who not only bend themselves, but all rules and laws, to please the political masters. Sardar Patel had said with great force and fervour in the Constituent Assembly in 1949: "You will not have a united India, if you have not got a good all India service which has the independence to speak out its mind, which has a sense of security. "As a man of experience, I tell you," warned Sardar Patel, "do not quarrel with the instruments with which you want to work. It is a bad workman who quarrels with his instruments..." It is a praphecy that the teenagers selected after 12th standard will develop the necessary maturity or independence, in a protected atmosphere of Government sponsored education and training and will prove a better. It is impossible for the

Chief minister or any Central Minister who orders such mass transfers, to have the direct knowledge of the work and worth of most of the transferred officers. It is impractical for any chief minister to know personally the quality and standards of work or the reputation for fairness and honesty of hundreds of transferred civil servants. Such transfers are ordered because an influential MLA or party functionary wants a particular officer, in or out, for his own reasons. This pernicious practice, forces many officers to seek political patronage, to stay where they are or to get posts or places, which they wish to have. This in turn leads to the notorious politician-civil servant nexus, which is the main cause of corruption and poor governance in our country today and not the method of selection of civil servants. Fixing the tenure of bureaucrats with clean chit as their basic service privilege, will turn the table on politicians. They would curry for attenuate chair, being scary of signing on dotted lines.

The problem of mass transfers, is not so acute in Central Government as in the States, which have more than 80 per cent of the IAS and IPS working in the state governments. Central Government has only 3 million plus employees, whereas all the States put together cross 15 Million. The truth is that political master does not want to be shown the rule book. He regards anybody, who quotes the book as a trouble maker. There is a great danger in having twisted rules or law enforcement, as evidenced by scams which are galore in the country. The uprightness and integrity requires that, first the Political Master should decide, as to what governance, he wants to give to the country. With the best of men and worst of system, almost anything will work or can be achieved. But with the worst of men and the best of system, you can create a mess anywhere. Setting up committees and commission is no way to improve the system or governance. What is required is less of rules, lesser of Inspector Raj and more of transparency and a quick justice system, which delivers to the offenders promptly.

Poor governance and inefficient administration are the main reasons for poor regime and inefficient management. Since our Independence as a Nation, in the Government and Government Public Sector, we have almost destroyed the foundations of work excellence, work ethics and work culture. In the organised sector, there is a total security and there is no fear of loss of job. The country is short of over 50 million dwelling units, with 63 million people living in the slums. We do not have quality drivers, because you one can get a driving license without any test or even visiting the RTO office. This speaks ill of the quality and integrity of our transport system. The result is that more people are killed on roads than in muders. We have only 25 million tax assessees, most of them from the organized sector. However, the actual number of taxpayers is hardly 15 million. Of every Rupee one sanctioned for development, only 12 paise reach the intended destination and the rest is gobbled up in the corrupt delivery system.

Indian bureaucracy is straitjacketed. In fact it is a closed shop, unless you enter its sacred portals, through either a competitive examination or through other prescribed means or even through bribery. Taking advantage of the novices, as the political masters, the wily bureaucracy makes rules in such a way that all top jobs are reserved for it. A few crumbs are thrown to others. But all jobs which involve proximity to top political leaders of the Government, the Centraler State Governments, are cornered by the Government servants. The result is that, when it is a question of selecting a person for any job, like the proverbial mother voting for her son, the bureaucracy cannot look beyond its own boundaries. All efforts at reform have come to naught because the political master is a novice and the bureaucracy would resist any change in the status quo. As the Indian economy modernises and globalises, policy making and its implementation is becoming more and more complex. Quite often the political masters are either not able to understand the nitty gritty or are bored by the tedious details.

Indian bureaucracy exactly functions on Evelyn's Rules, which are as under: "A bureaucrat's castle is his desk . . . and parking place. Proceed cautiously when changing either. On the theory that one should never take anything for granted, follow up on everything, but especially those items, varying from the norm. The greater the divergence from normal routine and/or the greater the number of officers potentially involved, the better the chance, a never-to-be-discovered person, will file the problem away, in a drawer specifically designed for items requiring a decision. Never say, without qualification, that your activity has sufficient space, money, staff, etc. Always distrust officers, not under your jurisdiction, which say that they are there to serve you. 'Support' offices in a bureaucracy, tend to grow in size and make demands, on you out of proportion to their service, and in the end require more effort, on your part, than their service is worth. Corollary: Support organisations can always prove success, by showing service to someone . . . not necessarily you. Incompetents often hire able assistants."

The popularly accepted principle is that, the making of policy is the prerogative of the political master and it is the job of the bureaucracy to implement it. This is only a fairy tale. In our Parliamentary democracy, the Ministers are selected from amongst the Members of Parliament, who may not always have detailed and specialised knowledge, necessary to compose and make policy in complex situation and ever changing world. Such Ministers depend only on bureaucrats. The result is Ministers, necessarily have to depend heavily on bureaucracy. So whatever be the complexion of the party in power, the bureaucracy rules roost most of the time. The rules get reversed quite often. One Chief Secretary of a State Government told me that most Ministers in his State were interested only in transfers and postings. He said that he had brought this matter to the notice of the Chief Minister, who said, he will talk to them and did not or perhaps would not.

The chief reason for our problems is that, we protect our Government employees unfairly at any cost to the Nation. This protection is afforded to them by Article 311 of the Indian Constitution. There is no fear of loss of job whether you deliver or not! The U.S, U.K, and Chinese Constitutions do not protect employees of the Federal or Union and State Governments like the way we do. In our country, the Government employees, seek and get protection for lifetime employment, even if, (1) they work or not; (2) they are honest or corrupt; (3) they are absent but marked present; (4) they are efficient or inefficient; (5) they get their work done from others (subcontract their work); (6) wilfully destroy public property in agitations and protests; (7) take sick leave of 30 days/year year after year! It is impossible to be sick, every year, exactly for 30 days! (8) restrict and resist retraining, redeployment and restructuring, for productivity improvement within the same organisation; (9) disrupt work and damage or sabotage the fixed assets of public enterprises or wrongfully confine the management, in order to pressurise it to get some concession; (10) get facilities like free telephone and free travel in some departments, though the departments might be losing and financially bleeding.

There have also been allegations that, some Central Ministers in the past, tried to use vigilance for threatening the Chief Executives of the Public Sectors, to bend to their will for wrong doings. Ultimate responsibility lies with the political master as to what kind of administration, we should have and or will have. No bureaucrat would dare to go against the political master. What they do is to make each other cohorts in looting the exchequer.

In the annual Cannes film festival, held in France in 2003, India did not have a single official entry. But almost every official who counted for anything in the Information and Broadcasting Ministry, including its Minister and Secretary went for the film festival. This is a record of a different sorts which has beaten even the record of Sports, where officials outnumber the sportsmen in Olympic and other International Events.

We need Government sector, which should be accountable, responsible and which should give good governance. We need to link job retention with job performance. In other words, we should consider having a "Fire & Hire" National Policy, which should protect employment, i.e., maintain the same total number of employees but replace employees, who are corrupt, useless, and do not perform. However, there is a word of caution here. Only reform in bureaucracy would not be sufficient, unless there is a firm consensus and reform in the political class. Political masters need to realize that as ultimate repository of faith of the Nation and all power, which flows from the Constitution, they need to function maturely, responsibly and without tilt towards any caste, creed or religion.

The Prime Minister of India, while addressing a conference of the State Directors General of Police on 2nd November, 2004, announced that a new Police Panel will be set up to reform the Police. In the context of what Prime Minister has said, it is important to examine the issue of Police, Police Commissions and People. Police organisations all over the world, are managed in a semi-military fashion and are structured as such. The individual Policeman does not get the opportunity to express himself fully, as the organisations are run along authoritarian lines. These days, the Police Officers have to function promptly both in emergency and normal situations, in accordance with the policies of administration and directives and orders (mostly orally) issued. People expect a response to their problems, whether they are cognisable or non cognisable. Cognisable cases are such of which, the police can take legal notice and take action under the law without going to the court.

The Police have to do tight rope walking in India. Professor David

H. Bailey observes regarding the prevailing situation in India: "In India, a dual system of criminal justice has grown up — the one of law and other of politics. With respect at least to the Police, decisions made by the Police Officials about the application of law, are frequently subject to partisan review or direction by the elected representatives. The autonomy of the Police officials in specific and routine application of laws has been severely curtailed. This is not only true of law and order situation. People accused of crime have got into the habit of appealing to political figures for remissions from the sanctions of law. Police officials throughout India, have grown accustomed, to calculating the likely political effect to any enforcement action, they contemplate. Fearing for their career and especially their postings,they have become anxious and cynical...."

Several top police officers as well as retired officials of Mumbai, are of the view that the police force today is not concentrating on its main work. They also feel, that all posts from commissioner of police to a constable are on sale and transfers and promotions come only at a price and not merit. Naturally, policemen, who pay to get posting would be more concerned with, trying to get their investment back than perform their duties as enforcers of the law. Thus enthused, they would like to make something more for the next postings.

Regrettably, this is what most police officers feel, about the prevailing scenario all over the country. I had a taste of it three decades back, when I found as DIG Headquarters, in Karnataka State receiving letters from the Chief Minister's office for posting of Constables to some Police Stations and for transfer of some others. When I told my boss that, this is something which should be done by those, who have the authority under the rules. I was laughed at and told that, if he did not do so, there would be many more to take up his job and bend backward to please political bosses. I kept quite and waited for my time, when I made my views clear and preferred to face transfer, than to do something against which I had fought all the time. If the morale in the police force is high, they will have a better commitment to their jobs and the chances of malfeasance and of terrorism incidents, would be considerably reduced, if not totally eliminated. They would be more keen to show their competence and would be vigilant against any intowards happenings. Now the question arises, as to what can be done to tackle such problems. First of all, both the political masters and police leadership should ensure that, square pegs are not fitted in round holes. In other words, the sale of transfers and postings, either for kind, cash, favours or caste appeasement should stop. Job retention should be linked to the job performance.

Admitting the lapses in the Police, the Police Commission of 1902-03, more than a century ago also observed: "There can be no doubt that the Police Force throughout the country is in a most unsatisfactory condition. That this involves great injury to the people and discredit to the Government and that radical reforms are urgently necessary. These efforts will cost much because the Department has hitherto been starved but they must be effected". The National Police Commission of 1977-81 set up under the Chairmanship of former Governor Dharmvira observed, "The basic and fundamental problem regarding the Police today is how to make them function as an efficient and impartial law enforcement agency fully motivated and guided by the objectives of service to the public at large, upholding the constitutional rights and liberty of the people". What the Police Commission said in 1903 appears more or less equally applicable to the conditions obtaining.

The Police is only a part of the criminal justice system. It can only take the accused before the court of the law and it is for the Courts to judge the guilt and award punishment. The gathering of evidence depends only on the cooperation and assistance given by the people. This is a very old problem. About it, in 1830 the then Governor of Bombay, Sir John Malcom has observed: The task of seizing the most notorious criminal, is easy as compared to that of proving their guilt, according to the principles and the forms of our courts of justice. There is seldom that full evidence they require and the consequences is the annual discharge of well known plunderers, to recommence their career of guilt and to take ample vengeance, on those whom they suspect of having aided in their apprehension. If our laws are not modified to meet this evil., it can alone be mitigated by the change in the executive branch of the Police, in those provinces that are inhabited or subject to the in-roads of predatory tribes." Incidentally, the same laws govern the criminal justice system of our country.

The Punjab Police Commission said: "The evidence led before the Commission has disclosed that members of political parties, particularly of the ruling party, whether in the legislature or outside, interfere considerably in the working of the police for unlawful ends. We have been told that politicians accompany the complainants to the Police Stations and try to influence the Station House Officer to take down the reports implicating innocent persons against whom the complainant has enmity... no objection can be taken to politicians accompanying their constituents for lawful purposes, but the objection is that they approach the SHO for ulterior purposes and use their position to influence him.

The Tamilnadu Police Commission said: "The problem of political interference is not a new one... And it has grown inspite of the most explicit public declarations made by successive Chief Ministers (including the present one); that there should be no political interference and they expect the officers to do their duty, without fear or favour, in the confident expectation of the Government support..."

The West Bengal Police Commission said: "We have little doubt that such interference takes place, although it is difficult to say to what extent they are prevalent."

The Delhi Police Commission observed: "We have been informed that political interference is another rich source of corruption. Allegations have been made before us that some politicians resort to the device of securing the assistance of goondas and bad characters, who are given protection by the police. This protection is the result of influence, exercised by the politicians upon the policeman...."

Pressure on the police makes a variety of forms, ranging from a promise of career advancement and preferential treatment in service matters if the demand is yielded to and a treatment in service matters, if the pressure is resisted. While it is not possible to punish a police officer with a statutory punishment under the Discipline and Appeal Rules, without adequate grounds and following a prescribed procedure, it is a very easy to subject him to administrative action by way of transfer or suspension on the basis of an alleged complaint taken up for enquiry.

While suspension acts as a great humiliating factor, a transfer acts as a severe economic blow and disruption of the police officer's family, children's education etc. The threat of transfer/suspension is the most potent weapon in the hands of the politician to bend down the police to his will. We have been told in several states, about the frequent transfer of police personnel ordered on directly for the transfer of a large number of police personnel as desired by the political leadership when he felt that the transfers were not justified on normal administrative grounds.

It will be of interest to quote that Mayawati had set a record in 1997 by transferring over 1400 civil and police officers in six months of her rule. Kalyan Singh had transferred 521 officials in 1991-92 and the SPBSP government headed by Mulayam Singh, 814 official in 1993-95. Some officers were transferred thrice in a week. Problem in other States is almost the same. Independent India set up the first National Police Commission in 1977. It diagnosed the problems of policing and suggested solutions for the same. After that a number of Committees were set up either to examine the recommendations given or suggest new solutions. These include Reberio Committee, Padmnabiaha Committee and the last being the Malimath Committee. It is not that there is a deficiency of advice or input to the Government for improving the police. It is perhaps the lack of will or to be more charitable, the police reform is not on the agenda of any Government. The best way of policing the country would be to let the law take its course in letter and spirit and not punish those who do their duty by it. It is time, that Government saw the writing on the wall and dusted the old files for reforms which have been lying for over a century with it without implementing their recommendations.

15
Corrosion in PSUs

The Transparency International ranks several countries, in the world, on the basis of corruption perception index prepared by it. The World Bank had observed in the year 2000 that the Delhi Development Authority (DDA) was the most corrupt organisation in India. The World Bank report was based on the observations made by a former Commissioner of DDA. This led to a protest by the DDA officials, who felt that the World Bank was unfair. However, the public is in 100 percent agreement with the sentiments of the World Bank. Similarly, when it was observed that the Delhi Air Customs were the most corrupt and the CBI caught some staff with money at the airport on duty, there was a strike. It was ultimately called off after the striking, employees had their way. When the Chairman and other senior officers of the Customs were arrested in 2002, no body remembered the protest strike. Similarly, in March 2003, no body in DDA or Government, recalled when almost the entire DDA top brass consisting of its Vice Chairman and its Commissioners were caught with their pants down by the CBI, about "the unfair protestations against the world Bank observations". One odd thing in our country is that, while most people will acknowledge that, most Government organisations are corrupt, the moment anyone makes a statement or says something to that effect in public, the senior Government officials and Ministers deem it a matter of principle and fetish defending the "fair name" of the office or its officers, irrespective of the fact of how much they might have skinned the public alive. Another abnormal characteristic of our government systems and public dealings is that, almost every office or official, can put the common man or any body who has to come in contact with it, to an unusual degree, of harassment.

It is almost considered an accepted right in the Government offices, to go slow or not work in a time bound fashion. Any excuse is good enough to go on strike or protest. According to a survey released in December, 2002, the people of India found the police, health and power sectors, the most corrupt. The survey also revealed that while people "perceived" police to be the most corrupt, in terms of "actual experience" or the bribe they paid, the health sector earned the dubious distinction of being the most corrupt.

Among the corrupt practices, identified in the police, were political interference to subvert investigations; money being paid for filing FIR; to avoid false arrests; to get an accused arrested; to avoid arrest or not to send chargesheets to the courts. People identified, lack of accountability as the main factor responsible for corruption. The most corrupt sector in the public perception was Health. Others were in the following order as per the survey: Power, Education, Land, Judiciary, Police, Taxation, PDS and Railways. According to Transparency International, Rs.26,728 crore is paid in bribes, across 10 service sectors in India each year. The survey says that in health sector palms are greased the most. The health network according to the survey, garnered Rs.7,578 crore worth of bribes each year. The survey lists doctors as the main culprits who demands 77 per cent of the bribes. Hospital staff are a close number two at 67 per cent. There's a regional variation too: hospitals in Southern India demand the most bribes for admitting patients. But East or West, the figures show that 11 per cent patients paid bribes for proper medicines, 11 per cent bribed doctors for proper health care while 6 per cent bribed nurses.

The power sector followed health, with most bribes being paid for either not fudging excessive bills or simply ensuring that power was supplied in the first place. Around 10 per cent bribed for proper power supply, 8 per cent for settling excessive billing and 3 per cent for getting a new electricity line. The linesmen were at the head of the bribe taking pack, followed by officers (24 per cent), meter readers (23 per cent) and billing clerks (22 per cent).

In the education sector, which was third on the Corruption List, 57 per cent paid bribes in the form of donations, both in government and private institutions. Again, the southern states beat their northern counterparts: 70 per cent of students paid donations to gain admission in Southern India whereas in the north, 42 per cent did it. In the east, 19 per cent students found it "impossible" to get good results, if they didn't hire their own teachers as private tutors, while 7 per cent had to pay more money, to get the forms filled in. Around Rs.1,803 crore is paid in bribes to the police every year, according to the survey. Around 14 per cent had to be paid just to file an FIR, 7 per cent to avoid false arrests, 6 per cent for arresting accused in a case, 5 per cent for taking down complaints and 3 per cent for sending chargesheets to the court.

In the judiciary, which ranks fifth in the survey, the report said "The key form of corruption is predominantly paying money to the court official. Around Rs. 2,510 crore is reportedly paid as bribes". While the railway is corrupt alright but the corruption therein is less than others. According to the survey, every 12th Indian pays about Rs 621 per year while dealing with the health sector, every 16th Indian pays Rs. 669 per year in bribes in the power sector, every 20th Indian pays Rs.745 in the education sector.

Politicians and politics survive on cliches and slogans. It is surprising that, what is publicly known to every person in the street, it is not known to the Government, as to who is corrupt and dishonest. Bureaucracy survives on following the old traditions and has a system of Biradari or brotherhood, where effort is made to save and not to punish. The Government is not the bureaucracy but the political executive. We have continued with the British system of the permanent civil service, which stays in office all the time, while the political executive may change, based on the result of an election. The permanent civil service, which is supposed to be politically neutral, has ceased to be so. What we have now in actual practice, is the spoil system of the United States. You can see the spectacle of the bureaucrats getting aligned politically and labelled as belonging to this or that political leader. With every change of government, both at Central and State level, massive transfers of bureaucrats are done, with the objective of having most pliable bureaucrats in key positions, who will do the political master's bidding. The corrupting influence of the corruption has institutionalised it. It is important that, job retention is linked in the public services to the job performance, as it generally happens in the private sector. Then only, there can be any hope for the country.

Alexander Solzehnitsyn observations should be a guide to our government. These are as under:

"In keeping silent about evil, in burying it so deep within us, that no sign of it appears on the surface, we are implanting it and it will rise up a thousand fold in the future. When we neither punish nor reproach evil-doers . . . we are ripping the foundations of justice from beneath new generations."

Some time, in seminars, debates and discussions, a question is asked as to who wants a clean system? Is it the politicians or the bureaucrats or politicians and the bureaucrats? The perception amongst the common man is that most of them belonging to both classes, are corrupt. The CBI raided the residence and offices of the top brass of the DDA on 27th March, 2003 in New Delhi. Huge cache of cash recovered, showed that the public servants have reached abyss, so far as integrity part is concerned. Some of them are not even remorseful about corruption they practise. A few actually justify it as a by-product of the system of democracy. It does not suit the bureaucracy to end corruption, as it gives them an opportunity to make money, which if necessary can be used to get their dependents the plum jobs, as was done by a Superintendent of Police in Punjab, to purchase jobs in the Punjab Civil and Police Services, from a Chairman of Public Service Commission. There is also a political umbrella and selective enforcement for friendly corrupt and dishonest. It is for this reason that scams are galore. Ketan Parekh, the master mind behind the country's biggest share scam is reported to have told Kolkata Police that, ever since he decided to manipulate the value of the shares related to IT and telecommunication, SEBI (Securities and Exchange Board Of India) knew all the details, including who else was working with him. He ensured that SEBI officials looked the other way by paying some hundreds of crores to these officials as "Cut Money". It was because of these hefty payments that SEBI did not seek any official explanation either from him or his associates, even though it was aware of the manipulations.

The State Bank of India in UP, published a notice in newspapers on 16 February, 2003 giving details of the oldest lockers holders, who have neither been paying rent nor been operating their lockers. There is nothing exciting about the notice, except that in some cases, when Nationalised Banks opened similar oldest lockers, they found them full of diamond, gold, silver jewellery and cash worth crores. This is a case of easy come and easy go, where somebody after stashing the valuables, either died or forgot the locker number or failed to inform his heir about the same before his death. Where does this kind of wealth take you, is a question which has never bothered such worthies.

The Tax Amnesty Schemes in the past, which have hardly been successful, have only enabled the corrupt to convert their black money into white. The vicious circle of generating or even converting the white money to black money continues unabated in all sectors of life. Even the honest purchasers of houses and flats are compelled to pay in black to acquire any property, as nobody wants to pay the abnormally higher taxes or stamp duty. A simplified tax structure will go a long way in improving the tax compliance. The country's external debt reached $ billion 101.3 (Over Rs. 5 lakh crore) as on 31st March, 2002.

It is the right of every individual to spend his money in any way, he or she chooses. India is a country of contradictions. Despite crores being spend on health sector, the medical services available to the ordinary Indians, and especially in rural India, are almost non-existent. Despite talk of health for all, a recent survey showed that health sector was the most corrupt in the country, leaving behind Railways, Police and many others.

When the Consumer Protection Act (COPRA) was promulgated in 1986, the medical and legal professions were left out of it. It was only after a lot of agitation that the medical profession was brought under the purview of COPRA. In countries like the UK and US, the respective medical council regulates the medical services. But the medical councils in India are so weak that in their long existence exceeding half a century, they have not been able to take an exemplary action of revoking the licences of defaulting doctor, guilty of negligence or malpractices. In their hurry to make their millions, it is not surprising that some doctor, wield the scalpel, purely for economic considerations and not because it is essential or required. The fast-increasing number of black sheep in this profession is cause for worry. Only the fear of prompt and deterrent punishment by the medical councils and courts can make such people fall in line. For the first time in India's annals, two Kolkata doctors were jailed for criminal negligence 2002 May. The Indian medical system, like many other systems, including the methodology of governance, desperately needs a proper, well-fanged desperate remedies.

According to the Planning Commission, our roads and road system is no better or safer. Rs.55,000 crore is the estimated social cost of road accidents in India, according to the Planning Commission. It is just Rs 5,000 crore short of what our country spends on defence. 81,966 people were killed in road accidents in 1999, while the figure for 2000 was 78,911. It is no wonder because a study by the Institute of Driver's Training and Research found that 28% of the drivers, driving the Government buses of Delhi Transport Corporations were unfit. The Institute also observed that many drivers had poor eyesight and most of them had slow responses Timely response to impromptu situations are extremely crucial. It make difference of life and death. But in the multitude of problems, somebody getting killed in a road accident does not evoke as much of protest as being killed in a gang war. The picture is not arosy on the defence side either. During 2004, 2005, one thrity Indian Air Force Pilots were killed and 68 planes were lost in air crashes. This loss in terms of finances works out to be anything between Rupees 1800 and 2000 crore. This is what has happened during peace time and without any war. Regrettably, our country has witnessed a downturn on social, economic and governance fronts. A set mind of pro-reform and pro-people is missing in civil services, especially at the cutting edge levels. A serving Union Cabinet Minister hit the nail on the head when during the course of a lecture on 20th February, 2003 said. "Be it the poor, the middle class or the educated upper class, all of them have looted the Capital of its environment and beauty... A major problem in governing the Capital, was the presence of many agencies, working in different directions... As a result, we all work a lot and a lot of noise is raised but the end result is nothing... Let us not get caught in the slogan and jargon of the day, which are the handiwork of the propaganda machinery. In most such cases, we miss out on the content...Those at the helm should be sure of the direction to be taken...If you think you can win the elections with these kind of concessions, then you are wrong... For, if people will vote you to power, for allowing them to do certain things, then the same people will pull you down for bad health services, that the city will face as a consequence... You can't build a nation with negative forces... We have to keep the core issues and problems in mind and try to solve them". It is important to remember that nothing can be truly great, which is not right. The answer to all our problems lies in the right and good governance.

In 1992-93, electricity boards losses were Rs. 4,600 crore and today the combined state Electricity Boards losses stand at Rs. 26,000 crore. We cannot achieve the development objectives, unless anti-corruption efforts are made an integral part of the scheme of things. We cannot have both corruption and good administration together. An effective and practical legislative framework to prevent and combat corruption is an essential prerequisite. But more importantly, implementation capacity and funds are also absolutely necessary, apart from co-operation and commitment at all levels of the government as well as non-governmental organizations. Public authorities, civil society and the private sector have to complement and reinforce one another, in making public resources flow in a more transparent manner. The governmental organisations also need to be more transparent about their goals, results as well as about their sources of income and expenditure, as contemplated in the Right to Information Act.

One of the most regrettable features in our country, is the durability and long innings of the corrupt. Corrupt, whether in politics or in bureaucracy, has more than nine lives of the proverbial cat. Some people openly accused of corruption and malfeasance have bounced back as King or King Maker. According to one report, at least 10,000 files relating to individual property transactions are missing from Delhi Development Authority (DDA). 10,000 files vanishing into thin air is nothing short of a scandal. These are not mere files. These are 10,000 properties on which, people are living or earning their livelihood or are the ones, which are must for getting free hold conversion. The beauty of the system is that, it would be considered mere negligence and the defaulters would go unpunished. If a person were to claim ownership or not pay any dues to the DDA, there is no way DDA can legally prove its case in the Court. The files go missing or are traced for a price and not due to innocent negligence. DDA has roughly 10 lakh files, which pertain to flats, plots and industrial establishments. Tracing a 20-30 years old file or papers out of lakhs of applications for the conversion of property, is simply out of the question, unless there is a proper method of maintaining the records.

India has done it again. It is not that it has won any Olympic medal or topped in some invention or made any new discovery. It had also retained the position of being in the big league of the most corrupt in 2004. According to the 'Corruption Perception Index 2004 Report released by Transparency International India on 20th of October, 2004. it is one of the bottommost amongst 55 of the 146 countries where corruption is rampant. Nobody in the Government, like in the past, has shown any concern or expressed regret at the slide down. Even in the limited State Assembly elections, held in October, 2004, corruption was never an issue. Corruption as an issue, is periodically raised invariably by the political parties in wilderness, when they run short of any other idea or issues.

When I put a question to a contractor, he laughed. He said that if he paid 10 per cent only as a cut, he would not longer remain in business. He said that depending upon the 'honesty level' of the officials, he was dealing with, he had to pay anything between 25 to 45 per cent cut. He also added that 10 per cent cut was a thing of the past and only 'the honest' were satisfied with it. Gone are the days, when people were satisfied, with a few token gifts on new year or Deepwali day. Now they want cash down, in addition to the gifts on festive occasion. Sometimes, demand like the Television or Fridge or Music System or a Jewellery set, is also indicated in advance. Central Vigilance Commission had issued a circular, banning the acceptance of the gifts. I reminded a senior officer, whether he was aware of such a circular and how far it was followed. He chuckled and said: "Who will complain"? Neither the giver, nor the recipient is likely to kick up a shindy to it and what is the enforcement machinery for it? I said that CVC expects officials to follow its instructions. He said that such circulars existed dozen a times. In the absence of any mechanism, except the willingness of the officials concerned to implement it, their existence or non-existence, does not make any difference

Government rules are made on the premises that the public is thief. They create a web of complicated procedures, which gives birth to corrupt practices. An anchor of a TV channel told me her personal experience. She wanted to purchase some property. Her identity card showing that she was from the press, saved her from most demands of bribery. At the time of registration, she was told to bring the photo graph of the registering officer. She said that she had not brought her camera, as she was not aware of such a requirement. She was told to get the same from the photographer outside the office concerned. It cost her a tidy sum of Rs.1200 at the rate of Rs. 200 per photograph. The photographer had kept in advance the photos of all the public dealing officials. It is a novel modus operandi, where the officials, did not touch the money but used the photographer as a collection point. A number of Chartered Accountants have been arrested by the CBI, for acting as conduits of the revenue officials, either for settlement of the cases or for getting them transferred to the juiciest of the prized wet postings, where such people can line their pockets. If anything, corruption has grown up at the retail level, where public have to interact with the Government functionaries at the cutting edge level. In the past surveys, this type of corruption was not included in the above mentioned survey of Transparency International 2004. According to another survey, there is a price tag, which varies from person to person, as per his or her capacity to pay, to get the Government documents, which should be normally free. These include getting a Ration Card, Birth, Death Certificate, Driving License, Admission to school and college, bank loans, customs,

Excise and Income, Sales Tax, Pollution Tax Clearance, Insurance claims passed, admission to hospitals, Government or DDA Built Houses, Escaping Traffic Volation, getting married the same day in the court or compromising Examination System. The list is only illustrative and not exhaustive.

The corrupt takes on whistle–blowers. There have been cases, where such whistle–blowers as happened in the case of an Engineer of National High Way Authority of India, Satendar Dubey, were killed to prevent exposure of corruption in the system. Corruption in our country is hardly a new phenomenon. Surveys after surveys, cases after cases in CBI, have documented a widespread pattern of corruption and racketeering prevailing in several departments of the Government. Corruption has been more than a problem for India. The Supreme Court of India has observed how efforts were made, to change the prosecutor in Bihar Fodder Scam case and it correctly found fault with how things had been done, under the influence of the powerful politicians.

Extortion and not corruption have neither disappeared nor reduced but grown more sophisticated, with the help of lawyers and accountants. The reason for all malaises in the country is that, some wrong sort of people are always in power. Perhaps, they would not be in power, if they were not the wrong sort of people. Many a times, people question as to what can be done, to improve the situation and root out corruption. To this Carlyle replied: "Make yourself an honest man and then you may be sure that there is one less rascal in the world". Said Cicero: "Be a pattern to others and then all will go well; for as a whole city is infected by the licentious passions, and vices of great men, so it is likewise reformed by their moderation."

16

Governance by Default

One of the recommendations of the 5th pay commission was to increase the retirement age of the central government employees from 58 to 60 and in the case of technical personnel from 60 to 62. A government within weeks of its taking over suddenly increased the retirement age which had been turned down by the previous government. One argument put forth was that the government would save about Rs.5,000 crore in deferred payment to its employees. The increase in retirement age benefited 3.5 million civilian employees and 1.3 million armed forces personnel. Such was the hurry in implementing the decision, that on the next the day orders were issued after the Cabinet decision. Total numbers of employees both in the public Sectors and Central and the State Government is more than 1.75 crore. A fat chunk of Government revenue goes in paying of salaries, allowances and post retirement benefits.

Conceivably, a the number of arguments would have been given in favour of increasing the retirement age. One could be, that the tenure at the highest level was too short. It was the most misleading argument put forward. There had been the Heads of the Departments and the Secretaries, who had a long tenure. Some of them held their office for over five years. But still the performance of the administration was not only disappointing but also dismal. By the time a person becomes the secretary, he would have put in over three decades of service. It is expected that he knows the rules of the government. Irrespective of any Government or political party in power, the bureaucrats retain their position. It is their interpretations of the rules and regulations, which is final.

The pressure for increasing the retirement age came from the Secretary level officers, who were to benefit immediately from the increase in the retirement age. It is not for the first time that so many number of persons would have retired but it was because the pressure was so much and perhaps the government headed by few bureaucrats, it would win the internal gratitude. A senior officer from the accounts service met me. He said one of the probationers came to him and said he had given his joining report and he wanted one month leave. When asks the reason for asking for the leave, the young probationer told him that he is working for three companies and earning Rs 40,000 and it was not possible for him to do a government job. Then this officer asked him why he was doing a government work. He said that was a kind of security which he had been getting. For him it was nothing. He also offered to the officer concerned his entire salary as bribe every month. When further pressed he said, this officer will be for a year or a two and when a new officer comes he will have a better negotiation with him and may be take his half the money home.

This is one of the worst decisions taken in total disinterest of the administration. It has not improved efficiency and it has not improved better working and it has blocked the opportunity to weed out the dead wood. The arguments that the experienced people are lost does not hold good. Efficient people are always in the pipeline. There has to be somebody to replace somebody.

Some state governments like Rajasthan have reversed the decision to increase retirement age. They have pegged it to 55. There is good case for not only keeping the age of retirement not only to 58 but to bring it down to 55. It will enable more and more people to get employment. I was told that in one of the most progressive State, 62% of budget goes to the payment of salaries. 32% for maintenance of roads, hospitals, schools and government buildings, cars, telephones and only 6% is spent for development. The way government has been going about proliferating the bureaucracy, a stage is likely to arrive soon, where like Uttar Pradesh, where 110 per cent of revenue earned, goes for the establishment charges.

The key purpose and goal of elected representatives in the Centre or in the States as well as Government employees, of Central and State Governments are, to administer and govern, in the best interest of the citizens. The basis for the governance of our country is our constitution. All institutions are formulated, regulated and run as laid down in our constitution including the fundamental rights and the appointment of constitutional authorities. The Constitutional Institutions include all judicial appointments of the High Court and Supreme Court, appointment of Election Commission and Governors. Article 153 of the Constitution says that there shall be Governor for each State... The Governor of a State shall be appointed by the President by warrant under his hand and seal and will hold office during the pleasure of the President. A Governor shall hold his parts for a term of five years from the date on which he enters upon his office. However, the Inter State Council, which consists of all the Chief Executives of the State Governments, the Chief Ministers or the Governors, where the State is under the President's Rule as well as the Central Government headed by the Prime Minister, has accepted Sarkaria commission recommendation about the gubernatorial appointments. It has accepted a code for the appointment of governors in future, under which the governors would be barred from entering active political life after they lay down their office. They however can be appointed for a second term. Another commission's recommendation, which has been accepted by the Inter-State Council is that, the appointment of Governors would be in consultation with the respective state government. Governor's office has long been looked upon as a kind of interfering agent of sorts, in the affairs of the state governments by the central government.

Technically, all holders of the Constitutional posts, hold their offices during the pleasure of the President, which in reality means, the Government of the day. But in actual practices, some of these Constitutional posts, especially like that of the Governors of the States have become sinecures to reward the faithful and all others who have toed the party line or Government's biddings all along. Largely, such appointments have now become political. In the era of coalitions, it is not uncommon for the ruling partners, to demand a share of the pie of gubernatorial appointments. The Raj Bhavans have occasionally been reduced to refuge of the dead wood of some political parties. It would not be wrong to say, that there is no criteria or minimum qualification for the appointment of the Governors. The more nearer such a worthy is to the grave, the better are his chances of appointment. It is nothing unusual, to see a few Governors having kicked the bucket, despite the best medical facilities.

A number of Raj Bhavan jobs are held by the retired bureaucrats, police officers, judges and army officials. The rest are headed by the appointees, who at one time or the other belonged to the ruling party or parties or were other sympathisers or supporters. Once a Joint Secretary, who was my batch mate told me that, for two posts of Joint Secretaries, in the Commerce Ministry, 153 recommendatory letters had been received from a couple of Chief Ministers, Union Ministers and Members of Parliament.

It is easy to perceive the number of recommendations for such appointments, which might be received by the Prime Minister of the day. After the election in 1977, the first shot in this direction was fired by Janta Party Government, which asked all Governors to resign. It went a step further and asked all State Government to quit and ordered fresh elections to the State Assemblies. This exercise was reciprocated when Mrs. Indira Gandhi returned to power in 1980.

It has become a well established norm and a practice, that when a Government of different party assumes power in the Centre, all the former governors call it quits. They see the writing on the wall and find, that voluntarily leaving their jobs is a more honourable option than to be dismissed, in the euphemism of having the Presidential pleasure withdrawn. The drill in the Home Ministry, for withdrawing the Presidential pleasure is almost set. A senior Home Ministry official rings up the Governor or Governors to be removed and requests him or them to send in their/ his resignation. A political party of NDA Government, had urged the UPA Government not to remove the Governors appointed by it. In America, all Presidential appointees sink or swim with the incumbent or successfully elected President. Though we do not have a Presidential form of Government, in actual practice, most Governors are political appointees. It would raise the standard of public life, if all political appointees resigned on their own, with the change of the Government, as the Lieutenant Governor of Delhi has then done, when NDA was voted act. It would save embarrassment of being asked to leave post haste and sometimes unceremoniously. When the innings is over, it is time to clear the field and say graceful good bye. It is time to remind, what Lord Krishna says in Gita that it is the wonder of wonder, that people should see others dying, but somehow feel, that death would not touch them or forget them. It would be a good idea, to have a law, instead of a code, which has no authority or legal sanction, that once a person has held the office of the Governor, he would be debarred from participating in active politics and for holding any other office in the Government.

Mr. George Fernandes was strip searched twice at Washington DC's Dulles Airport when he was the defence minister, once while on an official visit to Washington and another time while en route to Brazil. The former Deputy Secretary of State Mr. Strobe Talbott in his book: Engaging India - Diplomacy, Democracy and the Bomb, has written that in July 2004, he was told this by Mr Fernandes himself when he had visited India as part of a delegation assembled by the, Asean Institute and CII: "Just as we were saying goodbye to Fernandes, a member of our delegation innocently asked him when he would next be coming to Washington. His demeanour abruptly changed. It was as though he was glad to have an excuse to tell us how he really felt about our country....Fernandes regaled us with the story of how he had been strip searched... when he arrived for an official visit in early 2002 and again in mid-2003, when he was passing through the US on his way to Brazil". United States Deputy Secretary apologised to the then Defence Minister, for what, some may call overzealous checking. To understand the US position, it is essential to recall my personal experiences, when I had visited the United States, for an official bilateral meeting with the State Department Officials on Narcotics Cooperation, in my capacity as Director General Narcotics Control Bureau. I was received at the State Department in Washington by a Deputy Assistant Secretary of State, who had invited me for the meeting followed by a lunch. As I was a Director General of Police, I had never or rarely been subjected to a any security check in India. If any check was done, it was done with a lot of apologies and at the top of it very perfunctorily, to comply with the rules and not the spirit of the law or rules. Policemen feel, that it is a fringe benefit of the job, like free telephone for telecommunication employees, free travel by the Railway Officials. When entering the State Department building in Washington DC, both I and my host were subjected to a thorough security frisking and X-ray screening. I was a bit surprised, when my host, who had the highest security clearance, was not spared. I asked him out of curiosity, as who were these people doing security check and whether they did not know him. He replied that that they were from a private agency and were not United States Government Employees. It was a part of the agreement, that they would not spare anybody from the security checks and if they did so, they would be guilty of breach of contract. He clarified that nobody minds these checks, as exccpt for the terrorists or other undesirable elements. Nobody in his right senses would object to them.

In our country, anybody who is or has been somebody, feels that he or she is above law and exempted from all checks or restrictions. It is more so with the Ministers, who feel that people of all ranks or categories should recognise them and fawn on them. Indeed, one MP belonging to a North Eastern State, when told that she could not take her car, or her supporters to the tarmac and to the plane stairs, was enraged. She wanted the Central Industrial Security Force, to which the security of all the airports had been entrusted, withdrawn. Her ground was that the officials were rude, as ostensibly, they wanted to go by the rules in the book. Security is both thankless and unrewarding, apart from being difficult. Security people are damned, if they do and damned, if they don't.

Every time an Indian VIP travels by road, everything stops. Once he goes past, all hell breaks loose. A five-minute stop during peak hours on any road in Delhi, could mean a pile-up of about 5,000 vehicles, which have to negotiate serpentine traffic and compete with snails, as to who is faster. Whether entitled or not, even petty dignitaries including officials, flaunt a blue or a red light atop their vehicles, as nobody dare check whether the person displaying the light is entitled to it or not. The episode involving the former Defence Minister shows, how in India, security checks are considered offensive, when it is all part of a drill, laid down by the Government itself. It goes to the credit of the United States, that they do not spare even their own high and mighty from checks. Law makers in United States are routinely subjected to the same security checks, as I and you would be. When a US Congress man, John Dingel was subjected to a thorough strip, by stripping up to his under wear, as the metal detector set off an alarm, he felt hurt as the Security would not be believe that he had a metal hip replacement, due to a fall, two decades back. He later joked about his search saying that "they felt me up and down like a prize steer". When the Transportation Secretary telephoned him to express regret, he replied: "Make sure that the security do, what is necessary and that he gets the same treatment, no better or not worse than anyone else. The rich and powerful there, get the same treatment, like Azim Prem Ji of India, Pakistani Army Corps Commander, The Jan Orakazai who after thorough security check, vowed never come to US again.

If any Indian VIP going on Government account is subjected to a thorough security check or unpleasant frisking, then it is the direct fault of the Indian Embassy Officials, incharge of protocol and reception, who failed in their duties of ensuring, that proper courtesies are extended to the visiting VVIPs. Defence Ministry has Colonels and Generals in some places posted as Defence Attaches. Also the Americans like many Indians would, by the unstarched and unpressed or crumpled dress, as well as unkempt hair style of George Fernandez, (with due apologies to Mr. George) would have doubted, whether he was really the Defence Minister of India. It happened with him in India also when Police in Mangalore, his home town did not, permit him to go to a function with the then Chief Minister of

Karnantaka, as he was without any fanfare or security hooting sirens. Customs and Police officials were transferred from the airport, for checking the baggage of VIPs who would come loaded with dozens of bags of dutiable goods. Security officials are generally at the receiving end, for their so called highhandedness, which is only complying with the rules.

17

Dictatorship of Cabinet

As constituted at present, automatic promotions and security of service, whether you perform or not, whether you are active or a dead wood, is the hallmark of a large majority of bureaucracy. The present system does not match the competence or qualification and work experience, when officials are posted to any assignments. Prime Minister Vajpayee was eloquently talking about downsizing of government, but in spite of promises and exhortation, very little was achieved.

The Government suddenly woke up to the weeding out of the dead wood. Railway is introducing a Voluntary Retirement Scheme, so that 20,000 old engine drivers could be retired. This has been done due to a spate of Railway accidents. If the past is any indicator, this will be a non starter. To a question her in Parliament in 2003, the government had replied, that out of a total employment of 3.3 million, only 23 had opted for the voluntary retirement scheme. The Expenditure Reforms Commission, which looked into the working of 36 ministries/departments, had arrived at the conclusion that there was 42,200 surplus manpower in a total sanctioned staff of 8,65,000. That is, nearly 5 per cent of the manpower is redundant and their exit would make no difference to the working of the government. Nothing has been done to get rid of even the idle hands. Senior ex-bureaucrats never retire. They angle regulatory or other post retirement jobs. It is amazing, how the governments after governments recycle retired bureaucrats, whether for commissions or committees, irrespective of their track records. There is no doubt that some of the retired people appointed to such jobs are talented. But in all fairness, it is for the Political Executive, to take a decision in this matter. Sometimes back, a former Commerce Secretary and a Company Affairs Secretary, were appointed as chairman and member respectively of the proposed Competition Commission of India. Consciously or unconsciously, it is bound to further reinforce anxiety and uneasiness of trade and industry that the Government does not want to part with bureaucratic control over any economic activity, inspite of liberalisation and globalisation. Almost all regulatory jobs, whether it is the Central

Election Commission, State Election Commissions, Central Finance Commission, State Finance Commissions, Ombudsman of the Banks, Insurance Regulatory and Development Authority, the Central Electricity Regulatory Commission, the Telecom Regulatory Authority of India, the Securities and Exchange Board of India, the Central Vigilance Commission or the Union Public Service Commission, are cornered only by retired bureaucrats. Post retirement jobs mean another two to five years of extension in service. Even post like India's Executive Directors with the World Bank and the International Monetary Fund have been entrapped by the retired bureaucrats with or without economic specialisation.

It is amazing as to why, the political parties which are governing the country, cannot find any talent in the rest of the country, except in the retired bureaucrats. In USA and some other countries, economists, lawyers, bankers and financial experts shift freely between the academia, business and think tanks and the bureaucracy. In the United States, individuals with the relevant professional expertise, fill about 2000 top bureaucratic positions. The President of the country can fill up those posts by nomination. US President is free to appoint leading experts directly into the Cabinet. There have been instances, where top economist or professors have been appointed as Treasury Secretary (finance minister).

In India, corruption, has become a part of the system. Justification is given that, political parties need funds, which are collected in cash and not by cheque. Black money is generated, only by black transactions. Black transactions and corruption sustain each other. This is generally done by showing favours at a price, for bending or twisting laws or giving sanctions with the help of obliging civil servants at decision making level.

Central Vigilance Commission Bill 2003 was passed by Parliament on August 7, 2003. According to the Bill, a three-member Commission, each with a fixed tenure of four years, will be appointed on the recommendation of a high-level committee, for overseeing the working of the CBI. The Central Vigilance Commission has been in existence since 1960s as a result of the recommendation of a Committee headed by Shri K Santhanam, which went into the whole gamut of circumstances leading to corruption and steps required for curbing it. The Santhanam Committee recognised the malady of corruption and observed in 1962: "The tendency to subvert integrity in the public services, instead of being isolated and aberrant, is growing into a well-organised, well-planned racket". The Committee also observed then, that corruption had increased to such an extent that people have started losing faith, in the integrity of public administration. Corruption in certain areas had spread even to that level of administrative hierarchy, from which it was conspicuously absent in the past.

The Supreme Court in the Vineet Narain case, popularly known as the Jain Hawala case, looked into the entire gamut of purifying public life and controlling corruption, in its judgement dated 18 December, 1997. It also looked into the question of validity of several executive directions, including so called Single Directive, which required CBI, to take the prior permission of the Government, to start any inquiry or look into any malfeasance of the officers of the level of Joint Secretary and above. This permission is separate, from sanction for prosecution, which in any case is required in case of all public servants from the peons to the Cabinet Secretary, should it be decided to prosecute them.

The Supreme Court held: "Obviously, where the accusation of corruption, is based on direct evidence and it does not require any inference to be drawn, dependent on the decision-making process, there is no rational basis, to classify them differently. In other words, if the accusation be of bribery, which is supported by direct evidence, of acceptance of illegal gratification by them, including trap cases, it is obvious that no other factor is relevant and the level of status of the offender is irrelevant...It is for this reason that it was conceded that such cases, ie, of bribery, including trap cases, are outside the scope of the Single Directive"... "No serious attempt was made by the learned Attorney General to support inclusion within the Single Directive of cases in which the offender is alleged to be in possession of disproportionate assets. It is clear that the accusation of possession of disproportionate assets by a person is also based on direct evidence and no factor pertaining to the expertise of decision-making is involved therein. We have, therefore, no doubt, that the Single Directive cannot include within its ambit, cases of possession of disproportionate assets by the offender. The question now is, only with regard to cases other than those of bribery, including trap cases, and of possession of disproportionate assets being covered by the Single Directive."

Thus the protection enjoyed by the higher echelons of the bureaucracy till December 1997 against investigation by CBI was held illegal, as the Government's power of superintendence did not include the power to interfere with CBI's power to investigate. The classification of offenders on the basis of their rank was not rational. Hence opposed to the right to equality guaranteed under the Constitution.

In the new CVC Bill, the field of choice of appointment is restricted only to the retired bureaucrats and retired officers of public sector undertakings. It would have been better, if the field of selection could have included eminent public men, jurists or judges of the Supreme Court. Otherwise, CVC appointment would mean an extension of service by four years, like the UPSC or Election Commission. The Central Vigilance Commission, as per the Bill, will exercise superintendence over the functioning of the CBI in so far as it relates to investigation of offences under the Prevention of Corruption Act or an offence with which a public servant can be charged.

What Supreme Court had declared as illegal has been smuggled back and the position is almost the same, as it was before the Central Vigilance Commission Bill was passed. The Supreme Court in its judgement had laid down the following guidelines for the functioning of the holders of the public offices:

Holders of public office should be as open as possible about all the decisions and actions that they take. They should give reasons for their decisions and restrict information only, when the wider public interest clearly demands.

Further, holders of public office are accountable for their decisions and actions to the public and must submit themselves to whatever scrutiny is appropriate to their office. Supreme Court held that "It is trite that, the holders of public offices are entrusted with certain powers to be exercised in public interest alone and therefore, the office is held by them, in trust for the people. Any deviation from the path of rectitude, by any of them, amounts to a breach of trust and must be severely dealt with, instead of being pushed under the carpet. If the conduct amounts to an offence, it must be promptly investigated and the offender, against whom a prima facie case is made out, should be prosecuted expeditiously so that the majesty of law is upheld and the rule of law vindicated. It is the duty of law and therefore, to guard against erosion of the rule of law. The adverse impact of lack of probity in public life leading to a high degree of corruption is manifold. It also has adverse effect on foreign investment and funding from the International Monetary Fund and the World Bank who have warned that future aid to underdeveloped countries may be subject to the requisite steps being taken to eradicate corruption, which prevents international aid, from reaching those, for whom it is meant. Increasing corruption has led to investigative journalism, which is of value to a free society. The need to highlight corruption in public life through the medium of public interest litigation invoking judicial review may be frequent in India but is not unknown in other countries."

The government has since amended, Section 33 (B) of the Representation of the People Act. It is declared that "no candidate shall be liable to disclose or furnish any such information in respect of his election, which is not required to be disclosed or furnished under this Act or the rules made there under". This provision was to be effective, notwithstanding any judgement or directive of the Election Commission to the contrary. The court struck it down on March 13, 2003 on the ground that, the new law violated the fundamental rights of citizens guaranteed under Article 19(1) a, as interpreted by the court. Interpretation of the Constitution is within the domain of the judiciary. There is no doubt that a law creating two classes of public servants, one Joint Secretary and above and other lesser mortals below, will meet the same fate as the amendment to the People's Representation Act met. The Single Directive was held as violative of the fundamental right to equality in the year 1997. It cannot become legal in 2003, (Section 6 of the CVC Bill) when big fish like the Vice - Chairman of the DDA and Chairman and other senior officers of the Income Tax, Customs and Excise other Services have been caught indulging in blatant corruption.

Office of Profit Bill returned by the President for reconsideration by the Parliament has been returned to the President without any change. The flawed Bill has been steem rolled to protect 40 MPs and hundred of MLAs whose membership is held unconstitutional by emenint law experts. Most of the affected MPs belong to rulling parties. Legislators who cannot be accommodated in Ministries, are given these appointments as compensation. Being head, of such offices, they enjoy many benefits in kind if not in cash. The President has signed the Bill unchanged on the stipulation that JPC would be constituted to resolve the issue.

18

Low Breakers to Lawmakers

The Delhi High Court in November, 2000 gave a far reaching ruling, to decriminalize the politics in which, it sought to help the electorate in securing information, about the antecedents of candidates.. The Court also said, that if criminalisation of politics is to be prevented, the fundamental right to information, for the benefit of the citizens, must be enforced in letter and spirit. All candidates seeking election to Parliament or a Legislative Assembly, must submit relevant information about their background, at the time of filing nomination papers. The Bench said: "Furnishing of false information will result in prosecution of the candidate. Persons with questionable background, do not deserve to be occupying seats in Parliament and the Legislative Assemblies, adding "such persons need to be eliminated from the race."

There has been a crying need to ban history-sheeters, bad characters, extortionists and harbourers of criminals from contesting and holding any elective office. Earlier, the criminals used to support some candidates in election, as a kind of insurance against their past and future misdeeds. The criminals, later on became emboldened and started using their money and muscle power in getting elected to State Assemblies and National Parliament. The result is, known dacoits and criminals have occupied seats in the Parliament and Assemblies. Some of them have held or are holding Ministerial offices, both in the State and Central Governments. The irony is that, those who lived by breaking the law, catapulted themselves into the position of the law-makers.

People are generally lured to enter politics or contest elections for becoming rich overnight. Holding an elective Legislative Office has been turned into a kind of insurance against any legal action. The Central Government filed an appeal in the Supreme Court against the orders of Delhi High Court, which not only confirmed the orders but also asked the Election Commission to take steps to comply with its orders. Consequently the Election Commission issued the following Poll guidelines on 28th June, 2002 and asked for the following details from candidates, wishing to contest elections. If he/she has been convicted/acquitted/discharged of criminal offence in the past and if so, the sentence fine imposed. If prior to six months of filling of nomination the candidate was accused in any pending case of an offence punishable with imprisonment for two years or more along with assets (immovable and movable) of spouse and dependents. Liabilities. If any, particularly details of dues to public financial institutions or government and educational qualifications of candidate.

Instead of coolly and passionately examining the guidelines, an all-party meeting on 8 July, 2002, rejected the EC guidelines on the following counts: Ground realities are ignored. Filling of nominations becomes cumbersome; and detailed information on criminal antecedents has potential of political misuse and the MPs prefer to file details of assets after the elections and educational details as unnecessary since media publicises it. Some professional politicians objected at that time as now that, it was only their privilege to make law. But what does the country do, when no action is taken for years together. The Supreme Court order at that time was nowhere close to the judiciary, encroaching on the powers of the legislature. It was a simple plain order enforcing the right to information.

There was a suspicious unanimity and cohesion amongst our political parties, which only gave an evidence that politicians come together only when they have much to gain. In fact, there was no public support or letters to any Editor supporting the political Biradari's stand. People expected a major clean up of the political process. The election of well-known mafia dons only showed that our political class bothered only about the winning numbers and not about the background of individuals. The Political parties should have evolved a consensus that those with criminal records will not be given party tickets.

The implementation of the Members of Parliament Local Area Development Scheme (MPLADS) has not escaped the culture of all-round mismanagement and loot in Bihar. The AG report for the period of 1999-2000 has revealed grave irregularities in implementation of the scheme involving allotment of Rs 2 crore to each MP for execution of local needbased development programmes through district magistrates (DMs). The MPLADS was grossly mismanaged as there was "absence of monitoring, reporting and misutilisation of funds, irregular, illegal and inflated payments, incomplete projects, doubtful execution of works, execution of works beyond the scope of the scheme", according to the report.

The Election Comrnission's orders implementing the Supreme Court judgement of May, 2002, was nullified by passing/amending the law thus undoing the judgement.

The Supreme Court's main concerns in its judgement, were the ending of criminality and corruption. The Supreme Court of India in a petition filed by an NGO in its judgement dated 13th March, 2003, struck down as unconstitutional the Electoral Reforms Act passed in 2002 after an all-party consensus in Parliament. The Supreme Court declared the electoral reforms law, as unconstitutional and restored its earlier order, making it mandatory for the candidates, to declare their criminal antecedents, assets and liabilities and educational qualifications at the time of filing nomination papers. "Voters have a fundamental right to know about the criminal antecedence of their candidates. There is no scope for interpreting this right since it was a constitutional one and not statutory", the apex court held, while striking down a provision of the Representation of People (Amendment) Act, 2002, enacted after all-party consensus. "The legislature cannot declare that the law declared by the Supreme Court is not binding", observed the three-judge Bench, who held that the law enacted by Parliament curtailed the right to information of the people, vital to choosing proper candidate to the legislature. The court, after quashing the amendment to the Representation of People Act, directed the Election Commission to issue a fresh notification for implementation of its judgement, which would be applicable prospectively and not retrospectively.

Given the well known and well documented malpractices in elections, the SC order is just one step in ending criminalisation of the politics. In the State of Bihar, which has an important presence in Parliament, crime and politics go hand-in-hand. It is not a matter of surprise that then, some candidates contested the general election while being behind bars. While the Election Commission orders make it mandatory for candidates to give all details about themselves including the details of criminal cases, they were facing or have been convicted of any crime, the criminals found ways, in connivance with the local authorities, to run the election, even while they were officially in the prison. The Patna High Court feeling exasperated, at the gross violations of the law, directed the Bihar government, in the last week of April, 2004 to send back to jail those under trials who were ostensibly undergoing treatment in hospitals, but in reality were running their election campaigns from there. Observing that jails were the right place for criminals, the court said: "Criminals have no role in politics."

Patna High Court also directed the Election Commission to consider countermanding elections, in constituencies contested by prisoners. It was a well-intentioned order, issued by the High Court, keeping in view the need to check the entry of criminals into Parliament and state legislatures. It was discovered after the 1996 elections, that as many as 40 MPs and 700 MLAs had criminal antecedents. This menace has grown deeper and deeper. A committee set up in 1992 under the chairmanship of the then Home Secretary, which had the Director CBI and others as members, had exposed the nexus between criminals and politicians. Regrettably, successive governments, whether at the Centre or the State, have done nothing to check the influence of criminal gangs, drug mafia, caste senas, smuggling gangs and economic lobbies and their extensive network of contacts with politicians, bureaucrats and others. Many legislators were reportedly, involved in cases of extortion and murder. A number of them or their kindred have either served jail sentences or were in. Crime is one of their source of livelihood and they use political activities to build influence to get the necessary safety or insurance cover from the law.

The Election Commission, while agreeing with the larger need for tougher laws to keep the criminals out of politics, challenged the Patna High Court order, directing it to countermand polls in constituencies where candidates have been disenfranchised due to their being in jail. In a special leave petition filed in the Supreme Court, the EC questioned the Patna High Court's "interference" through such an order, even as the election process was on at that time. The EC cited Article 329 of the Constitution which bars any court from interfering with the elections, once the process is underway. The Election Commission felt that it was just not feasible for them to scan 'the list of candidates for each constituency for criminals, who have lost their right to vote. The Constitution required the Andhra Pradesh assembly to be in place by May 13, 2004 and they had no time to countermand polls and start the process afresh.

However, the Commission, agreed in principle with the need for tougher laws, to keep criminals out of electoral politics. The EC also felt that the right forum, to decide upon tougher laws; to end criminalisation of politics, is the legislature and not the judiciary. At present, the RPA provides for debarring of only those candidates, who have been convicted of an offence and sentenced to more than two years of imprisonment.

The Patna HC had, in an order, directed the Commission to consider countermanding elections in constituencies contested by prisoners who have been disenfranchised. On an appeal from the Election Commission, against the order of Patna High Court, the Supreme Court has stayed the order. Regrettably as present, the Representation of People Act does not disqualify an under trial from contesting an election. It only bars him from exercising his franchise. As per the existing criminal law, even a known murderer or a dacoit, irrespective of the offence, for which he is an under trial is considered innocent, until he is proved guilty in a court of law. Moreover, the crux of the question is, whether a law or an order can be applied retrospectively, after the election process has been set in motion. For instance, when the High Court order was issued, out of the 40 Lok Sabha seats in Bihar, elections for 28 seats were over on April 20 and 26, 2004.

Moreover, this is an All India issue and it would be best to carry all political parties in sorting out the problem of criminalisation. There is no doubt, that you cannot maintain the dignity or sanctity of the legislatures, in the presence of the criminals. There are no two opinions, that law breakers should not be allowed to become lawmakers. By criminals, we normally treat dons and those using brute power as criminals. The truth is, that white collar criminals, are as dangerous to the polity and perhaps sometimes more than the dons. We had a spectacle of a former Prime Minister along with his Home Minister being convicted in JMM bribery case. However, on appeal they were let off. We have a case of former Communication Minister, who was wooed by major political parties, so that they could form a State Government. We have a spectacle of a Chief Minister of a South Indian State, who was disqualified from contesting due to conviction for corruption charges in criminal cases. The party of that Chief Minister has been wooed again by the National Parties turn by turn. Similarly, an influential former Bihar Chief Minister, who is facing court trial in fodder scam, is allied with a major National Political Party. It is these type of politicians or rulers of the country, who are responsible for slanted governance. According to a report, an MP of the state ruling pary from Siwan, who is accused in several criminal cases including murders, has vowed to kill the Siwan Superintendent of Police (SP), after the district police force, under the !eadership of the SP, raided the village of the MP. A huge cache of arms including an AK-47, was recovered from his village house. In the crossfire between the supporters of the MP and the police, two cops including a sub inspector and 11 others, allegedly the men of don MP, were killed. Criminalisation of our polity had ceased to be a news, much earlier before a lady dacoit, facing trial in several cases of murder and dacoity was elected to sit as a people's representative in the National Parliament. The elections in our country in April May 2004, have thrown the criminalisation of the polity to the fore.

The present scenario is that, assorted and a varied group of ambitious contestants having money and muscle-power, want to enter the portals of power. For them, it does not matter, even if it is the subversion of our democracy. The solution lies in political parties not putting up such candidates. It is not an impossible task for the political parties to find the best talent or the best people, out of a population of over billion people. Stringent laws are the only answer to this situation. Laws, coupled with a voluntary restraint, by the political parties and their having a Lakshman rekha or bottom line, about the suitability of candidates, is the only workable solution. It should be remembered, that heavens won't fall, if the crooked and criminals, who have the free run of the country, are neither given a chance to enter the Legislatures and nor allowed a free run of the Legislatures.

The Chief Election Commissioner in an interview, in December, 2003, is reported to have said that politicians are like cancer to the society. He is not the only one, to have such views. Abraham Lincoln said: "If ever this free people.... if this Government is ever utterly demoralised, it will be, from this incessant human wriggle and struggle for office, which is but a way to live without work". To be a doctor, you need to study medicine, to be an engineer, you need to study engineering, to be a lawyer, you need to study law but to be a successful and a triumphant politician, you only need to be an expert, in the art of winning elections. It is a paradox but too true that two kinds of men, succeed best in politics. The first category is of people of no principles but of great talent. The second is of no talent, but of one principle, that is, implicit obedience to their political party bosses. An amiable but correct or right politician, is no match for a loud mouthed politician, who might be tenaciously and persistently wrong.

William Shakespeare said: "A politician is one, that would circumvent God. There are no rules or conditions either fixed variable or the requirement of a degree, to become a politicians. The only thing that bars a person from becoming a politician is imbecility or insanity". The Chief Election Commissioner was damned for saying, what is public knowledge. But where he erred is, the tarnishing of all politicians with the same brush. There are more honest and dedicated politicians, than those whom the CEC had probably in mind. Bashing of the election processes and politicians is normal in any democracy, as they are the most visible part of the governance. Compared to what Americans think of their politician, what the CEC had said about Indian politicians was just short of a tribute to them or calling them angels.

William Anderson once wrote: "Political elections do not choose leaders of society. Rather, they are an exercise, in which groups of people, choose individuals, who will assist them, in looting other groups of individuals, those folks, who were unfortunate enough, not to be able to elect their own political strongman. The process can be downright blatant, as is the case in African and Asian countries, or it can be relatively subtle, as it is in the United States, where the trappings of constitutionality and rule of law, hide many of the more nefarious goings on."

What is your view about the politician of today?

Vielw	*Agree*	*Neither agree nor disagree*	*Disagree*	*Dont't know/ Can't say*
Most Politicians are Corrupt.	76	17	6	1
Politicians are above the law.	36	17	44	3
Politicians with Criminal charges would be bannedfrom public life.	86	8	5	1
Politicians contribute to the country's economic growth.	35	25	38	2
Politicians, as public servants, are excessively concerned about their personal security.	79	13	8	-
We are spending too much on protecting our politicians.	82	12	4	2
Women politicians are better than men.	55	28	15	2

Vielw	*Agree*	*Neither agree nor disagree*	*Disagree*	*Dont't know/ Can't say*
There should be reservation for women in Parliament/state assemblies.	79	13	7	1
Politicians should be accountable to the public.	87	10	2	1
There should be minimum educational qualification for politicians.	90	4	5	1
Media devotes too much airtime and space to politics.	76	18	6	-
Politicians are publicity-hungry.	85	9	5	1
There should be a retirement age for politicians.	83	11	6	-
The bureaucracy makes fools of politicians.	51	27	18	4

While politicians are 14th in the terms of liking or approval of public, the bureaucrats share honour with them in the next rung. Obviously, people feel cruelly short-changed by their rulers, whether they are the bureducrats or politicians.

Another significant cause for this abhorrence of the political class, is the entry of law breakers, as lawmakers, in the portals of our legislatures both at the State and central level. In the elections held in December, 2003 to four State Assemblies, all paraties put up candidates with criminals cases pending aganst them. In Madhya Pradesh, 153 candidates with criminal antecedents contested election and 43 of then won. The matching figures for Rajasthan were 104 and 23, for Chhattisgarh 73 and 11, and for Delhi 70 and 25. I asked a senior politician as to why his party gave tickets to people with criminal background. He explained that, in the last election, his party had religiously declined to sponsor andy such candidates. On being rebuffed, such candidates were sponsored by another party and won. After all, politics is about being in power and not morality. So, all parties decide on the candidates, on their being winnable. Hence, they are reluctant to say no, to winning candidates. With the passing of the amendment to the Anti Defection Laws, the party bosses should definitely be, in a position to resist any arms twisting by the tainted legislators. What is morally wrong, cannot be politically right. There are greater expectations from our leaders to rid the country of poverty and misery and be a role model. While we cannot have all angels as our politicians and rulers, let us as the citizens and voters play our role, to keep cancer out of the portals of power. It will force the political parties to put their house in order.

The world we live in is not ideal. The rulers are not ideal and not for that matter people, who send criminals to the portals of power, as their mouthpieces and representatives. The following information about our Legislators in 2000, is an eye opener about the level of our rulers.

29 had been accused of spousal abuse.
19 had been accused of passing bad cheques.
117 had bankrupted at least two businesses.
3 had been arrested for assault.
71 could not get loans dues to bad credit histories.
114 had been arrested on drug related charges.
8 had been arrested for shop lifting .
21 are current defendants in various lawsuits.
84 were stopped for drunk driving in 1998 alone.

At least, 100 MPs faced criminal charges ranging from minor misdemeanors like disturbing peace, rioting murder, rape and dacoity.

Nearly 33 per cent involved in heinous crimes.

About 12 were charged with murder, 10 with attempted murder.

11 are known as dons.

Even before the UPA Government secured a vote of confidence from the 14th Lok Sabha, the Manmohan Singh government, faced embarrassment over the induction of Mr Mohammed Taslimuddin in the Council of Ministers because of his criminal antecedents. Infact, it was the RJD President, who secured him a berth in the Cabinet. He was the Chief Minister of Bihar, when seven cases had been filed against him, during his tenure Chief Minister of Bihar. There was no stopping or lessening of the cases against him, even after the wife of The RJD Chief succeeded him as the Chief Minister. There are 11 heinous crimes, cases filed against the MP from Kishangunj, of heinous crimes, including the attempt to murder, extortion and violation of the Arms Act and the Cheating. The Minister, like his RJD chief, himself a Union Minister, got bail, which can be revoked by the competent court. In all fairness to the tainted Ministers, it is safe to assume, that some cases could be the result of personal vendetta or rivalry, by their rivals or disappointed opponents.

There is little in the hands of criminals in position of power, to help the fellow criminals; if they too go much out of the way. With a vigilant press and an effective judiciary, the criminals have little chance of escaping, if the evidence against them is marshalled and it stands in the court of law. On the insistence of Bihar Unit of Janta Dal Mr. Taslimuddin was earlier included in the H.D. Deve Gowda led United Front government in 1996 as Minister of State for Home. Following an uproar over his criminal antecedents, he was forced to quit his office. With friendly Governments in power, who prefer to look to the other side of the criminal activities of their activists and political supporters, some of them have enjoyed full freedom to roam about, though technically in jail or hospitals or in police or judicial custody.

The Supreme Court ordered on 20th July, 2004 that Bihar's tainted politician Rajesh Ranjan aka Pappu Yadav to be "immediately" shifted from the Patna Medical College Hospital to the Beur jail. In a related development, Patna High Court had ordered the dismissal of a fast track court judge in Siwan for granting bail to RJD MP Mohammad Shahabuddin and allowing him to attend Parliament, in violation of an earlier HC order. The Apex Court had also ordered Janta Dal (United) MP Prabhunath Singh to surrender in a court in Bhagalpur in a case related to the murder of four persons. Prabhunath evaded arrest for several years.

Thanks to a spirited judiciary committed to upholding the highest values and an equally alert and watchful press, the going is to be tough for the criminals masquerading as successful politicians. Criminalisation of politics is not something, which started in 2004. In the last elections to the 13th Lok Sabha and State Assemblies, as many as 700 legislators, including 40 MPs with criminal background, secured berths in the Parliament and State Assemblies. In the 1996 elections, 1,500 out of 13,950 candidates had criminal cases against them. In the year 2002, as many as 15 MPs and 635 MLAS had cases pending against them. It may appear outrageous that 21 major national and regional political parties of dissimilar and separate ideologies and bitter foes of each other, joined hands to reject the Election Commission's directive, in pursuance of the Supreme Court order seeking information of a candidate's possible involvement in any criminal case. They went a step further and passed a law as such, which was declared void by the Supreme Court.

The truth is that, all lamentation on the criminalization of politics by the politicians both inside and outside the Legislatures, whether at the State or the National level is seasonal and opportune. Almost all the political parties, except perhaps the Left, believe and practice the motto that, power at any cost, even if it means embracing the devil to get a pie of the power. They are not bothered about the past of their associates, but what their association can fetch them now and in the future. Even in the 14th Lok Sabha, as per the affidavits filed at the time of contesting elections, 100 elected MPs from the States had cases pending against them. They are the eventual winners. They are 1/5 of the 543 Members of the Lok Sabha. State wise, they are:

AP 2, Chhattisgarh 2, Bihar 2, Punjab 5, Rajasthan 3, WB 14, Maharashtra 12, Kerala 5, MP 7, Gujarat 5, Jharkhand 6, Karnataka 6, Haryana 2, Goa 1, Orissa 3, TN 3 and Delhi 1.

It is true that most cases may be old and minor, in the perception of the accused but it does not take away the odium from them.

The World's largest democracy has nearly one fifth of its law makers, who at one time or the other broke the laws, which they bad sworn to uphold. Compliance with the law is done as per the convenience and not what should be taken as a serious duty. Earlier there used to be censure, disapproval and denunciation about anybody involved in the Court cases being given a party ticket for election to the Parliament or State Assemblies. Now the Lakshman Rekha or boundary line has been stretched, by several political parties to say that, while there can be no objection to a criminal becoming a Legislator, It is a serious impairment of values, if such a person is made a Minister. It is because, all political parties have such worthies, in the rank and file as well as in the State and Parliament legislatives. There is an Urdu saying that Iss Hamam Men Sab Nangey Hain (In this bath, all are naked). It happened once that a Prime Minister was also chargesheeted in the infamous JMM bribery case. It might well happen, if we let the things go on, as they are going on now. Even here an accused in a number of serious cases, who is a Union Minister, has declared that one day he would like to occupy the Prime

Ministerial Office. One UPA Union Minister was absconding to evade the execution of an arrest warrant, so that he can get the whole matter stayed from a higher court in appeal. His house had to be searched by the Police to trace him. It beats everything. Said William Shakespeare: "If to do were as easy, as to know, what were good to do, Chapels would be Churches and poor men's cottages prince's palaces. It is a good divine that follows his own instructions; I can easier teach twenty, what were good to be done, than be of the twenty to follow mine own teaching". The political parties, which make noise will do well to keep the above observations of Shakespeare in mind.

It is a journey down the hill, partly because of the atmosphere of casteism, money power and muscles prevailing in the country and partly due to the indifference of good citizens, who chose not to vote to keep criminal elements out of power. It is time for a concerted drive by the enlightened citizens and media to expose the menace, to which our country is falling prey. Opportunity has hair in front; behind she is bald; if you seize her by the forelock, you may hold her. If you let her escape, there is no way, you can catch it again. Shall we let this opportunity slip? If we don't, what is there to prevent Abu Salem, Chotta Rajan or Dawood to get a berth in the Rajya Sabha or even Lok Sabha, as some dacoits earlier got elected or even people with money power have succeeded in entering the upper house? Let not the wake up call be too late.

19

Coalition Revisited

It appears that after 1990 the politics of coalition Government has come to stay. Every coalitions Government — there have been half a dozen of them — has come to power on the plank of social justice, to raise the lot of deprived sections of society. Coalitions are of course, more representative of diverse political parties, interests and groups in the country. There are no chances of imposing any emergency or authoritarianism in the set up, as no one party is in a position to ride roughshod over the Parliament. However, the price of keeping any coalition government afloat, whether in the Centre or the States, is becoming increasingly exorbitant and almost unaffordable. Anybody, who is in a position to topple the coalition Government, can demand any price and almost get away with it. More precarious the coalition, more will be the clout of individual legislator or a group of legislators. Despite all talk of Dharma, whether rajya Dharma or Coalition Dharma, the only Dharma, which is being followed is how to stick to rajya at any cost; hell with Dharma. Politics has simply become a game of sticking one day more to power and nothing else. It is for this reason that the credibility of the politicians is so low. The thought of governance, what to talk of good governance is far from anybody's mind. Nobody even talks about it, except during or near the election times, so as to garner votes for election. Cabinet systems entail collective responsibility of all ministers. For some coalition partners, it is not their accountability to Parliament or to the State Assembly or national leaders of the country, but to their party bosses, who decide as to what line to take. However, fortunately there are only a few coalition Governments in power at the State level. All coalitions are born out of compulsion of sticking to the power or keeping somebody else out of power. For instance, when the coalition Government was formed in UP by the BSP with the help of BJP, the Chief Minister functioned almost as if it was a single party Government. Politics brings strange bed fellows together. Enemies of yesterday become friends of today. Then the Chief Minister went on a suspension spree. District officials, whose districts were visited by her, were not sure whether they would be in service or under suspension, during the visit of the mercurial Chief Minister. As soon

Taj Heritage Corridor controversy came within the public domain, the then UP Chief Minister demanded the resignation of the Tourism Minister Jagmohan, for allegedly misleading Parliament over the Taj corridor issue. UP coalition partner, BSP forced the adjournment of the Parliament on 29th of July, 2003. The BJP sought to pacify the BSP in Lok Sabha, but without any avail. It was alleged that Mr. Jagmohan had all along known about the construction of the corridor and that it was only now he was trying to pin the blame on the Uttar Pradesh Chief Minister. Actually, in the perception of the general public, the then Chief Minister as a pro quid, though not said in words, wanted to be bailed out of the Taj imbroglio. It was neither feasible nor, desirable nor possible for the Central Government to do so, with a vigilant press and an equally alert Supreme Court keeping a watch on every move. When the Supreme Court has ordered the case to be investigated, the Government ceases to have anything to do with that case as if it is a matter between the CBI and Supreme Court. It was the Apex Court which ordered the initial inquiry and subsequent registration of the case against the former Chief Minister and others.

Within one day, Chief Minister Mayawati was forced to retract her demand for Union Tourism and Culture Minister Jagmohan's resignation. The climb down, was the result of the BJP stand, which felt that enough was enough. Politicians, irrespective of their party hue, do not like anybody calling them to question. Big scandals whether Bofors, JMM or criminalisation of politics were first raked by the press. Nevertheless, even the most sensational exposures in the press, do not cause any ripple, unless the same are raised in the Parliament.

Miss Mayawati, stand was extraordinary, as she was almost dictating to the Prime Minister, whom to remove or keep in his Cabinet. No self respecting Prime Minister would allow his authority to be whittled down like this or allow himself to be cowed down. Being used to riding roughshod over coalition and electoral partners, ranging from the BJP to the SP and Congress, she had her bluff called off.

In August, 2003 the Supreme Court of India, reminded Gujarat Government of its Rajya Dharma of ensuring that all citizens are treated equally and get justice. But Dharma is possible only, if those who believe in Rajya Dharma are in power. According to a newspaper report, out of 403 Members of UP Legislative Assembly, 205 of them had criminal cases against them. Some of them may not be victims of vendetta or cross criminal cases. Yet it is a disturbing figure. If the country has been ruined by the selfserving politicians. It is still the politicians on. Whom the onus lies for reforming and giving good governance to the country. We are in for a long era of coalitions. With the right person in place, almost any system however bad will work and be a success. But with wicked, corrupt, immoral and depraved, even the best of system and best of laws would be a failure. Nothing can be politically right, which is morally unethical, immoral and wicked. Montesquieu rightly said in this context that: "We should never create by law, what can be accomplished by morality."

For elections to the 14th Lok Sabha, the focus shifted to the dynastic rule. Democracy has no scope for dynasties, though some sort of dynasties have been thrown to the top, both at the State and central level in our country. Thomas Paine said. One of the strongest natural proofs of the folly of hereditary right of Kings is that, nature disapproves it; otherwise she would not, so frequently turn it, into ridicule by giving the mankind, an ass in place of a lion". The fact remains, that all elections are about seizing power in a democracy. The power won by popular consent is reportedly for the good of the people.

There is a kind of fascination for a dynasty or dynasties, all over the world. In democracies. political parties tend to zero on anything which will fetch them votes. Dynastic rule is common where Kings or Queens are still reigning, though not necessarily ruling. Democracies have also not lagged behind, in creating myths around some families projecting them as the dynasties ordained to rule. The Bush regime is reportedly spawning such a huge forest of spouses, sons, daughters, siblings etc, in positions of power that some columnists in that country call USA, as at present, a Nepotocracy. In Sri Lanka, after the assassination of Bandranaike, his wife Srimavo succeeded and now his daughter is the democratically elected President. Similarly the widows and daughters of the former rulers of Bangladesh have been taking turns to rule that country as did Ms. Benazir Bhutto, who became the Prime Minister. Earlier her father, Mr Bhutto, was the Prime Minister of Pakistan, who was executed by the military dictator Zia. In India, Jawahar Lal Nehru, in the absence of a son, made his daughter Indira Gandhi, the Congress President and later on she succeeded him as Prime Minister after the demise of Lal Bhadur Shastri. A congress President, DK Baruaha had proclaimed, at the height of sycophancy, that Indira is India and India is Indira.

The trouble with full blown sycophancy is that the object of sycophancy comes to believe, what his underlings tell him. Indira Gandhi was grooming her younger son Sanjay to take over the reigns of the country, when he was killed in a plane accident. Having no other alternative, she brought her elder son Rajiv in the main stream of politics. He was reportedly an excellent pilot with the National Airline, in the main stream of politics. He ultimately succeeded her, after her unfortunate assassination, by her body guards, who were upset, like other Sikhs all over the country, over the army's attack on the Sikhs' holiest shrine Golden Temple in Amritsar. There was a small interregnum, where after the assassination of Rajiv Gandhi, his widow Sonia Gandhi remained behind the scenes. It was only a question of time, before she dethroned the old war horse, Sita Ram Kesri and took over the reigns of the Congress party. Now in the family tradition, her son and daughter have made entry into politics, as primary members of the Congress Party. It is only a question of time, before they are given an active role, to be groomed for possible occupation of the ultimate and the highest office, which Indian democracy can offer. However, nature does not always work as per the best laid plans and nobody knows, what future has in store for any individual.

It will be unfair, to single out only Nehru dynasty as ambitious and power centric, which wants all the highest offices to go to its closest kins. Kashmir has been having, a three generation of Abdulla rulers, starting with Sheikh Abdulla, Farooq Abdulla and later on, Omar Abdulla. Haryana also had Sh. Devi Lal and his son Om Prakash Chautala had become Chief Minister. His one son is a MLA and anothera Member of Parliament. Similarly, the former Chief Minister of Punjab, Partap Singh Kairon's son was MLA and later on Minister. former Chief Minister Prakash Singh Badal's son is also a Member of Parliament. Similarly, the son of Chief Minister of UP, Sh. Mulayam Singh Yadav, is also a Member of Parliament. Mrs. Laloo Prasad Yadav succeeded as Chief Minister of Bihar, after her husband had to leave the job of Chief Minister due to reasons beyond his control. Many former Chief Ministers of Madhya Pradesh and Maharasthra, Gujarat, Orissa, Andhra Pradesh, Karnataka, Kerala, Tamilnadu and a number of other Stares have ensured the presence of their closest kiths and kins or their caste parsons either in the State or Central Legislature. The names of NTR Ram Rao, Biju Patnaik, Karunakaran readily come to the mind. The effort is to pass on the mantle to the son, daughter or wife.

Academically, there is nothing wrong in a Doctor's son becoming a Doctor or IAS and IPS Officers' son following in the foot steps of his father or mother by joining their service. There have been cases where almost all the members of a family have either become civil servants or doctors or even teachers. But academics apart, the sons and daughters of the high and mighty, start with an advantage of hangers on, which their close proximity with established leaders gives them. Getting elected does not require the same expertise, or hard work as is required for entering Civil Service or for becoming a Doctor.

The powerful families traditionally have ruled down from one generation to another in India, China, and Japan. Of course, in democratic countries, dynasties are not like the Mughal, Gupta dynasties. They are subject to the will of the people. People can reject them right at the very first electoral battle. There is no such thing as automatic succession in free democracies. However, some selfserving sycophants and hangers on, for their personal benefit, create dynasties of any ruler. It is so, all over the world.

Any aspirants to future leadership has to base his or her claim, not on promises, or on belonging to any family, but to the past records and credentials. There is no need, to be obsessively preoccupied with any dynasty. We need not raise any new dynasty to beat any other dynasty. Of course, Nehru and his progeny called Gandhis, though they are no relations of any Gandhiji, have ruled the country, with the electorate's consent for over 39 years in Independent India.

Winning elections is selling movie tickets, declared Governor Schwarzenegger in his first, state of the state' address, pledging to carry California out of its imminent bankruptcy. For him, running a state is like selling movie tickets. "If I can sell tickets for my movies like Red Sonja or Last Action Hero, I can sell just about anything. California is the easiest sell I've ever had." I beg to differ with Mr. Governor Schwarzenneger. Politics is not all about showmanship, though good looks and good speeches matter. There may be a few odd fellows, who might be lured, by the dynasty tag or public school polish. These things do not create charisma. Neither charisma can be invented, nor faked.

Chairman or owner of a company has an advantage of starting the members of his dynasty almost from near the top; the political dynasty members generally do not have to start their political career at the block or district level. They, by and large start either as

Members of the State or National Legislatures or as number two or three in the party. Besides, on being elected, they claim that it is their merit or nation-building activities, which has got them elected and not dynastic connections. Nevertheless, the dynasty factor does not disappears with the elections, as such people who may have been former rulers, never fail to remind others as to their status of Maharajas. For instance, present Punjab Chief Minister is still referred to as Maharaja. For want of icons or role models in the country, people will make a hero out of zeros. We have had the spectacles of film stars, being catapulted into the role of top political leaders or Chief Ministers, on the basis of their performance as heroes or noblemen or noblewomen's role in film.

20

Crime Craft

Times change and so do theories of governance or working. There was a time, when the National leaders thought that everything should be done by the Government, right from the building of the toilets, to the construction of steel factories. The concept of controlled economy through quotas and permits led to a situation, where everything was at a premium. Even the rickety and defectively manufactured cars, were not available off the shelf. You had either to buy the same on a premium or wait for decades for your turn. Another way to possess cars or scooters, was through the Government quota, as the Government had laid down in its orders, that it could allot upto 3% of the manufactured vehicles, at its discretion. A Supreme Court Judge, while inaugurating a conference, observed that a crime related to property took place every minute, a violent crime every two minutes, burglary every four minutes, robbery every 14 minutes, murder every 15 minutes, rape every 52 minutes, molestation every 26 minutes, kidnapping and abduction every 43 minutes and eve-teasing every 51 minutes in our country. Criminal law or criminal justice system, is no more deterrent for the crooks and criminals. It is so, because of long delay in the disposal of cases along with the declining rate of conviction. At present, the conviction rate stands at 6.4 per cent, of all cases brought up for prosecution. The same judge rightly advocated an all over change in the criminal justice system, as it was cumbersome, expensive and cumulatively disastrous preventing the poor from reaching the courts for the redressal of their grievances. The civil laws relating the property and commerce are not costly; but they involve lengthy procedures that result in delays. An Attorney General Of India said: "The Criminal Justice is on the verge of collapse. Because the justice is not dispensed speedily. People have come to believe that there is no such thing as justice in the courts. Justice delayed will not only be justice denied, it will be the rule of the law destroyed. This perception has caused many a potential litigant, who has been wronged, to settle out of Court on terms, which are unfair to him or to secure justice, by taking the law into his own hands or by recourse to a parallel mafia dominated system of 'justice', that has sprung up in metropolitan centres like Mumbai."

Delays are primarily caused by the outdated procedures and abysmal shortage of judges. Judiciary has also not remained immune from corruption, as observed by a former Chief Justice of India, who said that at least 20 per cent judges are corrupt. Though Supreme Court is the highest Court in the country, it has no power of punishing superior judiciary, which can only be impeached in Parliament. High Courts have powers over the judiciary working under them in the State. But a similar power, does not vest with the Supreme Court. A moneyed man by spending tons of it, can delay justice, going in for layers after layers of appeals. Our laws and systems have not moved with the time, nor kept pace with them. Unless radical changes are brought about in our institutions, there is no way, we can usher into the 21st century with a sense of dignity and pride. On the contrary, there is ample evidence, that phenomenon of making impracticable laws and bloating bureaucracy, is expanding.

The more laws we have, the more loop holes we create, to enable the escape of the corrupt. Rackets after rackets, go on unpunished and undealt with, or dealt with perfunctorily. The Taj corridor investigation by the CBI have led to the registration of a number of cases against officials and politicians in 2003. But none of the accused is considered a pariah, either in political or official circles. All political parties are keen to embrace any body, who can add his or her party's numbers to their kitty. The biggest swindle, which has been going on right under nose of the Central Government, is the rampant encroachment on Government or public lands in Delhi. When complaints are made, the standard reply is that, it is not possible to determine, when the land was encroached upon. However, the real problem of vote bank politics in encouraging slums and occupation of government property, cannot be tackled by the government officials. It is something to be tackled, at the political level. Delhi Police did an excellent job in detecting the leak of CBSE AIPMT paper leak in April, 2004. The CBI arrested two Delhi policemen, including the investigating officer of the case, for allegedly accepting bribe of Rs. 2 Lakhs from the father of prime accused. The accused were caught red-handed while accepting the money. This was the first instalment of the money, which was being handed over to them. It is a very disturbing feature that the law enforcement officials themselves have become partners of law breakers. Earlier, the former Commissioner of Bombay Police, as well as an IG of Maharasthra Police and some other officials were arrested. A DIG of Tamil Nadu and a DSP were arrested in July, 2004, for colluding and soft pedalling the accused in infamous Telgi stamp scam.

About some journalists, former Prime Minister AB Vajpayee put it, "Journalism started as a mission turned into a profession, now it's but a mere sensation". Notwithstanding what politicians may say about the media, it is largely the media, which keeps the Government and public servants on toe. If it were not for the media, many scams, which are now hitting the front line would not have been exposed.

Almost total lack of accountability and transparency are the main reasons, for the growing corruption in India. Bureaucracy is accountable to its own hierarchy and politicians to the Parliament, on which the public has no control. Even the replies to questions raised in Parliament, are prepared by the bureaucracy and Ministers have to go nilly willy with them. Once, when the Present Prime Minister was the Finance Minister I happened to be present, at his briefing for the replies to Parliament Questions. As Director General of Narcotics Bureau, which at that time was a part of the Finance Ministry (1993-94), I had gone to see Dr. Manmohan Singh, in connection with my portion of the work relating to the Parliament. Another section of the Ministry, which had a lot of public interaction had prepared replies to a question, which amounted to saying that it (Finance Ministry and Banks) had done a tremendous public service. Dr. Manmohan Singh said, that it was all lies. He said that he would not tell lies. But the bureaucrats pleaded with him that as the Minister incharge, he must defend his department. He said that the Government must focus on improving services, rather than finding alibis.

Metal scrap is imported to recycle and reconvert the same as original metal, by many factories in our country. Imported scrap in India from all over the world, including South Africa, Europe, Asia and the Middle-East, includes spent cartridges, used bomb shells, ferrous and non-ferrous materials like steel, copper, zinc, brass and lead. One estimate puts the import of scrap to a figure of 1,500 tonnes daily. Imported scrap is, in great demand, since it is used in the manufacture of secondary products, such as steel ingots, billets and bars. The demand for such scrap is estimated at about 6 lakh tonnes. Only half of this, is actually imported.

Scrap is a good source of making money. There is a great requirement of it from low-grade manufacturers of steel, who are unable to make do with the scrap that is locally generated. Metal scrap is obtained from source like the old used machinery items or even from shells and projectiles used by the defence forces or by the countries engaged in hostilities against each other. War metal scrap is cheaper. Estimates indicate that 60,000 tonnes of stainless steel scrap, resulting from the September 11 attack was imported into India, for recycling and use as building material, furniture and household utensils. Even by a conservative estimate, nearly 315 million computers became obsolete in the US between 1997 and 2004, two third of which reportedly reached Indian shores, as a scrap for reconditioning. 1.38 million computers generate 1,050 tonnes of electronic scrap every year. There are about 40 to 50 major computer scrap dealers in and around Delhi roughly importing 1,500 tonnes every day as compared to about 100 tonnes of domestic scrap collected by the Kabaris from all over including the individual houses.

Even Indian Defence Forces, as well as Police and Para Military Forces sell fired shells, which can be recycled by the industries. A case under the Explosive Material Act was registered on the 6th of October, 2004 against the Chairman and Directors of a Steel Company in Gaziabad, UP following the recovery of munitions and explosive materials, from the scrap it imported from Iran. Amongst the explosives found in the steel scrap, was a light machine gun, a tank chain, and some shells of missiles. Earlier, in explosions from metal scrap, which was a part of the consignment, imported from Iran, 10 workers were killed and 9 injured on 30th September, 2004, at the same factory. The scrap dealers and scrap recyclers, have lived a relatively low profile business life. It is only were, due to rocket explosions in Ghaziabad, where 10 persons died lost their lives and scores were injured in a junk recycling factory that the unsavoury and dangerous side of the trade was exposed.

The metal scrap, which exploded in Ghaziabad, was imported from Iran via Dubai. Customs officials claim that it underwent "thorough" checks at Teheran, Dubai, Kandla Port in Gujarat and then at the Tughlaqabad scrap yard in the heart of Delhi. That nothing incriminating was discovered at so many checkpoints, shows that either the officials neglected their duty or were in connivance with traders to hurry up clearances and checks, for considerations other than efficiency. In fairness to the Customs or other checking agencies, they do only a visual examination, before clearing the entry of the scrap. Nobody has bothered, to equip the inspection agencies with container-scanning machines, which can detect live shells in scrap.

Our country has the only contance scanning machine in Mumbai. The writing on scrap dump, is portentous. Without any check or a thorough inspection, any scrap could contain explosives, which can trigger off mishaps. However, the bombs and rocket seized were reportedly so rusted, that it is difficult to decipher their country of origin. The rockets and missiles, as scrap have also been found in Khurja, Bulandshahr, Mussori, Meerut, Aligarh and Mandi Govind Garh in Punjab, Rajasthan, Mumbai and Delhi

All is well with our rules, procedures or methods of importing and handling such materials. It took ten deaths and scores of the injured to wake up the Government, in October, 2004 to streamline the procedures, under which the import of scrap would be permitted only in shredded or compacted form. Now unshredded and uncompacted waste only would be allowed after total inspection through major ports and ICD, Tughlaqabad only. For imports from war-affected countries, documents would have to be furnished to the customs department. Must a few unfortunate tragedies occur to wake up the slumbering Government? There are many more areas, in the field of imports or hazardous or unsavoury substances, where constant streamlining and vigilance is required. In 1970s, a vegetable oil manufacturing industry near Gaziabad had imported a lot of beef tallow for mixing in the Hydrogenated or Vanaspati oil. It created a lot of problems and some hard explaining on the part of the then Government. Also in the name of rags, for recycling, fully stitched and cheap clothing had been imported.

21

Surfing the Scams

A duo posed as a Minister of State for Home and his private secretary and allegedly spoke to a gangster in a jail in Uttar Pradesh. CBI investigation and laboratory tests proved that the voice was not that of the Minister. The same duo had reportedly tried to enlist the help of a district police chief, which was declined as the area fell beyond the jurisdiction of that police officer. They cooled their heels in the jail.

Impersonation is not uncommon for obtaining pecuniary and other benefits. A good actor can pose as somebody important, impersonating voice of someone else to get a favour done or to take some other advantage. The first big case of such fraud after Independence was when a man mimicked the voice of then Prime Minister and asked the chief cashier of a nationalised bank to deliver an amount of Rs 60 lakh to a specified person. The cashier, without verification or crossexamination, delivered the amount to one Nagarwala. The police traced the recipient of the money who mysteriously died in police custody and the chief cashier was dismissed subsequently.

Once I received a phone call when an Inspector General Police, CRPF, on the eve of recruitment, purportedly coming from late Rajesh Pilot, the then Minister in the Home Ministry. I was told to take down the names and details of persons whom the so-called Minister wanted to be recruited. Again the person on the end asked me to repeat the names and make sure that all the 10 persons were recruited as constables. Later, I promptly rang up the Minister's house and wanted to speak to him. His staff told me that the Minister was on the visit to the North-East and was expected to return after two days. Then I told them that I had received a call from him, asking for some persons to be recruited. I told them that the recruitment would be done strictly on merit. I was told that even his office could not contact him and were sending only wireless messages to keep him apprised of whatever was going on and so his speaking to me was not possible.

The Central Government has received nearly 36,000 complaints from across the country. Some of the complaints, incidentally, show that pension has been granted to some 'freedom fighters' who were infants at the time of Independence in 1947. Incidentally, the number of freedom fighters in much more than the official figure recorded by the British. With the passage of time, the number of such worthies should be getting reduced due to natural cause like death but it shows no signs of abatement.

The Income Tax Department has also unearthed a huge scam running into crores of rupees of withdrawal of tax refunds by fake companies issuing fake Form 16. The cheats had floated bogus companies and had claimed refunds on the basis of tax deductible at source (TDS), supposedly deposited by the company. The Income Tax department's investigations have revealed that the names of owners and employees mentioned on the TDS certificates were bogus. Such fraudulent companies that had paid no taxes and did not even exist, had succeed in robbing the national exchequer of crores of rupees.

There are an estimated 30,000 quacks in Delhi alone. Their number in the country would easily cross a million. As against 30,000 quacks in Delhi, the number of registered doctors is about 26,000. Impersonation, for personal financial benefits, is emerging as a new type of crime, which has affected almost all sections of society. With fake doctors around, fake drugs are far behind. According to the World Health Organisation, 35 per cent of fake drugs come from South-East Asia, which had a Rs.4,000 crore spurious drug market.

These cases do not merely make a matter of deceit or impersonation. In certain areas like the counterfeiting of currency, they are capable of affecting adversely the economy of the country. In the last five years, false currency worth Rs.20 crore had been recovered, which is only the tip of the iceberg.

New technologies like mobile phones and the Internet, accessible to common citizens, is also available to criminals and terrorists. Nowhere in the world, access to latest technologies been denied on the ground that crooks would misuse it. We are living in a world that has shrunk due to modern communication tools. The boundaries are irrelevant for impostors in the fast moving world. We can only take precautions so that, we are not taken for a ride.

No preventive strategy is guarantee against cheating. However, positive self-regulatiory measures can minimise temptation. As the proverb goes, "Who will not be deceived must have as many eyes as hair on his head". When faced with a problem, one must use one's head and not the heart. If it is not possible to do so, then one must remember what George Bernard Shaw once said, "A fool and his money are soon parted."

According to the Supreme Court: "A person, who studies one system of medicine, but practices another is a quack". According to the same Court, a practising allopathic doctor should register with the Medical Council. Ayurvedic doctors need to be registered with the Bhartiya Ayurvedic Chikitsa Parishad and homoeopathic doctors should be registered with the Homoeopathic Board. The government's anti quackery drive is many years old but there are no tangible results yet, despite the orders of compulsory registration. It is doubtful, whether quacks register themselves, with their respective councils and if they do not, there seems to be no mechanism to ensure that they do. A few Inspectors are too willing to be compromised for a price. Homeopathic doctors freely prescribe allopathic medication, as the Police themselves do not know the difference in the fine print or even the law or the Supreme Court judgements. Registration being mandatory to check quackery has not made any difference.

There have been cases where the father passed the MBBS and is no more. But his son, a homeopathic continues the business in his name or vice versa, where father is a homeopathic, but son is a qualified allopathic doctor and both practice in different places. A man used to openly give advertisements in the name of Delhi Degree College. By the time he was arrested, he had reportedly sold over 5000 fake degrees. In one case, when a decomposed body of a woman was found in a clinic, the fake doctor owning the clinic had simply fled after the woman had died. Many MBBS, BAMS, RMI degrees were sold for hug amount.

Many drugs, including those commonly used for headaches and common cold, are fake or substandard. Of them, 60 percent have no active ingredient and 16 percent have harmful ingredients. Spurious drugs are a major threat to people's health and well-being. The web of fake medicines spreads from Kashmir to Kanyakumari. In the northern India, Bhagirath Palace in Delhi reportedly the hub of fake medicine trade. Other places, which are the breeding ground of fake drugs include Lucknow in UP, Ahmedabad in Gujrat and Indore in Madhya Pradesh, where like in other places, small-scale fake or substandard drug manufacturing units operate from garages, shanties and hovels. Most so called medicines but really fakes, are being churned out in slums under the most unhygienic conditions. They are positively harmful and cause complications leading to fatalities. Fake medicines have a thriving market in South Africa, as well as in neighbouring countries like Mynamar, Nepal and Bangladesh as well as in Russia and Uzbekistan.

Unofficial figures, assessed by the consumer bodies estimate that more than 40 per cent of the medicines which are sold in the rural market are fake or substandard. That means, three out of 10 fast moving consumer goods (FMCG. a collective term for cosmetics, toiletries and processed food products) in the market could be fake. The rough estimate is 10-30 % of cosmetics, toiletries, packaged food are counterfeit. 10% of soft drinks sold as major brands are spurious; Rs 4,000 crore worth of spurious drugs are sold every year; 61% of computer software and 40% of music sold are pirated and Rs 10,000 crore revenue is lost to the fakes industry annually.

The AC Nielsen survey estimated the annual loss to the FMCG industry at Rs 2,600 crore and to the government, in unpaid taxes, at Rs 900 crore. An ORC survey of 12, 500 retail stores completed in January 2002 found the counterfeit market to be 5.15 percent of total annual sales of the Rs 60,000 crore for PMCC industry. That's between Rs 3,000 crore and Rs 9,000 crore a year. Our drug regulatory authorities have no teeth, few inspectors and even fewer experts. The law lacks for the manufacturing fake drugs is not a cognisable offence. It means that Police cannot register a case against such fake manufacturers. Fake drugs come under the Drugs and Cosmetics Act, 1940 or the Copyright Act. An accused can only be punished for two or three years after the case drags on. Often he is let off with a fine of a few thousand Rupees.

The identification of fake or substandard medicines is not an easy task. It is now a mandatory requirement, to mention the key ingredients, date of manufacture, date of expiry, price including all taxes and the batch number of the product on the label or the container. Printing, packaging, design and colour of a fake will be inferior and may come off. Pay close attention to advertisements regarding the packs. Similarly, chances are that in the case of look alike products, manufacturer's address will be missing. But fakes in most cases carry full details as in the original. It is wiser to be beware of undue huge discounts by retailers that are not backed by the manufacturer. Often this is to lure an unsuspecting buyer. The Mashelkar committee, set up in 2002 by the Government of India, recommended amendment of the Act and the setting up of a National Drug Agency with some teeth to it.

The consumerism has so much infatuated a certain section of society, that they want all good things of life without earning them by the sweat of their brow. The lust of avarice has so much possessed that the desire to get rich at any cost has become the ruling principle. Greatness through money whether earned by crooked means or any crime, is the craze. The latest scandal of leakage of examination papers, right under the nose of Union Education Ministry, which has been trying to control IIM's five member cartel that leaked the CBSE Pre-Medical Test papers, was caught for the examination slated on 10th of April, 2004. The gang involved in the leakage would demand a total price between Rs 7 Lakhs to Rs 10 Lakhs from the intended beneficiaries. Advance payment between Rs 50,000 and Rs 1 lakh was required. Complete payment was to be made only after the candidate confirmed the examination did have all the questions shown to him/her the night before. The gang had claimed that they had the genuine question papers in their possession. Instead of parting with the papers, another condition laid down was, that the students desirous of availing the facility of knowing the question paper in advance, would have to spend the night at their place in Delhi and mug up the answers. The candidates would have to stay there, till the examination day that is 10th of April, 2004 Sunday morning and proceed straight for the test centres from there. When Police, acting on the information raided the house, they found eight boys and five girls, busy mugging the answers. The police discovered that most of the 13 students, were children of government officials and doctors. So bold and confident were the criminals that they placed advertisements, well in advance, in some newspapers in Rajasthan.

Students and parents were asked to reach the specified house in Delhi, to memorise the questions and answers. They were not allowed to take away anything in writing. Four of the seven parents in Delhi contacted, were ready to pay money to secure a seat for their sons. The other three contacted the accused through newspaper advertisements. The wards found the randezurous of the accused persons, belonged to an official working in MTNL Delhi, in the meteorological department and DDA in fairly junior positions. How they could collect such huge amounts for payment, when working at the level of supervisors or junior engineers required unravelling of a further mystery. Around 2.4 lakh students appeared for the preliminary examination, again to be held again on 17th April at 424 centres in 31 cities across the country. Of these centres, 75 were located in

Delhi. The leakage this year, is again a repetition of what happened last year in the CAT as well as of 2003 CBSE pre-medical papers. Like the investigation into CAT examination, this case also was handed over to the CBI. The arrest of half a dozen accused persons in Delhi is only a tip of the big iceberg, as such leakages are masterminded for sale to hundred of aspirants all over the country. In the 2003 CBSE premedical examination, questions papers were printed at a Jaipur press. They were sent 15 days before the examination on April 27, 2003 to Canara Bank branches all over the country. Paper leak mafia was able to identify a Manager of the Bank in Bokaro, who for a financial consideration got the paper out from the bank locker..

The condition of availability of the jobs and opportunities for advancement is like *ek anar, an bimar*. In our country jobs have been sold by leaking the question papers even of the examinations conducted by the State Public Service Commission as it happened in Punjab and Maharashtra in 2001 and 2002. The net result is the same, with the only difference, that in the case of Public Service Commissions, the accused betrayed the trust reposed in them by the Constitution. Such episodes and occurrences reveal the hollowness of the system and how casually, we as a Nation take them. The real problem lies in the fact that neither our Government, politicians nor those charged with the responsibility of safeguarding the integrity of the affected institutions, take such problems seriously. Evading taxes, misusing or pinching the Government property, copying, cheating in examination, bribery, underselling or selling fakes, are not considered crime. Otherwise, how could such social criminals can start as the veneer of respectability.

As money can buy respectability and if some body opens his lockers, he can even become a legislator. There is no shame attached to the means of making money. The truth is: what has been revealed in the CBSE examination in April, was already transpiring. There is a case investigated by the CBI, which revealed how a postal official, working in Bihar had developed an expertise in abstracting papers for top UPSC examination sent through the post. His close relations made it to the top civil services through his malfeasance. He was prosecuted and sentenced. But such prosecutions, do not have the desired impact, as it takes a long time for the trials to be over, with the options of layers of appeals after appeals. Considering the money, that can be made in leaking examination papers, the sleaze experts develop newer and newer techniques to beat the system. In many places, open copying goes on, where either examiners are intimidated or are bought with money or proxies appear for others. The net result is the same as the leakage of papers for CBSE or CAT examinations.

This is not the only leak of papers which has occurred in our country. In 2003, Punjab Police had busted a similar scam in which by approaching, a politically connected rice miller was involved. A decoy after a tip-off, was sent to him, who struck a deal for getting the CBSE paper leaked, a day before the entrance test for a payment of Rs I1 lakh. The accused after his arrest made several disclosures including as to how he was duping the candidates for the entrance test for the past two years. He used to get list of aspirants of PMT test from senior officials of the CBSE, who were obviously involved in the scam. The Jammu and Kashmir Vigilance Department had unearthed leakage of papers of 2002 MBBS entrance test in the state. This fact came to light when the investigators were probing 2002 paper leak of MD and MS 2003 entrance tests. The accused in the MD and MS test paper leak told the investigators, that they had sold papers of the MBBS entrance test, held on July 14, 2003, for lakhs of rupees. It is reported that the needle of suspicion points to the candidates who topped 2003 merit list. According to the investigators they were named as beneficiaries of the leak.

There has been increasing mess in the system of conducting examination. Hardly a year passes, when the papers of one examination or the other, do not get leaked. At the drop of a hat, the Government sets up an Inquiry Commission, an Inquiry Committee or a Joint Parliamentary Committee. It had offered to set up a JPC to inquire whether any soft drinks sold in the country were healthy or not. Leakage of question papers, strikes at the root of our education system and it renders any talks of academic excellence a sheer rubbish and garbage. Such a Committee or Commission should also have a representative of the investigating agencies and not only educationists who are responsible for the mess. The examination system as at present, is only a test of memory and not of any in depth knowledge or comprehension of the candidates. Says Falconer. "Do not talk about disgrace from a thing being known, when the disgrace is that the thing should exist."

Bofors case is, now to the second decade. Out of the five recipients, Win Chadha and his wife are no more; another, two

Quotrochi and his wife are abscending. There seems to be no possibility at present of their being extradited from the safe haven of native Italy. At every election, Bofors guns boom in the electoral field. Government of India was on the look out, from 1980 for a suitable 155-mm gun system to meet the country's defence operational requirements. The choice was short-listed to M/s Sofma of France, M/s AB Bofors of Sweden, M/S IMS of UK and M/S Voest Alpine of Austria in December 1982. In November, 1985 here was further short listing of Sofma and Bofors. The Ministry of Defence had earlier set up a seven member negotiating Committee in May, 1984 with the defence Secretary as the Chairman, to deal with the entire matter of purchase of gun. At the meeting of the committee held on 12th March, 1986, the Committee felt, that the offer of Bofors was the better of the two. It recommended that pending finishing touches to the contract, Letter of Intent might be issued to Bofors, to the effect that the government was willing to award the contract to them. It was subject to their satisfying the Govt. of India, on all aspects of the purchase, license production, credit and other arrangements. These recommendations of the committee were approved, first by Ministry of Defence and then Ministry of Finance by about 10 officials followed by four Ministers, including Defence Minister, Sukh Ram and Arun Singh on 14th March, 1986. The Letter of Intent was promptly issued to Bofors on 14th March 1986 after above approvals. Further negotiations were continued. It was an unusual case, where negotiations continued even after a letter of intent was issued. Bofors submitted revised offers on 21st March 1986, as a hurried exercise. Correct procedure was to issue any final letter, after all the negotiations were over and not half way. The then Defence secretary sent a note to the Prime Minister stating, "it is now requested that permission may kindly be accorded to sign the agreement with Bofors. I had discussed this matter with Raksha Rajya Mantri (A) at the Airport before he left for Bhutan on 21st morning and he gave his blessings that if Bofors eventually agreed to give 10 guns free of cost, we should go ahead and clinch this deal". On 24th March 1986, Prime Minister, Rajiv Gandhi approved the proposal to conclude the contract with Bofors.

Finally the order was placed by the Govt. of India with Bofors on 24th March, 1986 for supply of 410 numbers (400 plus 10 free) of 155 mm field Howitzer 77-B gun system/spare guns for a total amount of Sek 8410.66 million (Swedish Kroner is the official currency of

Sweden). In Indian Rupees, it was equivalent to about Rs. 1437.72 crore. It is a well known fact that nothing moves in the Government, till it is moved with love, money, influence or contacts. The bigger the deal, the larger number of middle men will promise to swing the same. Dens of corruption rule roost, right from the lowest municipal organisation to the highest level of governance. We had the spectacle of a former Prime Minister and his colleagues being prosecuted for purchasing votes of the Parliamentarians. Government of India had made it clear that it would not have any middle men and this fact was well known to Bofors and other companies. Before getting the contract, they all confirmed that they had no middle men or brokers or agents. As claimed by the Defence Ministry the "agents" did not do any purported service to get the contract in favour of Bofors, Yet they were paid large sums as commission. When the total commission payable to Svenska Inc. and Anatronic General Corporation was reduced, AE Services Ltd. (Quatrocchi's company) suddenly entered the scene with an agreement with Bofors on 15th November, 1985, virtually guaranteeing the execution of the contract in favour of Bofors before 31st March, 1986 and achieved this with 7 days to spare. AE services Ltd. themselves had acted as trustee for CIAOU Anstalt, Vaduz. The payment made to AE Services Ltd. (Quatrocchi's company) by Bofors in September 1986 was exactly 3% of the 20% advance amount received by Bofors. This was as stipulated in the agreement dated 15th November 1985 between AE Services Ltd. and Bofors... Bofors paid an amount of Sek 50,463,966 to AE services Ltd. on 2/3 September 1986.

Obviously, no businessman pays any money, without a pro-quid. The Bofors company consistently and unjustifiably declined to disclose the names of the actual beneficiaries of the remittances made by them to the above three companies. The Government of India had set up a Joint Parliamentary Committee to look into the question of kickback in Bofors. In the report of Joint Parliamentary Committee, Thulholm, Chairman of Nobel Industries had also stated that he could not guarantee that bribes had not been paid. Bofors being a subsidiary of Nobel Industries, this statement of Tulholm is self explanatory. When contracts dated 24th March 1986, were awarded to Bofors, it was done without ensuring, that there was no agent or middlemen to whom any commission was payable by Bofors. By not ensuring these, the Defence Ministry did not obtain from Bofors corresponding reduction, at least to the extent of the commission payable by Bofors to the so called agents, from the contract amount payable by the government of India to Bofors. There has therefore been dishonest or fraudulent diversion of the funds of the government of India to Bofors at least to the extent of over Sek 319.40 million, which was the commission paid by Bofors to several agents, including Ottavio Quotrochi, an Italian power broker.

Arun Singh, Minister of State, in the Ministry of Defence, during that period had this to say to the CBI: "Shri Vohra informed the Cabinet Committee on Political Affairs (CCPA), as to how he put pressure on the Vice President of Bofors to give out the names of recipients of bribes and managed to get a reply from them that the President of Bofors would fly to India on the following Monday with the details of the recipients and bribes, etc. The members of CCPA (Cabinet Committee on Political Affairs) at the meeting were S/Sh. Buta Singh, N. D. Tiwari, P. Shiv Shankar and probably Shri V. P. Narasima Rao also. Some of those members present like Shri Buta Singh were very vocal and questioned the proprietary of taking a decision to summon the Bofors chief. It is possible, they were acting in such a fashion based on the mood of the PM. Immediately, the PM also expressed his anger and displeasure at Vohra An (Additional Secretary in Defence Ministry at that time) and demanded to know from Vohra on what basis and whose authority he had initiated this matter to discuss with A. B. Bofors. To the best of Arun Singh's recollection, he told the PM that Vohra was acting under his instructions. Arun Singh fell from the grace of PM instantly. Apparently there was a difference of view between Arun Singh and others. The PM agreed with his fellow members of the CCPA. The meeting concluded with the instructions that a future investigation in this matter would be under the JPC... Instructions were issued to inform the President of Bofors, not to come until summoned by the JPC. Mr. Vohra, was asked to ensure that Bofors team which would start on 4th July, 1987, should be stopped forthwith from coming to India until summoned by the JPC. The only way to get the Bofors not to reveal the names of those who received kickbacks was to threaten to cancel the contract. Arun Singh also felt that Quotrochi could not have wielded influence in this matter, without the involvement of somebody in the Government of India. It is not likely that any influence could swing the contract in favour of Bofors in the MOD without the influence of at least the Defence Secretary or the utter negligence of the MOD. Defence Secretary was not known to be a negligent man.

On being asked, by the CBI as to why did he not go for an F.I.R. on the bribes, when he had came to know of the matter, Arun Singh said: "As far as he remembered, there was no investigation required. Bofors would have suffered Rs.1400 cr. Loss, if we had cancelled the deal. We could have pressurised them to reveal the names. He also told the CBI that he was convinced that with the threat to cancel the contract, we could have persuaded them to give back the money they had paid as kickbacks". But the fact remains, there has been no evidence of any direct receipt of money by either Rajiv Gandhi or his other family member including Sonia Gandhi. Any suspicion or knowing even a thief or a crook is not a good enough reason to tarnish any body. In investigations, any suspicious role of any individual has to be converted into a legally sustainable evidence, which can stand the test of truth and examination in a court of law. It is totally different, writing impressionistic journalistic stories. In Bofors case, the evidence is foreign based, which has to be sustained in the Indian Legal Evidence. Our systems believes that let nine crook escape, rather than one guilty be convicted. It looks as if, the crooks of Bofors fall in the category, who have got away or will get away. It does not appear that Bofors case would be buried that easily, despite the absence of the main players, either due to death or due to other causes. Rajiv Gandhi was well aware of the commission already paid by Bofors and wanted to suppress its leakage by using his authority. He had alerted intelligence agencies in advance for any sensational news from Sweden. One mid /night news breaker was awarded for prompt interception of Swiss Radio news, night. The other having no news/ had to put in his papers.

Says Seneca: "Money does all things for reward. Some are pious and honest, as long as they thrive upon it, but if the devil himself gives better wages, they soon change their party". The CAT examination in November, 2003 once again proves, that men are seldom innocently employed or self employed, when they are honestly making money. The Centralised Admission Test became a gold mine and made not only millionaires, but some billionaires out of it. Surprisingly, the land of Ashoka and Buddha, that is Bihar, has become quite fertile in giving birth and rearing of scamsters. It is reported that such was the expertise of the leaker, that one student who appeared for his CAT admission for becoming a doctor, passed the same and made it to the first list, while he failed in his 12th standard examination on the anticipated passing of which, he had appeared for CAT examination. The evidence of the power of the scam can be seen from the fact, that in 2003 CAT examination of 1200 seats for medicine, nearly 600 went to the people from Bihar. For the first time in the 42 years-old history of the premier Indian Institutes of Management (IIMs), its Common Admission Test (CAT) for the MBA programme was cancelled on 23rd November, 2003, because of the alleged leakage of the question paper, a few hours ahead, of the examination. The question paper had about 150 questions running over 40 pages

For placement year 2003, the average salary at IIM Bangalore was Rs. 6.11 lakh. The average salary for the 2003 batch was Rs. 6.2 lakh and Rs. 6.18 lakh for IIMs at Ahmedabad and Lucknow respectively. At IIM Calcutta, the 250-odd candidates found final placements within the first four days of the placement season. Not only the students studying in IIMs benefited, but also the scamsters. The top pin king of the racket is roughly worth over 100 crore. Scamster along with six others who were arrested, was reportedly involved in the Bank's Probationary Officers, Medical Entrance Tests and other examinations. Reportedly, the scamster's rate for leaking various examinations papers was as under: MBBS examination Rs. 10- Rs. 12 lakh. All-India Medical PG, Rs. 12-14 lakh (higher for surgery, lower for anaesthesia). CAT rate was for Rs. 5 lakh. Engineering was around Rs. 10 lakh". Of course, the rates could be negotiated. Obviously a leak of this nature is no local and isolated matter. It is the result of an organised, countrywide racket. Whatever has become public knowledge may be only a speck and a small tip of the iceberg. The scam must had been going on for the past several years. Most people in education sphere, both in and out of Bihar, were aware of it.

A morning fellow walker commented to me, rather uncharitably that despite the saying that Bihar had a lot of fake Colleges and Universities, which were no centre of excellence, how is it a lot of Biharis have made it to the top All India and other services. He also said that the maximum number of Universities, black listed by the UGC, were in Bihar and how is it that Bihar is disproportionately highly represented in the jobs all over the country. I told him that Bihar also had produced Sikh Guru Gobind Singh, apart from National Leaders like Jai Prakash Narayan. I also mentioned that there are bad hats in every State and it will be unfair to single out Bihar, where perhaps there is maximum acute poverty and so conceivably people will do anything to get a job.

Such incidents reveal the hollowness of the claim of having a foolproof and time-tested system, with adequate checks at every level. The factual publicity surrounding the CAT examination is bound to affect the future of the candidates. Many job recruiting agencies do not accept as gospel truth the degrees given by some Universities. UPSC regularly publishes the list of many fake universities periodically. The trouble is neither the Government nor the affected institutions, take such malfeasances seriously, except some token action. The truth is, that social crime like stealing taxes, or copying or underselling or selling fakes, is not a reputation tarnisher. Millions stacked through malpractices are considered more than enough to buy respectability. The reality is that what happened in CAT' examination, was already happening.

The goons develop newer and newer techniques to beat the system. In some places, there is an outright copying, by intimidating the examiners, while at others it is done stealthily, by passing on slips or carrying possible answers to the questions by the examinees. If invigilation is strict, bogus applicants are made to send their test or examination forms along with the genuine candidates. They get seats close by and the answer sheets, written correctly by the dummy candidate are exchanged/ replaced with that of the other candidate. Still in other places, the examiners openly help the candidates either for love or money. New methods are needed to be devised to face the new challenges from crooks. The Principal of a College, told me that he had received a request from one of the State Ministers, to help a candidate in copying, which he had flatly rejected. The Principal was threatened with dire consequences. Another Vice Chancellor, of a deemed University, told me that he had also received a request for admission of a candidate to MD from the highest quarters in the Government of India. When he regretted his inability, to violate any rules or norms, he was threatened with a sack. Sacking could not be done under the rules straightway. By the time, the exercise to do so started, the Government fell and his job was saved. It is reported that Ministry of Human Resources had set up a single man committee headed by a retired IAS Secretary, who got a sinecure of a job of CAG, to look into the leakage for six years after his retirement . The only legal power to investigate the leakage of CAT's examination lies with the CBI. Many retired or serving IAS officers are working as Vice Chancellors, which has not resulted in any visible or appreciable improvement in academic fields. Says GF Train: "There is no credit in knowing how to spell, but positive disgrace in being ignorant on that point. So there can be no credit in doing right, while it is infamous to do wrong."

A young girl of 16 years of age, suffering from stammering, was reportedly operated upon by a quake, in the first week of June, 2004. The operation was to cure her stammering. The quake an 11th class passed had displayed his name board as MBBS. The so called Doctor had assured her parents, that to prevent any embarrassment to the stammer, by her colleagues and friends, a small operation would cure her. He reported cut off her tongue resulting in profuse bleeding. She had to be shifted to a Government hospital, where she was declared brought dead. We have no law in the country, which can prevent a person from being called a Doctor, without even having qualified. The result is that, Registered Medical Practitioners, (RMP) also style themselves Doctors, though they are basically trained in rendering first aid and possess only rudimentary knowledge of the medicines. There are others who call themselves Madrasi or Bengali Doctors, as they claim, that they can cure some specific diseases. There are others, who are only Ayurvedic Doctors. Some such doctors put advertisements advising young people to meet them for extra vigour or energy either before or after their marriage.

Laws if any existing, are of no deterrence to the quack or potential hit and miss street killers. It may appear strange, but the fact remains that, some of the penal provisions, pertaining to the fake drug trade have been toned down in the 1982 amendment. According to the 1940 Act, sale of drugs without licence could be punished with a jail term of a year extendable upto 10 years. But in the amended version, the crime is punishable with a prison term of a year extendable upto 3 years only. Very rarely, any conviction of a jail sentence of three years has been noticed. Most people get away with lighter sentences. Since 1982, no offender has been charged by the drug controllers under the Section that holds life imprisonment as punishment. Even if drugs are seized and got tested, it is next to impossible to connect the death of a person to fake drugs. This can almost never be proved due to the high standards of proof required, which is never available or possible to get. A social crime like the fake drugs or Doctor is not treated on par with murder and dacoity, though the result of fakes are no less dangerous and murderous.

State Governments say they do not have the manpower to check whether every 'doctor' has the requisite qualifications. It is the job of the respective Medical Council. The Medical Councils naturally and understandably cannot and do not want to get involved in policing their own fraternity. The result is that common man is the victim.

22
Monstrous Mafia

Those who live by gun, are bound to die by gun. You cannot always live for ever, by stealing sandalwood in the tropical forests of southern India. The lush tropical forests there, are vast lands having prized hardwoods, like teak, mahogany and rosewood. Veerappan, the brigand killed in Police Encounter on 18th of October, 2004, dealt not only in sandalwood, but also in ivory. For nearly eighteen years, he was a dreaded hunter of elephants, sandalwood and men. For over two decades he had avoided successfully, from being trapped. Crafty and suspicious by nature, as his calling required, he ended up in the Police lap, when he used an ambulanced driven, by an undercover policeman, who masqueraded as a taxi driver. The, called taxi driver was driving him for being taken to Dharmapuri for medical treatment. His final journey ended at 10.15 pm, when his ambulance emerged from the forest, 11 km from Dharmapuri. A Police party, which was standing by and had been tipped off, trapped him. The van was surrounded after the police constable, who was doubling as a taxi driver had jumped out. The police appealed to him to surrender but seeing the writing on the wall, Veerappan and his three companions decided to fight it out. This was a chance, which no policeman worth his salt will let go and thus the bandit was outmanned, outgunned and outmanoeuvred. At the end of the twentyfive minutes fight, it was curtains for Veerappan and his three accompanying henchmen. One non-ballistic 12 bore Remington pump action gun, which can spray bullets effectively for bush fighting, two AK-47s, a self-loading rifle (7.62) and two hand grenades and about Rs. 3.5 lakh were also recovered from the dead bandits. A lot of inputs, like the policemen in civilian clothes, moving about as taxi drivers, bus conductors, hawkers and masons, reportedly settled in the villages on the fringes of the forest, were deployed. Thus, the planted personnel had won confidence of the gang. Four policemen were also planted in the Veerappan gang.

The cost of manhunt, for a phenomenon called Veerappan, did not come easily or cheap one of the longest, bloodiest and costliest anti-dacoity operation, which was to cost approximately Rs. 700 crore and 119 lives, including 47 police and forest officials of both Karnantaka and Tamil Nadu States and 72 civilians. This is a small amount compared to the crores the bandit must have made in ransom and by smuggling ivory tusks and sandalwood. At the last official count, Veerappan (57) had butchered over two hundred elephants for their ivory. It is reported, that he had smuggled over 200 tonnes of sandalwood worth Rs 100 crore. In black market it must have fetched highly lucrative prices. The brigand had 106 cases filed against him in Tamil Nadu, 70 in Karnataka. There was a prize money of Rs 5 crore announced by the Karnataka government and Rs. 50 lakh by Tamil Nadu for Veerappan's capture. The reason for this prolonged and slow operation is that Veerappan had evaded the law for decades, in the shelter of the thick and literally impenetrable forests. Barring a brief capture in 1986, he remained elusive and sneaky. He was the craftiest of the renegades in the country's criminal history. Even today, it is a mystery where he has stashed away his money. His style was to roam the forest armed with a few machine guns and the barest of belongings and never spend more than one night at one spot or place.

Earlier, a joint-manhunt for over six years undertaken by a 324-strong BSF and Special Task Force formed by the two state governments had been unsuccessful and wasted. It had failed to nab the bandit, who continued to have a free run of over 6,000 square kilometres of forest area in both states. His killing spree commenced, in deadly earnest in July 1987 when he kidnapped R. Srinivas, a senior forest official into his lare, who he blamed for his sister's death and personally beheaded him. Two years later he murdered five men of a rival gang. In August 1992, to avenge the death of four of his gang members, he trapped STF SP Hari Krishna, tied him with grenades and blew him up along with five other policemen. Amongst his money making exploits, kidnapping of film star Rajkumar is reported to have fetched him Rs. 20 crore. This is stated in a book published by a former Director General of Karnataka Police but denied by the then Chief Minister of same State. However, a late Chief Minister of Karnataka, during his conversation with me, put the figure at Rs. 30 crore. May be, truth lies in some other figures, which will never be known, as the recipient is dead and the giver is never going to admit to any ransom having been paid.

The uproar about the dacoit's crimes had died down, after Kannada matinee idol had been released physically unharmed in 2001. The reason for a prolonged failure, is generally the mentality of only reacting to any given situation line kidnapping or other crime of Veerappan, instead of adopting a consistent down to business style to nab him. Another strike, killing a former Minister Nagappa; jostled the administration to some demonstrable action but this also ended soon. The thug held at bay, the police forces of Tamil Nadu and Karnataka and a special task force of the Border Security Force, echoing the might of the Indian state. Still credit goes to the officers and men of Tamil Nadu Special Task Force, who finally deliver a crushing blow to end the long standing regime of the outlaw. A legitimate question may be asked, as to why it took so long to deal the deserved desserts to the brigand, who had brought to heel the Governments of Tamil Nadu and Karnataka. They were willing to appease him to any extent to secure the release of Kannada matinee idol, Dr. Raj Kumar kidnapped in 2000 and kept in captivity for over 108 days. When any Government agency, has to deal with any situation, it is bound by the confines of law. Of course, occasionally even the Government agencies step outside the Lakshman Rekha, in the overall National interests.

A question is being asked, as to why and how so long, such a criminal could survive without any political backing. Karnataka Chief Minister had announced, that an "inquiry" would be conducted to expose the political patronage and financial support given to the brigand. It was a tall order, from which nothing emerged. It goes without saying, that all politicians and a number of bureaucrats, are too happy to accept any green bank notes, without asking too many questions, as to who is giving and for what reason. Telgi Stamp scam, is an eloquent proof of the possible involvement of some people having political contacts, if any proof is still needed, of the politician- criminal nexuses. However, it is doubtful, if any politician, either from Karnataka or Tamilnadu, was overtly or even covertly in league, with a dreaded criminal like Veerappan. May be some would have kept quiet, if only to safeguard their lives and limbs, even if they knew a lot about him or his whereabout. Both the Governments of Karnataka and Tamil Nadu, had gone over-board in showering largesses on the members of their Special Task Forces, running into crore of Tax Payers' money. The correct policy, would have been, to reward only those, (about 50 of them of Tamil Nadu Police) who actually took part in the operations, which saw the end of Veerappan and not all those 'who also ran' even from Karnantaka. One Veerappan has been too costly and some calculate the cost exceeding Rs. 1000 crore, if the salary, expenses and other costs are included for the operation against Veerappan, which went on since 1993.

India can boast of having possibly largest slum in the world, larger in population than many countries. It is Dharvi, with nearly 1.4 million population. Terrible slush, squalor, and mountains of garbage greet and glare the residents and others passing by it. A survey of school children in Bombay showed that nearly 70% of them wanted easy money by imitating the criminal gang leaders in the films. Rags to riches stories of the dons of earlier years, including that of Haji Mastan, Dawood Ibrahim, Gawli, and Vardrajan Iyengar gaining respectability by moving up and becoming politicians are there for every body to see. Their extortion, bullying, and manipulation appear to have paid off. The money accumulated as criminals came handy for them to secure social respectability in the society almost in most cases obliterating the fine distinction between politicians and criminals. The question naturally arises: "Why and who has allowed the situation to come to this pass? Could not timely action avert its". There is a lot of talk asking, "Who is this grabber, to make millions and acquire illegally many properties through the help of goons at his command. The nursery of his training has been Mumbai, which from 1998 to 2004 had 90 shootouts and over 90 Killings. The gangsters have been striking at will at Court and in Court premises and even in front of city Police Headquarters. Some gangsters attacked the police with hand grenades and killed the policemen near JJ hospital. A bold Police Inspector, who was responsible for the elimination of a number of dreaded and ruthless criminals was gunned down in Ghaziabad. Estimates vary about the level of extortion in Mumbai. It can be safely placed at nearly 500 crore. A colleague told me that there is price tag on every thing by the extortionists. His Gujrati businessman associate wanted to marry off his daughter in style in a five star hotel. He promptly got a demand of Rs. 25 lakh for safe marriage. Another builder, who had made millions, was killed because he refused to part with two crore demanded of him by the well known gangs of extortionists. A cassette industry leader, an hotelier, and those helping the police have been eliminated. The purchase of a car also has a price tag. A luxury car entails a demand ranging from one lakh to five lakh. More expensive cars like Mercedes, require an extortion amount almost equal to the amount of the car itself. Corrupt politicians and dishonest bureaucrats further assist them in their designs. A large number of Ramesh Sharmas and Prakash Shuklas are roaming around the country.

In the no war time, more policemen lose their lives, in fight against criminals than any other group. The fear has dawned on Delhi also with moneyed people making their houses secure with high walls, door chains, magic eyes, barbed wires, and erection of iron gates manned round the clock. They forget that for determined criminals and robbers, no obstacle is good enough. But strong physical security does mitigate a feeling of insecurity, though not that of the fear. As against the estimated requirements of 165 Police Stations to cope with the rising population, estimated after 1984 anti Sikh riots, the capital has only 105 Police Stations. It also has four Railway Police Stations and four Police Stations for specific type of cases. The public perception both in Mumbai and Delhi is that, people are living in terror. In an affidavit filed in Delhi High Court, the Union Home Ministry said that heinous crimes like dacoity, murder, attempt to murder, robbery and kidnapping for ransom had gone up in the Capital in 1998. It also admitted that the general feeling among public was that the situation had been deteriorating. Maharashtra has made an effort to issue a Presidential Approved Ordinance to combat the increasing under world activities in their Metropolis. The important features of the ordinance, is the reliance on evidence proffered by police officials. It will also enable the admissibility of taped conversations, including those on the telephone in between the gangsters and also between the gangsters and victims, especially in extortion cases. It is worthwhile to mention that non-compliance of the demands of the gangsters and kidnappers has led to reprisals in the form of killing. It also includes provisions relating to denial of bail. Witnesses deposing before the Special Courts would have the benefit of in-camera hearings. The objective of the Ordinance is to provide deterrence through higher punishment. At present, criminals like Shakeel, Chota Rajan, Abu Salem (A tailor cum driver), Dawood, Arun Gawli, Amar Naik (A vegetable seller) and few others operate from the protective environments of either Pakistan, Dubai, Malaysia, or even jails in India. At present, according to one assessment, Chota Shakeel Gang has over 20 killings and 150 extortion threats to its credit. Chota Rajan gang follows closely. The kind of crime indulged in by the criminals is such that victims prefer to buy off peace and security from the gangs than to complain to the authorities, in whom they have least faith and trust. A long list of victims including the politicians, exporters, contractors, hoteliers, people in video trade is sufficient to convince that the extortionists mean business. Each hit or a killing increases their credibility when they threaten a potential victim. Our policeman regrettably, has a bad name and he is accused of both tyranny and corruption, unlike the Police of England, which enjoy the whole-hearted support of their citizens. Everything flows from the top, including firmness of action and a desire to get the results in the overall interest of the people. Simple, transparent, accountable, responsive and transparent Laws and Procedures are required to redress people's grievances.

The question of getting our criminals extradited from other countries is linked with many other issues. It is not simply a question of a legal battle. First of all, the Indian Agencies or the Government of India, seeking the extradition, have no local standi in a foreign court. The case is to be presented by the Government Prosecutor or Police Department or ministry of External Affairs, depending upon the laws of the country, where a possible criminal, escaping from the Indian Laws might be residing or working. For whatever offence, a criminal, wanted by India, might be charged, for the purpose of extradition, it is essential to convince the court in that country, that there is a prima facie case against the accused. This will again differ from court to court and country to country. For instance, in the Bofors case, the Swiss Courts found ample and satisfying evidence, whereas the Malaysian Court did not accept the same evidence for extraditing Quotorochi, who had received 7.34 million Dollars in the deal. There are more than 11 fugitives, from Indian Laws, who are facing extradition proceedings. There are 38 Letters Rogatory (LRs) lying unexecuted in countries like the Bahamas, Chile, Gambia, Senegal, Paraguay and even the Ivory Coast. 113 of these unexecuted LRs have been sent by the Central Bureau of Investigation, for mutual assistance on criminal matters. Letter Rogatory is a request, sent by an Indian Judge to foreign countries through the Ministry of External affairs, at the instance of Indian Investigating Agencies. While the system of sending Letters Rogatory and asking for mutual assistance on criminal matters is good, the result is not even good enough. There are 43 LRs pending in 43 countries. The absence of response has delayed many crucial cases. There are 25 pending LRs in several countries for assistance in the Indian Bank scam and 23 more are for help, in chasing baffling international leads in the Rajiv Gandhi assassination case. Other requests for cooperation ignored by Foreign governments, include the Purulia arms dropping case and the IC-814 hijacking from Kathmandu to Kandhar, in December, 2001.

Extradition treaties are bilateral, with laid down extraditable offences, stipulated in such a treaty. Principle of double criminality, which is generally incorporated, in such agreements lays down, that the offence for which the extradition is sought be an offence under the national laws of the extradition requesting country as well as of the requested country and the requested country must be satisfied, that there is a prima facie case, made out against the offender/ accused. Also the extradited person, must be proceeded against, only for the offence for which his extradition was requested for and he must be accorded a fair trial.

A young engineer, working for the National Highway Authority of India was murdered by the mafia, in November, 2003, when he blew whistle on the corrupt practices going on in the Golden Quadrangle Project in Bihar. The furore created by his murder, led to the Prime Minister declaring, that guilty would not be spared, "wherever they were". The murder led to an outrage, wherein all political parties joined in a chorus, that would support the Whistle-Blower Bill. Unless there is a legal or departmental assurance the whistle-blower will face reprisals, either in the form of harassment, suspension or dismissal, as had happened in the case of former Director General Of Bihar Police, who spoke about the protection of the criminals by the politicians in that State, in November, 2003. The whistle-blowers, at least in India have reasons to suspect (rightly or wrongly) that, the corruption and the protection of criminals also implicates and incriminates, by the powers that be. In the present state of affairs, there is no respect for the confidentiality of complainant, as it happened in the case of killed NHAI engineer. Time and again, same similar messages come out of official inquiries by the Commissions or Committees, into major scandals and disasters. They expose that people who worked in or with the organization, had seen the problem but had either been too scared to sound the alarm or had raised the matter in the wrong way or with the wrong person. Quite often there is a tragic human cost. Whenever there is a scandal or a major disaster that could have been averted, there is pressure for new laws or new regulatory controls. The Committee of Independent Experts, while looking into the resignation of the European Commission in March 1999, remarked that the facts demonstrated "the value of officials whose conscience persuades them of the need to expose wrong doings encountered in the course of their duties. They also show, how the reaction of superiors failed to live up to legitimate expectations". The primary aim of a whistle blowing should be to use the whistle-blower as a witness, not as a complainant.

US legal expert, Thomas M. Devine says: "Whistle blowers, protection is a policy that all government leaders support in public but few in power tolerate in private."

23
Motivated Crimes

War in Iraq, which had broken out on 20th of March, 2003, again highlights the role of Intelligence Agencies of the Western war allies of the USA in general and CIA in particular. Intelligence agencies in the Western World, despite all talks of human rights, continue to play the cloak and dagger game. Marenches admitted that before he took charge, the French external intelligence agency seemed shocking in its activities. It intervened freely in the internal affairs of other countries. It was organising murders, assassinations, the kidnapping and disappearance of the Moroccan leader Ben Barka in 1965. French mafia was used just like the CIA mafia hitmen and various gangsters and gunmen. He claimed that he had introduced some degree of morality in his organisation. He went on to proudly narrate how the SDECE (as his outfit was then called) had succeeded in ousting Emperor Jean-Bedel Bokassa of the Central African Republic in 1979. He added that sometimes nations had to take actions which might be immoral or even illegal. Such decisions, however, could only be taken by the Executive Head of the State or the President. In his case, he said that the matter was of his discretion, whether to go ahead with an action on his own or consult the President. He says. "I could not make a unilateral decision to dispose of a head of state—and we always had certain ones in mind. In such a case, I would go to the President". In the US, disclosures have revealed that President Eisenhower himself authorised the CIA to scheme the overthrow of President Sukarno of Indonesia. President Kennedy too ordered the CIA to overthrow Dr. Cheddi Jagan of Guyana, which was achieved by surreptitiousness and manoeuvring. President Bush had ordered Saddam Hussein of Iraq and his sons to step down or face forcible removal through war. United Nations or no United Nations, world opinion or no world opinion, the USA after its success in Afghanistan embarked on a policy of selecting pot tin rulers of its choice in other countries. It has backed up its demands, with a mighty air power shower. It only shows that morality is used, as a façade when it suits and given up, when it does not.

The Soviets and their allies were no different, in the hey days of its power. Marenches, French Intelligence Chief said that the

Bulgarians were used by the Soviets frequently "for the worst kind of work — 'wet work' or assassination", as the KGB leadership considered them loyal.

The British had also tried to target Nasser of Egypt at the time of the Suez crisis. It appears that MI6 had developed a plan to kill him using nerve gas. The plan was abandoned when the then British Prime Minister Eden succeeded in obtaining French and Israeli approval to engage in joint military action against Egypt. However, when this alternative did not happen as expected, the plan to assassinate Nasser was revived. By this time, virtually all MI6 assets in Egypt had been rounded up by Nasser. Another operation using renegade egyptian officers was drawn up but failed lamentably, principally because the cache of weapons which had been hidden on the outskirts of Cairo was found to be defective. Wright with Green Grass, 1987.

In 1993 April, Kuwaiti police unearthed an Iraqi conspiracy to kill American President George Bush with a massive car bomb which was to be planted in Kuwait at the time of his visit. A senior Libyan intelligence official played a crucial role in organising the bombing of the Pan Am aircraft over Lockerbie on 21 December 1988. Various intelligence bodies in the Western World have routinely killed the opponents of their governments who have taken refuge in other countries. Libya, Iraq and Iran in particular have done it, almost all the time. After the murder of former Iranian Prime Minister Shahpour Bakhtiar in Paris in 1991, French investigations showed that Iranian intelligence services had effectively taken part in the criminal conspiracy to carry out the assassination. The West perceives Islamic terrorism, as great a threat as communism was fifty years ago. The NATO secretary-general Willy Claes and chief of the British MI5 Stella Remington had called radical Islam, the geopolitical menace of the future.

We, as a Nation, occasionally discuss the criminalisation of polity. The matters generally end there. Criminalisation is neither a new discovery, nor a new phenomenon. This phenomenon cuts across the entire country and all political parties. It is rather unfair to accuse only Bihar of electing tainted politicians to the portals of powers, both in the State and Central Legislatures. Almost all parties, with the exception of Left, have indulged in it. We need to have a look at Christian values, which allow only such persons to hurl stones at sinners, who have themselves been guilty of no sin. Neither criminalisation is likely to end with a few convictions, as it happened in the case of Jayalalitha or Narasimha Rao or his home Minister Buta Singh and later on, on their acquittal in appeal on technical grounds. Even conviction of Sukh Ram in a lower court was allowed to be in abeyance, till a decision could taken in the Higher Court on his appeal. Politicians talk about rooting out corruption or ending criminalisation, but are most of the time, party to the same, either by connivance, convenience or adopting the policy, of let the sleeping dogs sleep.

The induction of chargesheeted Ministers in the UPA Union Government, headed by the one of the cleanest politicians in India, and perhaps in the world, is only a confirmation of what has been a public knowledge for decades. Most politician owe an explanation to the public, as to how in the course of their 'so called public service' they have graduated from rags to the riches, beating the royalty of yore. No party has disowned the criminals or the corrupt, if they had even a remote chance of winning an election. In the last 59 years since India has been independent, with different parties ruling it, none has thought it fit to put into place, laws for dealing with political corruption or criminalisation.

The temptation of making easy money is too much for most people, when they can eat their cake and have it too. No corrupt with a potential to win, has ever become a pariah. On the contrary, some of them, floated their own political outfits and had or have become king makers. At present no party is either willing or has a mechanism to look within and identify and expel the corrupt and the criminal elements. Nobody is a pariah to any political party, if he or she is able to help a motley group of politicians to seize power and stay there. Pariah of one political party, easily become the darling of their rivals and a welcome guest.

A new culture has come to develop wherein no political party wants to condemn others, because the enemies of today, might become allies of tomorrow whether it is of Mayawati of UP, Jayalalitha of Tamil Nadu Badals of Punjab, Chautalas of Haryana, Yadavs and Taslimudins Shabuudins of Bihar. When there were discussions over the Supreme Court Orders on Representation of Peoples Act, almost all parties were opposed to any changes. They felt mere chargesheeting of a person was not proof of his guilt, whether he is chargesheeted for murder, dacoity, extortion, simple political rioting or agitation. When the Delhi High Court told the Election Commission on the basis of a petition that the antecedents of contestants should be disclosed, the government promptly filed an appeal. The matter had to go to Supreme Court, who held the amendment to the election statute bad in law and struck it down. The political parties go for winners, irrespective of their background. There are serious gaps in the law, to prevent criminals from getting into State and Central legislatures. Their entry to such houses amounts to treating law breakers as lawmakers.

A committee headed by Justice HR Khanna, Nani Palkhivala and Justice Lentin had proposed that the person convicted of a criminal offence as well as the one against whom a charge has been framed in a criminal court should not be eligible for election in any legislature. But their recommendations are gathering dust. Political parties have not shown the necessary seriousness in the matter, for obvious reasons. These days, politics is largely a matter of having enough of muscle and money power. Money politics, sustained on black money, naturally leads to strengthening the nexus of politicians with smugglers, black marketers, bootleggers and underworld dons. It leads to a perversion in the system. In the Telgi stamp scam, names of only some politicians have surfaced, with many more to come. One police officer indicated the involvement and association of the then Home Minister of a State, who ultimately resigned from his office.

No democracy is free from taints and deviations, which are but different tinges of criminalisation or a deviant behaviour. An American has this to say about his country:

"I have, in my life time of 79 years to date, lived through and with:

Two Presidents, who had mistresses unknown to their legitimate wives.

One President, whose mother didn't even know, who was the father of the President.

One President, who lied from top to bottom about the drugs he was taking daily.

One President, who accumulated illegal cash in his White House safe deposit box.

One President, who lied under oath to a grand jury.

Two Presidents who had sex in the White House with others than their wives.

One President, who had almost daily orgies in the White House with White House personnel.

A Vice President, who was found guilty of income tax evasion.

"A Secretary of Defense that lied to congress and was charged with improper conduct and got off only because a President pardoned him! What else can you expect from a generation of Americans who have lost their way? Our culture sponsors them; generates them and teaches them to be thieves, liars, cheats, crooks and thieves". Our politicians lie through their teeth day in and day out". Henry Miller (1891–1980), U.S. novelist said that "One has to be a lowbrow, a bit of a murderer to be a politician, ready and willing to see people sacrificed, slaughtered for the sake of an idea, whether a good one or a bad one."

The position is that, political tribes and their antics are totally discredited in the perception of the common man in our countryy. For one politician, standing exposed and disgraced temporarily, there are countless others, whose hands are perhaps more dirty, but have escaped public scrutiny. According to one political party, another major political party sponsored 78 persons with criminal cases pending in April, May-2004 Elections. A Committee headed by a former Home Secretary with Director of CBI and others as members in 1992/1993, confirmed the fact that criminalisation of the political and administrative apparatus had become all-pervasive. Linkages between the underworld, politicians and police were illustrated by the exposure of network in the Mumbai blasts cases in 1993. The committee report had brought out that the network of mafia gangs has been running a parallel system making the official machinery irrelevant in critical areas of public life. Unfortunately, these danger signals have not been taken seriously and continue to be ignored. In the present scheme of things, with a few exceptions like the Prime Minister Dr. Manmohan Singh, and a miniscule number of others, there is no premium on honesty and integrity in public life. Said Crosby. "To let politics become a cesspool and then avoid it, because it is a cesspool is a double".

The lure of money leads to strange situations. A new type of commerce, has recently flourished. It is the replacement of the organs for leading a healthy life. Said Voltaire: "The fate of a Nation has often depended on the good or bad digestion of a Prime Minister". Police in the National Capital has arrested three members of a gang, who were charging between Rs. 80,000 to 1.5 Lakhs for a kidney. The gangs used to go to blood banks, contact professional blood donors who are generally poor and persuade them to sell their kidneys.

Another hunting ground was the Government hospitals, including the well known ones, where poor people would come from all over the country for treatment. Gangs also collect information about the prospective recipients through networking with ward boys and technicians of super specialty hospitals. An agent contacts the recipient and then introduces the donor to him. Before striking a deal, the donor is asked to pose as a relation of the recipient. To avoid detection, the donor is asked to change his name. It is a requirement of the existing laws, that the Doctor performing surgery must counsel and warn the prospective donor about the dangers and consequences of the transplant. Gangs do the appropriate briefing of prospective donors.

The trade in kidney sale has its ramifications all over the country. A Delhi gang has reportedly sold over fifty kidneys all over the country. In Delhi alone, apart from Research and Referral Army Hospital, three more hospitals in Delhi and one in Gurgaon are reportedly involved. A similar scam was reported in Punjab, where some doctors were arrested, on the complaint of a Bihari migrant. Such offences have not only happened in Delhi, but replicated in many other States including Punjab, Karnataka, Kerala and in many other States. The Transplantation of Human Organs Act, 1994, is the existing law to "provide for the regulation of removal, storage and transplantation of human organs for therapeutic purposes and for the prevention of commercial dealing in human organs."

It makes the trade in kidneys illegal. It makes kidney-for-cash transactions a criminal offence, punishable with a term of imprisonment ranging from two to seven years and a Rs.10,000 to Rs. 20,000 fine. The Act defines persons who can donate kidneys as "near relatives", specifically spouses, mothers, fathers, sisters, and brothers. The Act also recognises the concept of brain-stem death. It also makes provisions for the development of a cadaver-based organ transplantation programme, so that the demands of gravely ill patients can be met. The aim of the Act, however, has been defeated by two built-in drawbacks. First, trade in kidneys, other human organs or any other violation of the Act is a non-cognisable offence. It means that neither the CBI, nor the police can start any investigation into such violations on its own. Under Section 22 of the Act, a court can take cognisance of offences, committed under the Act only on a complaint made by the Appropriate Authority or an officer authorised by it or by an individual who has given prior notice of not less than 60 days to the Appropriate Authority.

Despite this, large number of kidney transplants by unrelated persons have taken place. 19 suspected brokers and middle men were picked up from the premises of several prominent hospitals in Bangalore in 2002. Another grave flaw lies in Section 9(3), which permits unrelated donors, to give their organs for reasons of "affection and attachment towards the recipient or for any other special reasons". This means, that they can donate their kidneys to patients, provided they can convince the State Authorisation Committee, that they are 'donating' and not selling their organs. If the Committee is convinced, that money has not changed hands, it can allow the kidney donation. The willingness of the Committee to be convinced, that the unrelated live kidney donations, are being made on account of "affection and attachment" or for some other "special reasons" is a key factor working in favour of the kidney trade. Neither the improbability or doubtfulness of employees or unrelated dependants, donating kidneys, without money changing hands, nor highly questionable or unreliable factors such as recipients and donors, living away from each other, or any suspiciously doubtful connections, have stood in the way of the transplants. The Authorisation Committee interrogates the donor and recipient separately and asks them a standard set of questions about their relationship - how long they have known each other, a description of the area the other lives in, and so on. The donor must submit a ration card, a residence certificate from the police, an affidavit stating the donor's willingness to donate the kidney and basic hospital documents.

The Mandya District Police in Karnantaka found, that up to 80 per cent of the verification documents could be forged. In Mandya district alone, nine persons wear arrested for working as agents in the kidney transplant racket unearthed in January 2002. A member of The Karnataka Authorisation Committee says: "It is difficult to tell when a financial transaction takes place. Often the donor will say, that he has worked for the patient for many years that the patient has helped his family and that he is deeply attached to the patient."

An analysis of the reported cases highlights the following features of the commercial racket in kidneys. "Vested interests are promoting unrelated [live] transplants. Large sums of money are shared by doctors and hospitals that perform such transplants". According to a Doctor: A fourth of 274 cases of unrelated live donors, which went before the Authorisation Committee in Bangalore, were shown to be of dependant relationships, to the recipients or their families - as housemaids, watchmen, factory workers and so on. The kidney trade is exploitative of the poor and the needy. It is highlighted by the large number of cases where donors are shown, to be employees or unrelated dependants of the recipients.

Karnataka Authorisation Committee, a body set up under the Transplantation of Human Organs Act, 1994 gave clearance to 1,012 patients in Karnataka who, between January 1996 and March 2002, were officially cleared to receive kidneys from unrelated live 'donors'. The approval for all these donations was given, to ensure that no buying and selling of human organs takes place. Availability of the kidneys and hence kidney shortfall is the most acute of all organs. About one lakh people are being diagnosed with end stage kidney disease every year. Less than 10 per cent of them, can afford transplantation. Experts feel, that first relative donors are the first option, but in cases of a biological mismatch, the recipient may have to spend years, waiting for a donor. The solution lies in cadaver donations, like the eyes donation. "Live donation is great, if it is altruistic, but only cadaver donation can put an end to organ sale", says a Doctor heading transplant surgery. Globally, 90 per cent of all transplants done, are from brain-dead donors. The large-scale and flagrant violation of the law, is due to more demand and less supply. The Act, by allowing unrelated donors to 'donate' their kidneys after obtaining the sanction, provides legal cover to the buying and selling of kidneys. Unfortunately, in the kidney trade, the prevailing approach is that the poor can be bought by the rich.

What can be done to improve the situation is, hospitals doing transplants must (1) have an ethics committee, (2) maintain detailed clinical documents and indications for the transplant, (3) record the details of blood groups and cross-matching reports of all relatives of the patients, (4) ensure that all recipients of kidneys are residents of the same State, and known for at least three to five years, (5) notify the Appropriate Authority if a transplanted organ is rejected, or if a patient dies. So called emotional attachment and close association to the recipient, by the donor should also be verified by an appropriate authority. Such a trade is not possible unless there is a doctor-broker nexus, even assuming that some nephrologists and transplant surgeons, take a conscientious professional stand against the trade in kidneys. Lastly, it being a technical matter, it will be best, if the investigation into such offences is done by a specialist body, like the State or Central Medical Council, instead of the police, who have no expertise in the matter.

Bollywood has long been known to patronise musclemen for different reasons. One, they need black money, without which no film can be made and secondly the life span of a film actor or actress is limited and whatever he or she can earn in their hey days, is the only income for his or her life. When I raised this question with Mahesh Bhat, a prominent film maker in a TV programme, he gave me an impression, as if I was talking blasphemy or talking through my hat or should I say turban. He vehemently denied, that there were any black money dealings in film industry, though he did admit that extortions, black mailings or threats were possible.

The latest to allegedly join the bandwagon of using the gangsters is actress Shilpa Shetty's father Surinder, who has been trying to get an anticipatory bail, following an extortion case registered by the Surat police against him, on a complaint of Mr Prafulla Agarwal, the chairman of Praful Sarees. Agarwal had claimed that Shetty sent gangster Dinesh Shetty of the Mumbai-based Fazalur Rehman gang to extort money from him. Shilpa had done modelling for Praful Sarees. It is said that the company owed her nearly Rs. 25 lakhs for the advertisements. Agarwal had claimed that Shetty sent the gangster to force him to cough up the money. A case was registered at the Umra police station in Surat and Dinesh Shetty was arrested. Later on he has allegedly confessed he had been hired by Shilpa's father.

Shetty's counsel claimed Mr Agarwal was trying to implicate Shetty since he did not want to pay the money he owed to the actress. According to him, Agarwal had signed a one-year contract with Shilpa in 1998, who was a starlet at that time. However, the company continued to use Shilpa's image even after the contract had lapsed. It was claimed that Agarwal owed Shilpa close to Rs. 80 lakhs for continuing to air the advertisements, in the last four years. Shilpa on the contrary said, "The media is creating unnecessary hype on the issue. The information of my parents' involvement in the matter is completely wrong and is affecting my reputation. The issue should have been clarified first."

The fact remains that organised gangs, which is a parallel paying industry, has its own set of structure of strong and ruthless leadership, a kind of hierarchy and its own code of conduct for its members. The objective is either money; profit or to obtain political clout. The gangs back up their objectives with sharp-shooters, telecom experts, casino operators, computer wizards, corrupt policemen and politicians and anybody else, who can come handy to them.

Contrary to conventional belief, organised crime phenomenon, has existed in one form or the other in our country. The big landlords or moneyed people have always maintained their private armies or musclemen armed either with swords, lathis or illegal weapons. In Mumbai, Governor Aungier formed a militia of local Bhandari youths to deal with organised street-level gangs that robbed sailors in 1669. Thugee flourished in central India till the 19th century with armed gangs of thugs, masquerading as pilgrims or wayfarers, winning the confidence of unsuspecting travellers and then looting and murdering them. The British India government police officer, William Sleeman, through his campaign between 1831 and 1837, virtually crushed Thugee for ever.

Thanks to the introduction of prohibition after Independence. Bootlegging or illicit trade in liquor became a thriving and lucrative business. It led to the covetous attention of hitherto loosely organised street level gangs. Thus the seeds of organised criminal activity were sown in the commercial capital of India. The first of the recorded gangsters in Mumbai was Vardharaj Mudaliar, popularly known as Vardha Bhai. He ruled the roost for over a decade by organising bootlegging in a systematic manner; spreading an umbrella of protection to several lesser gangs dealing in illicit liquor. He soon diversified his illegal activities into gold smuggling, matkab gambling, extortion and supari killings. He had to flee Mumbai, under relentless police pressure. His near contemporaries were the gangs of Haji Mastan, Yusuf Patel and Karim Lala. Mastan and Patel made their millions in gold smuggling and Lala, a Pathan dealt in drugs. They were followed by Dawood Ibrahim and company. Only a bitter internecine gang warfare and the liquidating of all his rivals led to the emergence of Dawood.

The Mumbai underworld dons seem to have become role brand for other mafias in the country. Serial blasts in Mumbai in March '93, which left 257 dead, 713 maimed and property worth hundreds of crores damaged, forced the Nation to look at the menace and its use by Pakistan ISI seriously. It was for the first time that the country realised the immense potential of organised criminal groups to jeopardise its internal security.

The country's media shook up the Nation, by highlighting excerpts from film actor Sanjay Dutt's conversation on November 14, 2001 with an alleged gangster named Chhota Shakeel. These tapes were played by the prosecution before a special court, trying film financier Bharat Shah and three others in the underworld Bollywood nexus case. The tapes showed how Shakeel called shots from Pakistan and how certain film personalities were not only covering him but were also more than willing to oblige the gang lord.

At that time, the MCOCA (the Maharashtra Control of Organised Crime Act) Court had rightly advised the media to observe self-restraint, while reporting on the case, in view of the fact that for admissibility of tape-recording evidence, certain parameters like continuous recording and non-editing; with a view to giving a true picture, have to be observed. Those tapes, as well as the case involving the father of film actress Shilpa Shetty show, how the underworld continues to have a big influence on film industry and how it would not let go any chance of extracting or extorting as much as possible moolaha from the cash-rich personalities in the Bollywood. Reportedly, at least 60 extortion calls had been made to the people in Bollywood, by using the names of gangsters like Dawood or Chhota Shakeel or Chhota Rajan. The Shakeel-Dawood gang, Abu Salem gang and Chhota Rajan splinter groups are the ones, who reportedly intimidated the Bollywood. Among the people facing the threat are filmmaker Rajeev Rai, actor Aamir Khan, actress Manisha Koirala, Manmohan Shetty and Rakesh Roshan. However, nobody from film industry or even outside will come forth, to go public with their problems, because the affected parties felt that they had more faith in the words of gangsters than in the state protection. This menace will grow and not come down, with everybody concerned with solving his own problem and buying peace, by agreeing to be extorted. There is no Witness Protection Act in our country, where people deposing in sensitive cases, can be enabled to change their identities with the help of the State and settle far away from the place where they had deposed. The present legal system is too weak to deal with the gangsterism. The law needs to be changed, so that the onus that a person has no connection, with the gangsters or crimes like kidnapping for ransom or has used gangs should lie on the accused. Otherwise, what is happening at present is that, the victims and witnesses in most cases involving mafia dons, generally turn hostile at their first appearance in court. It would continue to happen as long as the present legal system continues. The ultimate decision in any case lies with the Judiciary. Any police officer deviating from the path of duty or getting mixed up with the criminals should be summarily dismissed. Last but not the least, the State should not become a party in encouraging dacoits and gangsters.

24
Irrational Investigations

Commissions and committees have urged the Government about the urgency to bring about reforms in the Police. Indictments after indictments have failed to move the Government to do something to set the Police House in order. Many a times there is a criticism of the police and its being used as a tool in the hands of the Government of the day. Police is a wing of the Government and no reform in this is possible, unless the Government changes the rules, laws or enactments. The fact remains that, no Government is willing to let go its control of the Police. But when it comes to criticism, it is the criticism of the Police and not of the Government. For reforms in the Police, the Central Government set up first Commission in 1977, followed by numerous committees, including Padmnabiaha Committee, Justice Malimath Committee and Reberio Committee. Each one of them made very sensible and positive recommendations to improve the Police and Policing. The bottom line, most of the recommendations was that, Police must be allowed to function as per the laws without interference. But beyond setting up Committees and Commissions and confining their recommendations to cupboards, things have remained where they were. Justice Malimath Committee had made 158 recommendations and none of them is unexceptionable. But one thing, which the Committee did not envisage is that in our country, reform is opposed, as it affects the vested interests. There is a lack of political will, irrespective of the party ruling the country or the State, to do anything, which will ruffle the feather and wake up the sleeping dogs. If the Government could consider and implement the following suggestion of the Malimath Committee, the matters would go a long way, in ameliorating the lot of the victims and benefit the country as a whole:

The Committee felt that "it is the duty of the Court, to search for truth, to assign a proactive role to the judges, to give directions to the investigating officers and prosecution agencies in the matter of investigation and leading evidence with the object of seeking the truth and focusing on justice to victims". It recommended the following changes in laws mentioned below amongst several other.

Section 54 of the Evidence Act be substituted by a provision on the following lines: "In criminal proceeding the fact that the accused has a bad character is relevant."

Explanation: A previous conviction is relevant as evidence of bad character. The victim shall have a right to prefer an appeal against any adverse order passed by the court acquitting the accused, convicting for a lesser offence, imposing inadequate sentence, or granting inadequate compensation. Such appeal shall lie to the court to which an appeal ordinarily lies against the order of conviction of such a court. Victim compensation is a State obligation in all serious crimes, whether the offender is apprehended or not, convicted or acquitted. This is to be provided in a separate legislation by Parliament. The draft bill on the subject submitted to Government in 1995 by the Indian Society of Victimology provide a tentative framework for consideration.

The Victim Compensation Law will provide for the creation of a Victim Compensation Fund to be administered possibility by the Legal Services Authority. The law should provide for the scale of compensation in different offences for the guidance of the Court. It may specify offences in which compensation may not be granted and conditions under which it may be awarded or withdrawn.

Most of the Laws, both substantive as well as procedural, were enacted more than 100 years back. Criminality has undergone a tremendous change qualitatively as well as quantitatively. Therefore, the apparatus designed for investigation has to be equipped with laws and procedures to make it functional in the present context.

About Godhra incident it is said that the police, were apparently under orders from Chief Minister Modi not to act swiftly; to allow the mobs 24 hours to carry out their violence. The weekly magazine *Frontline* reported that BJP Health Minister Ashok Bhatt sat in the police control room throughout the initial days of the violence. The federal government sent in the army, but only after a delay of one day as requested by Modi.

Even as the leaders of the mobs have gone unpunished, large numbers of Muslim youth were detained. Rather than arresting those responsible for the violence, police arrested the victims. All this had the complete support of the Gujarat state government with the complicity of the national government.

The role of police during Mumbai riots of 1992-93 came under severe criticism by various NGOs and above all, by Srikirshna Commission, which named 32 officers as guilty of anti-minority bias and also, Mr. Ribeiro, a former DG of Punjab Police, told a newspaper: "Apart from the usual complaints of inaction, people said that police were recording absolutely incorrect FIRs. I met a respectable Hindu gentleman who said that the police did not take down the names of the rioters he had seen and wrote that it was a group of unidentified people. If people who have seen their mothers and sisters raped and burnt before their eyes have no hope of getting justice, they will all turn into terrorists". And then, Ribeiro asks, "Why are we talking about ISI and Pakistan, when we are doing their job for them by creating terrorists". Even in Gujrat, many officers handled the situation quite professionally but they were, unfortunately, not given free hand by the political bosses. Such officers were instantly transferred and these transfers were either described as 'routine' or 'promotions'. It was more a culpability of political bosses than lack of professionalism among these officers.

In a landmark judgement on police reforms in the country, the Supreme court has directed the States to constitute a Security Commission to ensure that the Government of the day does not exert unwarranted influence or pressure on its police. Its functions would also include giving directions for the performance of preventive tasks and service oriented functions of the police, evaluation of performance of the State police and preparing a report for the legislature. This body shall be headed by the Chief Minister or Home Minister as chairman, with DGP as its ex-officio Secretary.

The Supreme Court has observed: "The DGP shall be selected by the State Government from amongst the three seniormost officers of the department, who have been empanelled for promotion to that rank by the Union Public Service Commission on the basis of their of experience. Once a DGP is selected, he should have a minimum tenure of at least two years, irrespective of his date of superannuation."

The court has also directed a fixed tenure of two years for IGPs, superintendents of police and even the station house officer, unless "cogent reasons" warranted their removal midway. It has also directed the setting up of several institutions, which include National Security Commission for the selection of Chief of Central police organisations, CBI, ITBP and CISF, with the chiefs having a minimum tenure of two years each.

The reforms in the police system have been overdue for over 100 years. The British, who had created the Indian police and the existing Police Act in 1861, set up a commission in 1902-03. After examining the performance of the police, the commission observed: "There can be no doubt that the police force throughout the country is in a most unsatisfactory condition, that abuses are common everywhere, that this involves great injury to the people and discredit to the Government and that radical reforms are urgently necessary."

The British did not have the police reform as priority, as they were in India only to rule. Thirty years after Independence, the Government set up a police commission under Dharam Vira, which observed: "Functioning under the constraints and handicaps of an outmoded system, the police performance has undoubtedly fallen short of public expectation. The present culture of the police system appears a continuation of what obtained under the Bitish regime when the police functioned ruthlessly as an agent for sustaining the Government in power. In public estimates, the police appears an agency, more to implement and enforce the objectives of the Government in power, as distinct from enforcing laws as such as an independent and impartial agency, The dividing line between the objectives of the Government in power as such on one side, and the interests and expectations of the ruling political party on the other side, gets blurred in actual practice and the image of the police as an impartial law enforcement agency, suffers in consequence."

A number of committees and subcommittees were set up to examine the reports of the Police Commission and almost all of them unanimously recommended that reforms were essential. Prof Bailey said: "In India today, a dual system of criminal justice has grown up – the one of the law and the other of politics. With respect at least to the police, decisions made by police officials about the application of law are frequently subject to partisan review or direction by the elected representatives. The autonomy of police officials in specific and routine application of law has been curtailed. This is not only true of the law and order situation. People accused of crime have got into the habit of appealing to political figures for remission from the law. Police officials have grown accustomed to calculating the likely political effect of any enforcement action they contemplate."

It is a fact that the police are being used by the political masters, irrespective of the parties in power, for their gains and ends. Transfers have become an industry. In Uttar Pradesh, for example, Mayawati set a record in 1997 by transferring over 1,400 civil and police officers in six months of her rule. Kalyan Singh had transferred 521 officials in 1991-92 and the SP-BSP Government headed by Mulayam Singh transferred 814 official in 1993-95.

An Administrative Reforms Committee appointed by the Government of Rajasthan, under the chairmanship of late Harish Chandra Mathur, had observed: "In the matters of transfer and posting of Government employees, there has been considerable undue interference by senior authorities in the powers of the subordinate authorities in this respect. The interference of this nature is one of the major causes of indiscipline and frustration and demoralisation."

In his first letter to the Chief Ministers in July 2004, Prime Minister Manmohan Singh said" "Maintenance of law and order is critical in providing an atmosphere, conducive to economic development and social harmony". Frequent transfers of public servants have a debilitating impact not only on their performance and morale, but also on the whole process of governance. Development administration also depends on the regularity of tenure. "Therefore, I urge you to ensure stability of tenure to officials in key positions in order to ensure effective administration and proper delivery of public services", he wrote.

Unfortunately, politicians of the day were loath to shed control of the police. As police reforms were not a vote-netting problem, nobody was interested in improving it. As swallow does not make a summer, so one Prime Minister, however honest and sincere, cannot transform the police governance. He, along with the people of India, should be thankful to the Supreme Court for doing something that nobody has been willing to do in the 59 years of Independence.

It is, however, not enough to insulate the police from political pressures. It is equally important to make its functioning transparent and accountable, which is necessary for good governance and sustainable development. In their absence, corruption and mismanagement is bound to rule the roost.

Since a few top officers were politicised in Gujrat they did not handle the situation professionally. Those who did, got transferred most arbitrarily. A highly respected retired police officer and former member of the National Police Commission recently wrote: "Senior officers pay visits to Police Stations and reserve lines which are too brief and they make no effort to find out grievances or examine defaulters. "How can discipline be maintained when nobody can be punished for his defaults?"

It is a fact that appreciation of situations, cases, events and persons differ from time to time. A former Union Petroleum Minister had been found guilty of "causing loss to the people and therefor he was asked to pay Rs. 50 Lakhs to the Government Exchequer for illegal, arbitrary and oppressive allotment of 15 petrol pumps from his discretionary quota". Later a Bench of three judges of Supreme Court held: "We are of the view that no case was made out against the petitioner...The earlier directions violate Article 21 (Right to life and Liberty) of the petitioner". (The earlier directions included the fining of Rs.50lakhs and ordering a CBI Inquiry against the then Petroleum Minister). It is worthwhile to quote Mr. Willoughby, a member of the Governor's Council and Madras Committee of 1806, set up by the orders of the Court of Directors of East India company: "The root of the whole evil is and was the useless expenditure on legislation neither homogenous to the Character of the People, nor suited to the conditions in the country, code of law, the delights of the thieves, rogues and Vakeels, a stumbling block and offence to all and grievance hindrance to the Administration of Justice...The people may have some confidence in our Honesty and wish to do justice. Look through the country and see who thrive and make fortunes. But a greater evil is that, the code is, Court of Sadder Ada lat and their incessant fault finding with the Magistrates and reversal of decisions for defects of form...And so it will be most of the time, as long as the Bombay Judge tries pursuant robber, and lets him off because his mother's name is said to be Ranjee, instead of Linjee; it may be very good law, but it is very bad Justice.... Penal laws loosely enforced are lotteries in which the offenders speculate and it is remarkable, how accurately they calculate their chances of prosecution and escape". Lieutenant Governor Grant of Punjab recorded during the British rule: "Dacoity is bad enough, but the subsequent. police inquiry is much worse. But after allowing for both these causes, no one conversant with the people, can have failed to remark how much of their strong unwillingness to prosecute is owing to the deep sense, which pervades the public mind of the utter uncertainty of the proceedings of our courts and the exceeding chances of escape which our system allows to criminals. Often I have heard natives express... Their inability to understand the principles on which the Courts are constituted, or so conducted as to make it appear... as if the object were rather to favour the acquittal than to ensure the ccnviction and punishment of offenders; and so often I have been assured by them that their anxious desire to avoid appearing as prosecutors arose, in a great measure, from their belief that prosecution was likely to end in acquittal, even as they imagined, in the teeth of the evidence, while acquittal of a revengeful and unscrupulous ruffian was known by experience, to have repeatedly ended in the most unhappy consequences to his ill advised and imprudent prosecutor.... No doubt, the badness of the police and inefficiency of the tribunals, act and react on each other and both are concerned in bringing about the deplorable existing consequences. But until the tribunals are reformed, I can see no use in reforming the police, and I think, it will be money thrown away to attempt the latter, unless we are determined vigorously to insist on the former."

It looks that the Authors of the above observations might as well be commenting on the existing system in our country. Despite the protests of the eminent Britishers during the British rule, the position did not change or was changed. It was for the simple reason that it was not in their scheme of things to provide an ideal administration. Their objective was to maintain their rule. The reforms in the criminal administration system was not a priority with them? The only and one priority for them was to exploit India and its resources for the mother country. However, they were very clear in their perception of what could be done and what people should expect. Mr. Elliot, a Commissioner of Northern Circars observed: "It must be surely unnecessary for us to dwell on the improbability that a native will obtain redress from a Tehsildar as Magistrate, for an injury inflicted possibly under his orders.... Or, in the discharge of a duty which.... relieves it of the odium or culpability, the collection of the Government revenues. It is a point. It is, in point of fact, to hand over the spoiled to the spoiler and ask the party most deeply interested in hushing the matter up, to display the impartiality of the Judge."

The British have left, but the legacy left behind by them continues to thrive. Delhi High Court has censured the police, justifiably for harassment and inconvenience caused to the general public due to the erratic VIP movements. The Court observed that: "What is the problem, if the Prime Minister travels like a common man. If there is a security threat to VIP, then take them by helicopters. But don't disturb the common citizen. ...Every Tom. Dick and Harry, is given VIP security these days. Every second car has a red bulb on it. Even an SDM is moving with a siren and red bulb on his car. Just because he is a bureaucrat, does not qualify him for such facilities. No VIP is allowed to flout traffic rules". Unfortunately, though such events get noticed in the National capital and taken note of, the position in the rest of the country continues to be same. The effective, and good governance in the country has been on holiday. Sycophancy and self-interests, instead of solid hard work, has become the ruling deity.

25
Hollow Human Rights

The subject of police arouses a lot of interest for an average Indian. In the perception of an average citizen, the police are neither successful in their assigned job, nor are they helpful, to a law abiding citizen. People also feel that as constituted at present, the Police are not even capable of maintaining law and order at the time of serious communal trouble and other partisan clashes.

In Ahmedabad a young girl from Bombay was killed during an 'encounter', along with some alleged LeT terrorists in the second week of June, 2004. Questions have been raised whether the 'so called encounter', was a fake killing. However, nobody tried to answer the question, as to what she, (an unmarried young woman, still studying) was doing in Ahmedabad with three other men. It is also claimed, that this entire show of fake encounter, was stage managed by Gujarat Police, to garner sympathy for Gujarat Chief Minister, who was to be the target of the killed terrorists. It has also been alleged that human rights of the killed have been grossly violated and the National Human Rights Commission has also issued a notice to Gujarat Government about this incident. A former Chief Justice of India, who has also been the Chairman of the Human Rights Commission, had castigated the government of India for state-aided terrorism: by saying that terrorism could not be combated by state sponsored terrorism as it would prove counter-productive. When Cornwallis came to India in 1786 he found, "abundant evidence of frauds, peculation, corruption, murders, dacoities and other serious crimes were daily committed with impunity and there was a general feeling that life and property were not adequately protected."

The Police is only a part of the criminal justice system in the country. Its job ends, with taking the suspect/accused before the court of the law. It is for the Courts to judge the guilt and award punishment. The gathering of evidence, depends only on the co-operation and assistance of the witnesses. In 1830, then Governor of Bombay, Sir John Malcom observed: "The task of seizing the most notorious criminal is easy, as compared to that of proving their guilt, according to the principles and the forms of our courts of justice. There is seldom that full evidence they require, and the consequence is the annual discharge of well known plunderers, to recommence their career of guilt and to take ample vengeance, on those whom they suspect of having aided in their apprehension. If our laws are not modified to meet this evil, it can alone be mitigated by the change in the executive branch of the police, in those provinces that are inhabited or subject of the in-roads of predatory tribes". Admitting the lapses in the Police, the 2nd Police Commission of 1902-3 also observed..... Neither do the Commission forget that much may be said in excuse for the misconduct of the Police, in the generally indifferent attitude of the people, in respect of crime, in the encouragement of corruption, by the readiness with which the people offer illegal gratifications and in the low pay and poor prospects of the Police Service. But honourable exceptions and mitigating circumstances cannot efface the general impression created by the evidence recorded. There can be no doubt that the Police Force throughout the country, is in a most unsatisfactory condition, that abuses are common everywhere, that this involves great injury to the people and discredit to the Government and that radical reforms are urgently necessary. These efforts will cost much,... but they must be effected". The 3rd Police Commission of 1977-81 set up under the Chairmanship of late former Governor Dharamvira observed: "The basic and fundamental problem regarding the Police today is how to make them function, as an efficient and impartial law enforcement agency fully motivated and guided by the objectives of service of the Public at large, upholding the constitutional rights and liberty of the people. What the Police Commission said in 1903 appears more or less equally applicable, to the conditions obtaining today". When another Police Commission Report was presented to the President, he remarked: If this report is implemented, even I cannot order the transfer of a Sub Inspector."

Incidentally, the same laws are operational even now when these observations were made in the past. Police job, partially due to society's hostile attitude towards police, makes the matters worse. Justice A. N. Mulla of the Allahabad High Court (in the 1960s) observed about police: "There is not a single lawless group in the whole of the country, whose record of crime comes anywhere near the record of that organised unit which is known as the Indian Police". Indeed, even killing of a policeman, does not produce any sense of shock and outrage in the public. The number of police fatalities has increased sharply due to eruption of terrorist activities in the country.

In all, 626 police personnel were killed on duty in 1996, 597 in 1997, and 638 in 1998. Of the 638 policemen killed on duty in 1998, 53 were gazetted officers. 517 where lower subordinate. In the year, 2001-2002 upto 21st October, 963 police men have laid down their lives in the call of duty. Police Accountability is one factor, which the Government of the day has not been able to enforce or is unwilling to enforce. The National Police Commission headed by late Dharamvira (1977-81) said: "We wish to emphasise that it is ultimately the people whose agents the police functionaries are and to whom they are ultimately accountable... We, however, find that the process of police accountability to the people has suffered considerable distortion in the recent past". The distortion goes on, with the help of electing representatives, some of whom themselves have criminal records. It is not unoften alleged, that the police, which is a wing of the Government and not independent like Judiciary or Election Commission, is used against political rivals. The distortions need to be ended.

Manipur, a land of exotic natural beauty with salubrious climate, continues to be plagued by internal conflicts and political uncertainty, which itself aids insurgency. Political instability, engineered by power hungry politicians anywhere, would incapacitate any Government. It has done so in Manipur. When Chief Minister Radhabinod Koijam of the Samata Party (SP) was sworn as Chief Minister in February, 2003, his government was supported by 58 of the total 59 legislators. There was only one MLA in the Opposition Congress. The horse trading left no administration or governance worth any name in Manipur. When such is the political scenario, then, whoever has the gun wields the power.

Manipur was under Armed Forces (Assam and Manipur special Powers Act, 1958). Under the Act, an entire state or parts of it or a union territory can be declared disturbed by the Governor of the state, the administrator of the UT or the Centre. The Act empowers a soldier, "if he is of (the) opinion that it is necessary to do so, for maintenance of public order to fire upon or otherwise use force, even to the causing of death, against any person who is acting in contravention of any law or order, for the time being in the disturbed area prohibiting the assembly of five or more persons... to arrest without warrant, any person who has committed a cognizable offence or against whom a reasonable suspicion exists, that he has committed or is about to commit..." Section 6 of the Act says "no prosecution, suit or other legal proceeding shall be instituted, except with the previous sanction of the Central government, against any person, in respect of anything done, or purported to be done, in exercise of powers conferred by this Act". The Act has been described by human rights activists, as draconian. Its Constitutionality was challenged in the Supreme Court, which upheld its validity in 1996. It also ruled that the declaration of an area as disturbed has to be for a limited duration and there should be periodic review of the declaration before expiry of six months.

The President of India, on 23rd of September, 2004, promulgated an ordinance scrapping POTA. The new law called The Unlawful Activities (Prevention) Amendment Act, 2004 defines terrorism exactly as in POTA. It has dropped Section 4, under which, independent MLA from UP, Raja Bhaiyya is charged. Now under the amended law, carrying of unauthorised arms in a notified area and possession of bombs, RDX, dynamite, biological and chemical weapons is not a terrorist act. The ordinance also has done away with POTA special courts, apart from doing away with the provision where an accused could not apply for bail for one year. Bail provisions as laid done in Criminal Procedure Code, will apply to those charged under the amended law. The POTA (Repeal) Ordinance, on the other hand, has also provided for setting up of one or more review committees to review all existing cases, whether at the investigation or trial stage, within one year.

The amendments to the Unlawful Activities (Prevention) Act also discards the POTA provision making a confession before a police officer admissible in court and shifts the onus of proof on the prosecution, besides providing for forfeiture of proceeds of terrorism. However, it allows any investigating officer (POTA only allowed officers not below the rank of SP) to make an order, with prior written approval of the DGP of the state concerned, seizing or attaching a property representing proceeds of terrorism. The Act allows evidence collected through interception of wire, electronic or oral communication as admissible evidence against the accused in the court during trial of a case. However, the POTA safeguards providing of one year punishment/fine to a police officer who intentionally intercepts communication or gets any person to do it have been deleted. There is a POTA like provision on checking funding of organisation . Similarly, banned-by-POTA terrorist originations remain banned under the amendment ordinance. There are no special Courts to try terror suspects.

There is no doubt that use of POTA against MDMK leader Vaiko might have been a big factor behind its repeal but the Unlawful Activities (Prevention) Amendment Act very much retains Section 21 of the scrapped anti-terror law, under which he was charged, with a rider that the offence should have been committed "with intention to further activity of a terrorist organisation."

The Unlawful Activities (Prevention) Amendment Act 2004 also retains the punishment for such an offence, imprisonment for a term not exceeding 10 years or fine or both.

However, BJP the main opposition party, feels that the newly promulgated Unlawful Activities (Prevention) Amendment Act to replace POTA, not only shows the government's political motives but also its "naive" approach towards terrorism. It says that "It is naive of the government to believe, that the Fidayeen will honour bail and judiciary". Under the new law, the bail provisions against terrorists would be much less stringent as against cases of other crimes like smuggling, black-marketing and narcotics. The normal rule that bail is the rule and jail is an exception, will also apply against the terrorists.

The Ordinance replacing anti-terrorist POTA has inserted a clause whereby organisations like Bajrang Dal and VHP, could be banned under provisions of the Unlawful Activities (Prevention) Amendment Act. The ultra Leftist extremist groups like Peoples' War or even to an extent, the outfit like SIMI, which was banned under POTA can no longer be declared unlawful under the new law.

The Human Rights violations take place all the time, in all the societies. The only thing common in such incidents is that where such violations take place, there is a common refrain in condemning them and called them "abhorrent". The very concept of State is based on power. If you take away the foundation of power, there is no doubt that there would be total chaos and lawless. It is for this reason, that State takes upon itself the onus of executing criminals by following the due process of law. A Young American soldier named Joseph M. Darby, blew the whistle alarm on abuse of Iraqi detainees at Abu Ghraib prison in Baghdad. According to a report , Darby, a reservist in the 372nd Military Police Company, placed an anonymous note under the door of a superior. In the note, he described incidents of sexual and physical abuse of Iraqi detainees by some unit members, documented by explicit photographs, The photographs have shocked the world. He later came forward with a sworn statement. The U.S. army has admitted there was evidence of widespread abuse of prisoners in military-run jails in Iraq and Afghanistan. A leading Democratic Senator has also called for a review of interrogation techniques at Guantanamo Bay. The Senator also demanded an investigation into the role of private contractors, the CACI International and the Titan Corporation) in questioning prisoners in U.S. military jails, after it emerged that hired interrogators from companies were involved in the physical and sexual abuse of Iraqi inmates at the Abu Ghraib jail, west of Baghdad. There have also been reports of abuses in military jails in Afghanistan, such as at the Bagram air base. In December 2002, two Afghan men died in U.S. custody at Bagram. Expressing deepest apology, the US Defence Secretary Donald Rumsfeld state that: "They are human beings, they are in US custody and the United States has an obligation to treat them right. It is this obligation to evaluate what happened and to make sure that those who did wrong are brought to justices, to make the changes needed and to see that this does not happen again". He had testified before the Senate armed Services Committee. British Prime Minister Tony Blair, issued a qualified apology to Iraqi prisoners who may have been mistreated by British forces, declaring that such actions - if true - were "absolutely and totally unacceptable. He expressed his regret at claims that soldiers beat and humiliate prisoners in Iraq, in breach of the Geneva Convention. Those who are responsible for this - if they behaved in this appalling way - they will be punished according to the Army discipline and rules". The US President said the abuse and sexual humiliation of prisoners in Iraq's notorious Abu Ghraib prison "was the wrongdoing of a few". Still believing to be the World's solitary conscience keeper and policeman, he added: "We have no intention of leaving the nation at the mercy of thugs and murderers. We're determined to help build a free and stable Iraq, a nation at peace with its neighbours and with the world". However, people in the field have a different story to tell. The US Brig. General Janis Karpinski, who was incharge of Abu Ghraib prison said that she was being made a scapegoat for the abuse of the detainees. She said that: "the current head, who now oversees prisons believed that prisoners are like dogs and if you allow them to believe at any point that they are more than a dog, then you have lost control on them."

Sadly in all use of force, the abuses of human rights, tortures, atrocities and violations of civilised behaviour do take place. In such situations, the victor or more powerful side cares a fig for the International Law or Geneva Conventions or basic democratic protection guaranteed in all democracies. When abuses occur in one area, they would quickly spread to other areas, if not checked in time and promptly. The difficulties faced by the forces and the daily attack on them, by the forces hostile to them and frailty and fallibility of the human nature to be vengeful are given as justifications for aberrant behaviour. It is also claimed that any organisation will have some rotten apples, who can bring a bad name to the entire whole.

The world has given itself, UN Charter—Declaration of Human Rights—Geneva Conventions—Rights of the Minorities. They are no doubt great documents, which provide guideline to what kind behaviour both humans and Nations should adopt. They were born out of the miseries of the past and showed a commitment to a newer and nobler ideals. Unfortunately, they are only guide lines and are more often broken in the perceived National or Sectional interests. There is no legally enforceable system of enforcement of International Laws and Good Governance.

However regrettable it may be, the torture is universally practised in the "interest of so called National Interests". In some countries, as in Israel till 1987, it officially existed though the Israeli interrogators denied it. In 1987 it came to light that torture was being used in Israel. Israel set up a commission of inquiry. This commission was convinced by the argument of the general security service that they needed physical pressure in order to get information out of detainees and so it recommended that interrogators should be allowed to use what they called a moderate measure of physical or psychological pressure. What this means is that from 1987, Israel is the only country in the world in which torture - or treatment amounting often to torture - is effectively legalised. But the methods permitted by Israel's legislation came in for international criticism. These methods, included prolonged sleep deprivation; putting hoods over prisoner's heads making them squat for long periods; keeping them for long periods in a painful condition and violent shaking. The objective of torture is to secure a confession. There are many countries in the worldwhere law and practice are not consonant on this issue. One of the most popular methods is called elephant torture. A gas mask is placed on the suspect's head and a police officer controls the flow of oxygen into the mask until the suspect loses consciousness or starts suffocating. A number of victims have lost their lives as a result of such suffocations in police custody. In 1999, Israel's Supreme Court overturned a 1987 Israeli report that gave the "Shin Bet" permission to use "moderate physical pressure" and banned the country's secret police from continuing to torture detainees suspected of plotting terrorist acts. Says the report: "The Court declares the Shin Bet [security service] does not have the authority to shake a person, to force him into a [contorted] position or to kneel in a frog-like position or deprive him of sleep.... Justice Matza said he and his fellow Judges had concluded, there was no legal basis for such practices, in response to a petition from human rights organizations". American constitution is one of the finest in the world, which declares that it is a self evident truth, that all men are created equals. Still its citizens in uniform have been found guilty of most flagrant violations of Human Rights. The silver lining in the whole episode is that it is the American soldier, who exposed the misdoings and the world media gave it sufficient coverage leading to the apology of the administration. It is wrong to say that the battle for Human Rights is over, over one exposure. There are many undisclosed violations going on, in obscurantist and fundamentalist societies. The world only wrings its hands on exposure after exposure. Still it is worth it to fight the battle for enabling man to live with dignity and honour.

The United Nation's General Assembly, in the Palis de Chaillot in Paris, adopted the Universal Declaration of Human Rights On December tenth 1948. The declaration has thirty articles which deal with a series of basic human rights and duties. It follows the principle that " the declaration is a common standard of achievement for all peoples and nations, to the end that every individual and every organ of society, keeping this declaration constantly in mind, shall strive by teaching and education to promote respect for these rights and freedoms and by progressive measures, national and international, to secure their universal and effective recognition and observance, both among the people of member states themselves and among the people of territories under their jurisdiction". However this is not always the reality of truth, as the violation of the human rights are all too often practiced, today as much as 56 years ago. War crimes in the former Yugoslavia, terrorist acts in the Gaza strip, political prisoners in China, the disappearances in Chile and Argentina, female genital mutilation in orthodox Muslim communities and American violations of the basic rights of Iraqi prisoners, are all too common. However the document conveys a noble message for the universe and for the entire humanity.

We need to ask whether there can there be a universal norm of human rights, when different societies and regimes are at different wave lengths? The United Nations Organization established in 1945, had a foundation and "faith in fundamental human rights". It is committed to promoting "universal respect for and observance of human rights and fundamental freedoms for all without distinction as to race, sex, language or religion". It has urged the member States "to take joint and separate action in co-operation with the Organization" for the achievement of that commitment. The United Nations in its human rights agenda concentrated on norm creation. The Universal Declaration of Human Rights (1948) is a kind of a Rule Book to the concepts of human rights and fundamental freedoms. Universal support for the agreement of faith in human rights, led to the declaration and "the idea of human rights is accepted in principle by all governments regardless of other ideology, regardless of political, economic, or social condition". President of the United States, Bill Clinton's visit to China renewed the worldwide debate on Human Rights, which forced Red China to review its stand and practice of human rights.

Trafficking in people has flourished as can be seen in the people migrating abroad in search of greener tragedy. In a horrible tragedy, in 1996 more than 250 youth from Punjab were transhipped in containers and a large number were suffocated to death. Only a few remained alive to come back and tell their tragic story in 1997/1998. The number of migrant workers and trafficking victims has grown with international commerce. There are a number of agencies doing manpower export as the recent exposure (April / May, 2004) of the illegal deployment of Indian workers to Iraq, via Middle East has shown. Some of them treated worse than slaves. The abuses against such victims remain largely ignored. Within the workplace, for example, factory workers often face poor wages, abysmal working conditions, sexual abuse, no social safety net, and no legal protection. According to a Press report, film actress Aishwariya Rai was paid over Rs. 2.50 crore to settle a deal of sexual harassment. Infoys paid several million dollars to settle a case of sexual harassment on behalf of its country Head in USA, who had left the job.

For war-torn nations, their survival is of utmost importance. India has been facing a unique problem in reconciling human rights and blatant terrorism. It has faced thirteen hijacking of its aircraft. The last one was on 25 December, 1999 of the flight of Indian Airlines, from Kathmandu to Delhi. The Kashmiri terrorists, aided by Pakistan succeeded in getting three of their colleagues, whom the then External Affairs Minister personally escorted to Kabul.

Self-appointed human rights activists have no thought or worry about the ruthless terrorists killing of girls for not wearing burqa, for going to beauty parlours, wearing dress of their choice or over children, being beheaded. Human Rights should be for the humans and not for demons, irrespective of their colour, creed or religion. It cannot and should not be only a one sided approach. Margret Thatcher, Former Prime Minister of United Kingdom had said that publicity is the oxygen of terrorism. It is best to deny it to them. Then only we can have a world, which is safe and where human rights can flourish.

A Central Reserve Police Constable recruited in 2003 and posted in Jammu and Kashmir, on his first posting, was absent from the roll call in November, 2004. Absence from duty, is a serious lapse in Armed Forces. Absence can mean anything, right from plain negligence to running away or mixing with criminal elements or escaping after committing a crime. Being a new entrant, he was reprimanded and given three days of fatigue duty, a kind of light punishment. On 28th November, 2004, he fired indiscriminately in the CRP campus, killing a company commander, a sub-inspector, a head constable and four constables, before he was shot dead. Misconduct and even killing of policemen by policeman and of the public men, is not uncommon. In the last two years, even an army Major and a Colonel, have been shot dead by the soldiers working under them. In October, 2004 a policeman was arrested for shooting dead, a truck driver, over the latter's refusal to bribe him. Public are entitled to know, as to why such aberrations take place in members of uniformed and disciplined services, and why some people, who should be a model of discipline, exhibit behaviour and conduct unworthy of the positions they hold. People also wonder, as to what has happened to our defenders in uniform, who instead of killing the enemies of the country are taking pot shots at each other.

I had some first hand experience during the hey days of insurgency, heading the Central Reserve Police Force in Punjab and Jammu Kashmir in 1988. Security forces fight an invisible enemy, who can emerge, from any where and at a place of his own choice. Unlike the terrorists, who can kill mercilessly, without any compunction, members of the security forces are required, to retaliate only when attacked. There is no compulsion of any law or requirement to ensure, on the part of the terrorists, that no innocents are killed. Terrorists' writ runs more effectively than that of the Government in some areas. Local people, with a view to purchase their safety, maintain strict neutrality. They rarely take stand against the terrorist. Most people are like sheep. They wait to see, which side is the drove going and then go with the drove. The result is security forces are exposed to indifference from the people, whom they are ostensibly and in reality, protecting from Improvised Explosive Devices, bombing, shooting and firing from the invisible enemy. The result of this scenario, which has so much changed that, being an Inspector General of Police of one of the largest para military forces, was not sure to return alive, patrolling and encouraging people working under my command. I was lucky to survive a bomb attack. This is not only my own feeling, but that of each one member of the force, deployed in terrorist affected areas.

Most lower level employees of security forces have no option, except to live in extremely substandard and stressful conditions. It is for this reason that, quite often, schools, rest houses or even hotels are used to accommodate security forces, much to the chagrin of the local people. In some insurgency prone areas, even green vegetables, TV or Radio are a luxury. When I was IGP CRPF one Union Minister who was asked to look after Kashmir, asked me before coming to Kashmir, as to what he should bring with him. I told him that a plane load of fresh green vegetables would be the best present to the men. He just laughed but did bring a few baskets of vegetables for the officers mess.

It can happen only in India, when the Prime Minister of India, visits J&K and announces a package of Rs. 24000 crore in November, 2004. His polite invitation, to talk to any secessionist leader, is turned down. The same terrorists leaders, come to Delhi within weeks of the Prime Minister of India's visit and wait for hours to meet even the second Secretary of Pakistan High Commission, and later on the Prime Minister of Pakistan in November- December, 2004.

26
Women's Woes

In our country, there is a general belief, bordering on the ridicule that reservations is, the panacea not only for poverty removal, but also for social uplifing. The present position is that initial reservation for Scheduled Castes and Scheduled Tribes, which was to last only for a few decades, has not only been put on permanent footing, but reservation for other categories has been included, taking the total reservation percentage to 50%. Left to themselves and to pander to the need for catching votes or sustaining vote banks, the political parties, would have gone to the outrageous extent of dividing the entire society on reservation basis.

One thing is very clear, that reservations has nothing to do with anything, except to create an illusion, in the section for which jobs are reserved, that a particular party espousing their cause is their true Messiah. No politician in the current dispensation, has guts to call a spade a spade.

The politicians of all hues feel, that, it is better to keep carrot dangling in front of the likely beneficiaries. There is no doubt that women for historical reason or for being so called weaker sex and otherwise have not gone ahead in many fields. The existing legal remedies have failed to protect women from India's most common crimes -dowry, bigamy, kidnapping, desertion, rape, refusal to shelter and denial of nourishment. It is not because of lack of reservation. Reservations or no reservations, these assigned by nature and society apportioned roles are not going to change easily, either in India or abroad. India, however, has made tremendous strides, in ameliorating the condition of women. Earlier, a woman joining the Indian Foreign Service could be asked to resign. The doors of Defence Services, Police and Para Military Forces were shut against them. But with more and more women, opting for these services, some women are there now on the basis of their own merit. Still, their presence in these service, where entry is by open competition, is slightly more than marginal. Even in service in the Private Sector and Government Sector, their total number is just less than 5 percent. It is worth noting that women belonging to reservation category of 50 percent, if competent and qualified, could corner all the 50 percent jobs, with an equal freedom to corner the rest of 50 percent on merits.

Reservation divides and does not unite the society. There has been a rising demand that women should have 33% elected seats reserved for them in the State Legislatures and the National Parliament. It could not be done due to no consensus of political or regional parties.

It is worthwhile to add, that Switzerland gave women the right to vote only in 1971. In the US, only 73 out of 535 - or 13.6 per cent - seats in the Senate and House of Representatives together are currently held by women.

Some women have done extremely well not on the basis of the reservation, but on their own merits. They were aided by the circumstance and a situation where women attained ultimate political office but in succession to a heroic male relative, usually martyred. Mr. S.W.R.D. Bandaranaike was assassinated in 1959 and his widow, Mrs. Bandaranaike, was swept into ultimate political prominence. Her daughter, Ms. Chandrika Kumaratunga become the President of the Sri Lanka. Jawaharlal Nehru died in 1964 and in 1966 Indira Gandhi, his daughter became prime minister of India. Zulfikar Ali Bhutto was executed in Pakistan in 1979 and eventually Benazir Bhutto became prime minister for the first time in 1988. She has continued to be in and out of power and is now in exile in UK.

In Bangladesh Sheikh, Mujibur Rahman of the nascent nation was assassinated long with his wife and five of his children in August 1975. Eventually one of his surviving daughters became leader of the Awami League and finally the Prime Minister in 1997. Again in Bangladesh, President Ziaur Rahman was assassinated in May 1981. Ten years later her widow was sworn as prime minister. Bangladesh is the first country to have had two women prime ministers in succession, belonging to opposing parties.

The Cooperative Republic of S Guyana is African member of the Commonwealth. Cheddi B. Jagan was sworn in on October 30, 1992, in succession to Hugh Desmond Hoyte. Cheddi Jagan died in March 1997. In December 1997, his widow Janet Jagan was elected president - amidst charges that since she was foreign-born, she was not qualified to be Head of State in Guyana. (Mrs. Jagan was born as a white American in Chicago). The one remarkable female leader who was in no sense a successor to a heroic male relative was, Britain's

Margaret Thatcher, who became Prime Minister in May 1979 and continued her top leadership for eleven years. Another female leader, Dame Mary Eugenia Charles of Dominica in the West Indies, was Prime Minister from July 1980 until 1994. Canada also had its share of a woman as a Prime Minister when Brian Mulroney resigned in favour of Kim Campbell in 1993. It was not an appropriate time to have the first woman Prime Minister ever in that country. In the election, her Party (the Progressive Conservative Party) suffered the worst defeat to any ruling party. Its seats in Canadian history shrank from 153 to 2 members in the House of Commons. She was Prime Minister for a mere 134 days. She resigned as party leader on December 13, 1993. No developed country talks of reservations, as they know that even nonreservation can take the deserving to the pinnacle.

According to a political thinker "Nothing can stop an idea, whose time has come". It is not the opportune time to have reservation in Legislatures for the women in India. Let us continue to experiment with reserving seats for women at the grass root levels, like in the Panchayats and Municipalities for the next ten to twenty years. If the experiment proves successful after two decades, it could be extended to National and State Legislatures, but by building up a consensus.

A former President of India during his address to the Nation, said as under on the position of women:

"one of the clearest indicators of the development of a society is the position and status women enjoy in that society. Even though women's rights are recognised as human rights and they are considered as best of human resources and central actors for development, their standing in our society is deplorable. While women's movement is gaining momentum and gathering pace, and reaching one milestone after another, the ill treatment and atrocities on women are recurring in regular and brutal manner. Dowry system is not only responsible for snuffing out lives of our women, at a very young age but is also primarily responsible for the growing incidence of female feticide in the country. Incidences of rape, domestic violence, sexual harassment at work places and trafficking of women have increased many folds. Half the number of women killed in India are murdered in their bedrooms. Rise in cases of sexual harassment by 40 per cent, dowry deaths by 15.2 per cent and smuggling of girls by 87.2 per cent in 1998, are indicative of their traumatised existence. No place is safe for them, not even their mother's womb. They are put to death even before they are born. The experience of Draupadi in the court of the Kauravas, has become symbolic of the ill-treatment of women in our country. I may quote from one of the poems of Sri Atal Bihari Vajpayee, "In every panchayat, Draupadi is robbed of her honour." She is today not only dishonoured in panchayats but also in the city transport buses, in the city streets and even in her own homes. It is high time that we got rid of this inequality and indignity to women in our country."

In Indian criminal law, sexual harassment of women has not been pronounced or articulated as a specific crime. However, there are specific ections like, 294, 354 and 509 of the IPC, which can be applied in case of offences against women, when a woman is sexually harassed. However, these related laws are framed as offences that either amount to obscenity in public or acts that are seen to violate the modesty of women. While section 294 IPC, is a law applicable to both men and women, the other two sections are specifically oriented towards women. Nevertheless, Supreme Court vide its judgement on Sexual Harassment of working women in the case of Vishakha vs. the State of Rajasthan (August 1997) has laid down, as to what is to be done, to deal with this humiliating feature in our society. Supreme Court has explicitly legally defined sexual harassment by laying down that "... sexual harassment includes such unwelcome sexually determined behaviour (whether directly or by implication) as: Physical contact and advances; a demand or request for sexual favours; sexually coloured remarks; showing pornography; any other unwelcome physical, verbal or non-verbal conduct of sexual nature". Supreme Court of India's Guidelines on Sexual Harassment, are significant in that, for the first time sexual harassment is identified as a separate category of legally prohibitive behaviour. Till now, no law has been passed, which considers sexual harassment as a separate legal offence. The fact is, that it is not less serious, but it is taken less seriously. The critical factor in sexual harassment is the unwelcomeness of the behaviour. It is the impact of behaviour, on the recipient, rather than the intention of the perpetrator, which determines the standards for sexual harassment. In other words, the complainant has to prove, the "unwelcomeness" of the behaviour. Anything less than a transparent rejection of sexual advances would not do. In actual practice, in the absence of witnesses or other concrete proof, it is the complainant's word against the sexual harasser. In India, according to one survey, every 51 minutes, a woman is reported to be sexually harassed and every 26 minutes a woman is sexually molested. Several studies indicate that the magnitude of unreported cases is several times over the estimate. The report of a study conducted by the Gender Study Group of the University of Delhi showed that in 1996, 91.7 per cent of all inmates of women's hostels and 88.2 per cent of all women day scholars had faced sexual harassment on the roads within the campus. According to a study by the International Labour Organisation (ILO) in the 23 countries, 15-30 per cent of working women had been subjected to sexual harassment, which varied from explicit demands for sexual intercourse to offensive remarks. One out of 12 women surveyed, had to quit her job. Some of them were dismissed. The issue of sexual harassment has been in the forefront of western women's movements for equality and in the efforts to make educational institutions and workplaces safer.

A study has found that 45 per cent of Czechoslovakian women had been sexually harassed in the workplace, yet the real numbers are probably higher. The Czech term for sexual harassment, "sexualni haraseni," implies a tacit understanding that whoever complains about harassment is making an unnecessary fuss. Sexual harassment is a widespread problem in post-Communist Europe, yet legal protection for the victims comes slowly. There is hardly a country where the problem of sexual harassment does not exist. France is the only country that has passed a criminal law related to sexual harassment, although some other form of criminal law in other countries can be applied to extreme cases of sexual harassment. During Clinton's Presidency, Franette McColloch, assistant pastry chef accused her boss, Roland Mesnier the pastry chef, of "severe sexual harassment" since 1991, culminating in stress-related medical conditions and retaliation for reporting the alleged harassment. For such assault or indecent behaviour sexual harassment lawsuit, McColloch is asking for a total of $2 million — $1 million from Clinton and $1 million from Mesnier. McColloch, who has worked at the White House since 1983, says in the complaint that Mesnier repeatedly made unwanted advances against her and demanded to know why she would not have a sexual relationship with him.

One would have a feeling that women lawyers would be most able to fight sexual harassment. But according to a recent survey and going by complaints lodged with the National Commission for Women (NCW), women lawyers across the country are subjected to sexual harassment, by their male colleagues. Some judges, magistrates and legal officers are allegedly reportedly guilty of turning more than a glad blind eye on their women juniors. A 33-year-old advocate practicing at the Andhra Pradesh High Court, committed suicide by consuming pesticide, as she could no longer bear the constant sexual harassment by her male colleagues and senior advocates. A judge of High Court in Rajasthan, was accused of soliciting sexual favour for rendering judicial favours. He reportedly resigned.

Till suitable law is passed, a few strategies for the victims are suggested, for breaking the cycle of sexual harassment. The possible victim should do something unexpected. Not many victimisers will be comfortable with a bold response as they expect all victims to take things lying down. However, some harassers will keep on harassing, no matter what you do or say. The possible victims should keep a notebook and write in bold letters on the cover Sexual Harassment Record. When an offensive behaviour happens, they should take out the notebook and say "Could you please say again, what you said just now? I want to be exact about it". Make a big show of asking the name, and address, of the victimiser and also write down the date, time, etc. Writing a letter to the person responsible for such behaviour: This technique has been extraordinarily successful in dealing with sexual harassment as well as other forms of interpersonal conflicts especially with the colleagues or even less known people. The writer of the letter, should describe what happened in a very factual manner and then her feelings and finally, what she wants, like "I want to warn about this behaviour, which should stop at once". Pretending Not to Understand. This approach is particularly useful with sexist or sexual remarks and jokes. Keep a severe and grim faced expression and state that you "don't get the point of this" or "I don't understand the meaning of this". The victim can use strong facial expressions of shock, dismay and disgust, if she cannot think of anything else to say or do. Never ignore sexual harassment in the hope that it will go away. It would not. The fact is that when women ignore sexual harassment, it is often construed as a sign of consent. In a working place, where chances of sexual harassment are plenty, the women should insist on their organisation to form a sexual harassment committee, for all inquiries. The bottom line is that, nobody can make you do anything against your will, if you do not want it.

In India, though position is not, as it should ideally be, women are occupying some of top-of-the-line manager's jobs including that of the Governors, Chief Ministers, Chief Secretaries to the governments, Secretaries to the Government, Additional Secretaries, Income tax and Customs Commissioners, Inspectors General of Police, Deputy Commissioners, the Superintendents of Police. However, in all sectors and government jobs, women will always have to prove themselves. They have to work doubly as hard as men, in order to carve a niche for themselves. It is a fact that, traditionally men have enjoyed greater positions of prestige and power than the women all over the world. The opportunities in the world, largely belong to men.

The National Family Health Survey (NFHS-2) conducted between 1998-99 by the International Institute of Population Sciences revealed following startling facts: 40 per cent women felt that neglecting the house or children was reason enough for the husband to beat up his wife. Another 36 per cent felt that if a woman goes out of the house without informing her husband, she needs to be thrashed. Others reasons, which women think justify domestic violence, include the wife's inability to cook properly or failure to respect her in-laws. The survey also revealed that women in patriarchal societies in India have been conditioned not only to silently accept and tolerate violence as part of their lives but also rationalise it. Interestingly, while women justify violence on trivial issues, like the wife not being a good cook, they feel that dowry related violence is unjustified. While 90 per cent of Meghalaya women had experienced domestic violence, 40 per cent of Tamil Nadu women said they had been physically mistreated by family members from the age of 15.

Women's exploitation, irrespective of their education continues. Sometimes back, a sex scandal surfaced in judicial circles in Rajasthan, where Deputy Registrar of High Court was suspended on the charge of seeking sexual favours for himself and a couple of judges from a woman litigant. The women suffer handicaps even after scoring high marks. They receive less approval and recognition from male bosses and are slower to be promoted. 91 per cent of women work in the private corporate sector and only nine per cent in the public sector. A survey shows that 46 per cent of women between the age group of 22-35 years work in the position of executives or assistant managers. Only 10 per cent are managers. Only two per cent are general managers while only one percent is vice– president. The data analysed shows 59 per cent of women work in Indian companies while, 41 percent work in multinationals. The reason for the small representation of women in the age group of 45-60 years, working in management positions in the corporate sector is, the non-acceptability of working women by Indian society at that point of time. In 1987, the percentage of working women was 13, two years ago it was 20, now it is 28. Entry of women in Armed Forces is now open. Gender discrimination in promotion for Short Service Regular Commission has been removed in the Army.

27

Jittery Jurisprudence

Broadly speaking, all crime is against the state because it disturbs public order and tranquility. It is not so only in India, where the criminal justice system is patterned after Anglo-Saxon law. Most countries, including the US, have adopted the system of public prosecution undertaken by a Government prosecuting attorney.

In India, any crime – from pickpocketing to murder – is regarded as having been committed against the state. The unfortunate and deplorable consequence is that the victim's version is only treated as evidence against the accused. He is at best, considered a witness to the crime committed against him. He is not even accepted, or acknowledged, as a party to the case. As the laws stand, the victim has little or no involvement in the process of bringing a wrongdoer to justice. A number of committees, including that of Justic Malimath, have urged that the victim's rights must be acknowledged. However, unlike the US, here we have no basic rights of the victims of crime and no state protection is extended to them.

The Prime Minister, Dr Manmohan Singh during the third Conference of Chief Justices and the Chief Ministers, urged the judiciary to weed out corruption existing within its system and suggested cut in vacations in courts to reduce backlog of over 20 million cases. He added on 18th September, 2004: "More than one retired Chief Justice has drawn attention to the growing incidence of corruption, among certain sections of the judiciary. The confidence of the public can be sustained only if, apart from efficient and effective justice, there is a firm belief that judgement will be rendered without any extraneous consideration" ... The framers of the Constitution placed a great 'onus and responsibility on the members and practitioners of our judiciary to maintain the highest standards of probity and integrity'... "Accountability and transparency norms cannot, and should not, be imposed, on judiciary from outside. It is, I believe, up to the judiciary to do some soul-searching and ensure how this can best be done."... "A simple way of improving the productivity, of the judicial system is, by increasing the number of working days".... Cutting down long vacations and reducing the number of holidays was estimated to be equivalent to increasing the number of judges by 25 per cent.

The former Chief Justice of India, Mr Justice R.C. Lahoti, said the year 2005 would be declared "the year of excellence in Indian judiciary"... "There will be no place for any corrupt or indolent in the system. I mean business"... The Chief Justice said, the financial crunch becomes acute as the Central grant was being made conditional to the effect that it would match the money given by the state governments. He did some plain speaking by clarifying that there was no money to make additional appointment of judges and to provide them with modern infrastructure... "We have diagnosed the ailment. The medicine is known, but we have yet to make provision for purchasing the medicine and administering it. We cannot leave the patient alone, to cure his illness all by himself." Incidentally, the Government is the biggest litigant in the Courts and quite often litigation goes on between the Government and Public Sector Organisations and some times in between the Government Organisations. The Prime Minister, during the same conference highlighted the need to reduce the number of Government cases in courts. He said, "a sample survey conducted by Karnataka found that in 65 per cent of civil cases, the Government was a litigant, sometimes on both sides. Government litigation crowds out the private citizen from the court system. Much of the Government litigation is, in the form of appeals and this survey again found that 95 per cent of these fail. In a way, they are appeals that shouldn't have been made in the first place."

The Prime Minister's statement that in 65 per cent cases Government is the litigant and sometimes on both sides and 95 per cent appeals which clutter the Courts and which finally fail is a damning criticism of the way Government functions. Having spent over 36 years in the Government, I can say with confidence, that Government cases are not only improperly prepared, but also improperly fought in the Court. About the quality of prosecutors, UP, the largest state in India had appointed a Police Commission, which observed: "It is a fact that appointment of the District Government Counsel and the Assistant District Government Counsel has in recent years become a matter of patronage of local people by the Minister. It has been unanimously found that recommendations made by the District Judge and the District Magistrate, particularly the District Magistrate are based on political influences... There have been cases in which a Minister appointed a person as District Government Counsel when there was no pending case in court either on civil or criminal or revenue side at the time of his appointment". (K L Misra page 54 UP Police Commission Report 1970-71).

The first UP Police Commission (1960-61 page 84) observed: "Several instances have been cited before us, the cases in which appointments of the District Government Counsel have been made on considerations other than those of merit. Occasionally, influence has been brought to bear over on the District Magistrates. Such cases have lowered the prestige of the office of the District Government Counsel in the eyes of the public and has done great harm to the criminal administration. Beside this, it has been complained that in some cases the District Government Counsel being local man, has been influenced on behalf of the accused."

The National Police Commission 1977-81 observed that well over 60 per cent of arrests in the country were unnecessary and unjustified. It also added, that about 40 per cent of the expenditure on prisons, was on those, who should not have been detained in the first place. The reality of manipulation of the power of arrest and detention, including the use of the defunct POTA, without trial requires no further proof. At the root of this state of affairs is the total lack of accountability on the part of the administration and the rulers.

The winds of falling standards of public life have affected all public institutions. There have been instances of judicial functionaries being involved in conduct and offences, which do not behove their high offices. The Government itself has not covered itself with glory, whenever an opportunity presented itself. In the only instance of impeachment in 1993, in the case of Justice V Ramaswamy of the Supreme Court, the Government developed cold feet, apart from the method of dealing with infractions proving cumbersome, dilatory and political. The only way, a Judge of the Superior Court, can be removed is by impeachment. It is a method, which is no longer a practical proposition. Due to rise in involvement of judges in conduct and crimes, the preset impeachment system must be made hussle free.

In the absence of a legally sanctioned method for chastising or punishing judges of superior courts, some optional extra constitutional methods have been used. On two occasions, the Bombay Bar Association called for the resignation of four judges. As a response, the then chief justice of Bombay High Court, did not assign any work to them, till they were transferred or retired. On the second occasion, the Bar called for the resignation of the Chief Justice of the high court, who ultimately resigned at the instance of the Chief justice. In this method, lawyers became the self-appointed disciplinary authorities over judges. This is certainly not a healthy approach, and has no legal basis.

Sometimes in response to some allegations made in press or even by the Bar, the Chief Justice appoints some Committees of judges to inquire into allegations of impropriety by other judges. As none of the Committees has the backing of law, no fruitful results emerge. In fact, as per the media reports, the judges of a High Court refused to give any explanation to the Chief Justice of their High Court, on the ground that he had no such authority. As a result, the Government has found a short cut, in transferring such judges to other high courts, which sometimes resulted in protests from the bar of that high court. A former Chief Justice of India, had said that corruption existed in 20% of the judges. How does the Government expect the Chief Justice of India, to maintain the highest level of integrity, when the Chief Justice of India has no power. In February, 2004, the then Chief Justice of India candidly confessed that he did not have the powers to curb the corruption rampant in lower judiciary.

"Give some powers to the Chief Justice. What powers does the Chief Justice of India have? Despite repeated requests nothing has been done. How do I control the situation and how much can be done to control such situations by passing orders on the judicial side. You (the government) do not know with how much difficulty I secured the resignation of the two high court judges earlier". These remarks by Justice Khare came in the wake of the Gujarat 'cash-for warrants' case - in which, an out arrest warrants for petty payment - and the second, CBI report confirming not only this racket but admitting to similar abuse of judicial powers elsewhere in the country. A Bench of CJI Khare and Justice S H Kapadia said: "We have to break this nexus. We must break it... 'I am exasperated that the CJI can't even ask for an explanation from deviant judges ...The framers of (the) Constitution didn't know that after 50 years, things will collapse". Justice Khare said in an exit interview.

A serving Chief Justice can press the Government only upto a point. The problem and remedy is also known to the Government. It is time for the Government to heed, before it is too late and give whatever withal is required to set the judicial deficiencies right, as projected by several Chief Justices of India. It is time to remind the

Government, what Pascal said: "Justice and Power must be brought together, so that whatever is just, may be powerful, and whatever is powerful must be just."

Said Montaigne; "Lying is a hateful and accursed vice. We have no other tie upon one another, but our word. If we did, but, discover the horror and consequences of it, we should pursue it, with fire and sword and more justly than other crimes". The Indian public and press grumble, whine and criticise incessantly, but rightly, whenever any high profile case ends in acquittal, or other serious crimes go unpunished. The crimes range from fraud, abuse of office, scams, looting the state treasury, corruption, embezzlement, rape, murder or criminal riot. But the cause of this state of affairs, that is perjury, has attracted no notice or attention from the quarters that matter. Perjury naturally affects the quality of justice, as a judge has to decide, only on the basis of evidence presented in the court. In fact, the law as it stands only casts a duty on the citizen to depose truthfully in a court of law. But there is no punishment for lying. The only way to make our countrymen, see the beauty of justice, is by showing them, in simple plain terms, the consequences of injustice.

Time and again, the prosecution in some of the most significant cases has failed, because the witnesses, initially gave evidence supporting a particular theory about a crime, have changed their mind when examined in the Court. This has happened in a majority of cases registered in many states under TADA. In sensational cases, like the BMW, where in a rich sibling had crushed to death some poor people sleeping on the road and the Jessica Lal murder case, wherein a bar hostess was shot dead by the brats of high and mighty. Most recently, in the Best Bakery case, wherein the Human Rights Commission intervened when the witnesses changed their statements in the Court, the same story of perjury has been repeated. While it is not possible to pin point the exact cause of turning hostile, there have been cases where money power, intimidation and fear for their lives, led the witnesses to change their stand. Both lying to sentence the innocent and dishonestly deposing to convict the guilty, are condemnable. However, whenever such cases are acquitted, the Police and CBI are blamed for poor investigation. It is not to deny that investigation can be occasionally slanted or motivated in some cases, because after all it is the same Indians who commit perjury and it is their brethren of the same category, who are a part of the criminal justice system. The expectation of the people is, that guilty should be arrested immediately after the crime, case investigated instantly, full evidence marshalled and by the evening the criminal should be behind the bars. This kind of crime, investigation, and punishment unfortunately happens only in the three hours film. Real life is full of potholes and is different from the real life. Perjury is a fact of life and more than perjury, technical acquittals, equally play havoc with the criminal justice system. Wherever the accused can take any technical plea to get off, they would do. Even former President of USA Clinton, took shelter behind the technicality to escape the charge of sexual misconduct, with one of his aides. He literally escaped the charge of perjury in the trial by Senate. Many believe that the results would have been different, if he had been tried in a judicial forum or if the trial Court, that is USA senate had not taken a partisan view.

The condemnation of either perjury, or poor investigation, is no justification for the malaise, which exists in our society. People have come to accept this almost institutionalised tendency to tolerate perjury. It is also that in some cases of extortion or where gangs are involved, the accused are able to intimidate the witnesses, because there is no law or a system, under which, after the assessment of the need for protection to a particular witness, the administration could give him/her the requisite security cover.

The Supreme Court has also observed that the incidence of perjury in India is widespread. In the latest reported case of perjury decided a few months ago, the apex court said that "unscrupulous litigants are found daily resorting to utter blatant falsehood in the courts", while "most of the witnesses ... make false statements to suit the interests of the parties calling them". The perjurer in the instant case was advocate R. Karuppan, the then President of the Madras High Court Advocates Association. Ordering a complaint of perjury to be filed against Karuppan before a magistrate, the apex court warned: "If the system is to survive, effective action is the need of the time". The perjury committed by Karuppan was that he filed a petition questioning the authenticity of Anand's date of birth in spite of knowing full well that the issue had already been settled by the President of India. Significantly, the Supreme Court even acknowledged that the perjury in the Karuppan case was "not an exception to the general practice being followed by many of the litigants in the country."

In our courts, any action contemplated on the charge of perjury, like contempt trial is only a derivative of the main case. Starting of perjury proceedings will mean burdening the system, which already has huge mounting arrears of cases. Only in an ideal situation, when we have a sufficient number of judicial officers can taking up of perjury cases is feasible. The offence of perjury and dealing with it expeditiously, can only be a part of the overall reform to speed up the justice delivery system. This approach will mean breeding more perjury, thereby causing immense harm to straightforward litigants.

In April 2003 a High Level Committee headed by Former Chief Justice V.S. Malimath was appointed by the Home Ministry to reform the existing criminal justice system. The Commission recommended a the Witness Protection Programme. It generally emphasised, the growing trend of hostile witnesses.

One simple way to check perjury for any charge by any person in a serious case is made a sworn depositions before a magistrate. If the witness then turns hostile, it should be treated as perjury, with no defence, and the judge should be free to convict such a witness on the spot. That will ensure that witnesses find lying far less profitable than truth. This simple legal reform can do wonders.

Police perjury in the fabrication of their reports, is done with a view to desire to see the guilty brought to "justice" should equally be treated as a criminal offence. The most charitable explanation, of this lying is, being the law enforcement officers, police do not want a person; they know to be a criminal, to escape conviction, simply because of a "technical" violation of the Constitution, a procedural formality, or a trivial "exculpatory" fact. For this a responsibility should be cast on the superior officers, that they will be held personally responsible for any misdemeanour on the part of their subordinates. Deterrence to lying, while testifying in court should lead to a stiff punishment. Government can make a rule that a perjury conviction would automatically lead to dismissal of a policeman from the force.

Police also needs to be sensitised, especially at the cutting edge level of the Constable and upto the Inspectors level, which is the investigating and intelligence collecting level, to the immorality and dangers of perjury. Prosecutors can also be warned to take their ethical duty, not to support any case, which in their view depends or rests on perjury, either by the Police or witnesses. At the same time, it needs to be emphasised that archaic laws coupled with anachronistic enactments have created the present anomalous situation. In short, our legal systems need a thorough overall, to meet the aspirations of the people. It is also timely to remind our countrymen, that justice is the great and simple principle, which is the secret of success in all Governments. It is, as essential to the training of the infant, as it is, to the control of a mighty Nation, like ours.

On March 2002, 14 persons in Best Bakery, Ahmadabad Marg burnt to death is the presence of Zahira Shaikh. In the witness box in a dramatic reversal of her alive testimony: "What I said in court was not true. I said it after pressure was put on me. In fact, I recognise all those who attacked us that night.... I am too scared to return to Gujarat and want to stay in Mumbai. I want the case to be re-opened and retired in Mumbai. The authorities in Vadodara are all hand-in glove and I don't see justice being done to my family" she said.

She said that she wasn't the only one to do so. In fact, out of the 73 witnesses who deposed, as many as 41 turned hostile. "Just as we lied, others also lied. Everyone lied. Who knows why? They may also have been under pressure. The pressure must have come from where we used to stay.. Nobody supported us."

The Indian public, Press, Human Rights Commission have been moaning and grumbling endlessly about this acquittal as a dastardly crime that has gone unpunished. The NHRC had filed a petition for retrial of the case outside Gujarat and Government of Gujarat would probably approach Gujarat High Court in appeal against acquittal of Best Bakery accused. But nobody had looked into the basic flaw of the defects in the Indian legal system. About the present criminal justice system, the British said as under; "It will be neutralised if all parties act in harmony together for the good of the public service. "(Minute 11-4-1851 Parliamentary papers 162 of 1853 pages 63 to 95). Mr Willoughby also quoted the Madras committee of 1805, the Courts orders of 1814 and Sir John Malcolm, Lord Falkland and other officers. One of the Magistrates mentioned therein that the police had been greatly neglected everywhere. The root of the whole evil is the useless expenditure in legislation, neither homogenous to the character of the people, nor suited a code of laws, that delights the thieves, rogues, and Vakeels. It is a stumbling block and rock of offence of all and grievous hindrance to the efficient administration of justice. The people may have some confidence in our honesty and desire, to do justice but they hold our courts in contempt. Look through the country and see who thrive and make fortunes; but greater evil than the code is the court of Sadar Adalat and their incessant fault finding with the Magistrates and reversal of decisions for defect of form and so it will be to the end of the time, as long as the Bombay

Judge tries the pursuant robber, and lets him off, because his mothers name is said to be Managua instead of Lingo. It may be very good law, but it is very bad justice. Some reliance must be placed in the judgement and discretion of the Magistrates and then the police may become a terror to evil doors and the praise of those who do well. Mr. Willoughby quoted Sir James Mackintosh who had said that new code should be adopted to the peculiar interests and usages of the people. Penal laws loosely enforced are lotteries in which the offenders speculate and it is remarkable how accurately they calculate their chances of prosecution and escape.

The British had toyed with the idea of changing the criminal justice system. But their priority was the maintenance of the British Raj and not providing justice to the people. Moreover, there was no separation of judiciary from the Executive. There were sufficient powers with the Executive to deal with any serious disturbance or law and order situation. In a flush of enthusiasm, judiciary was separated from the Executive after independence. The result was the demand of impossible standards of proof for proving and case. Indian Criminal justice system, which is based on the principle that let the nine guilty escapes, rather than one innocent be convicted, had led to the acquittal of all the nine guilty along with the innocent. Whenever any sensational case ends in acquittal, there is a hue and cry, and the matter is forgotten. Nobody had tried to solve the basic problem of improving the criminal justices system. There is no former Attorney General. The Criminal Justice is on the verge of collapse. Because the justice is not dispensed speedily; people have come to believe that there is no such thing as justice in the courts. Justice delayed will not only be justice denied, it will be the rule of the law destroyed. This perception has caused many a potential litigant, who has been wronged, to settle out of Court on terms, which are unfair to him or to secure justice, by taking the law into his own hands or by recourse to a parallel mafia dominated system of justice, that has sprung up in metropolitan centres like Mumbai.

In 1984 riots, 2733 innocent Sikhs were killed after Prime Minister Indira Gandhi was assassinated by her Sikh bodyguards on Oct 31, 1984. All the accused have been acquitted and only a few have been awarded some sort of punishment. Best Bakery case and other riots in Gujarat pale into insignificance, when compared with Anti Sikh Riots. Unless the basic law is changed to find out the truth and punish the guilty, the present state of affairs would continue in future also. But said type of remedies would not do. What is required is to bring about a balance between the rights of the society and the rights of the criminals and not go overboard over abstract concepts of letting the crooked and criminals, escape by hiring expensive advocates, who would quote devil's scriptures to prove their case, that the worst of the criminal is innocent. Other wise, one or many more Best bakery Case or Riots, which would be forgotten by the flux of time.

When Government of Gujarat filed an appeal in the Gujarat high court against the trial court judgment acquitting all the accused in the Best Bakery case, the Court said: "It appears to us that it (the appeal) is an eyewash. It is just eyewash and nothing else". The Supreme Court also said: "We will not be silent spectators... There is no cross-examination as to why so many witnesses turned hostile. This shows the nature of prosecution"... Democracy does not mean you will not prosecute anyone" said Chief Justice of India. When the Additional Solicitor General cited shortcomings in the criminal justice system, as a result of which not many rioters had been punished, including the 1984 anti-Sikh rioters, the bench asked him: "Are you saying that the rioters in Gujarat should also be acquitted. What else are you saying?.. Just because nobody had been punished for the last 40 years, it does not mean, that we should shut our eyes"... "We do not take any pleasure in doing so. But when we are forced to do, what else can we do?"

The Supreme Court reminded the State Government of 'Raj dharma' to protect the weaker sections and punish the guilty. Every single word pronounced by the Supreme Court is more than justified. However, so far as Raj Dharma is concerned, the political parties, irrespective of their complexion are following in a different way. Their's is the Dharma of sticking to Raj at any cost, and building up or retaining existing vote bank. The prosecution as well as investigation of cases has been far from satisfactory, as mentioned by various Commissions. It is pertinent to quote only a few samples below.

The Delhi Police Commission (1966-68) observed: "We have been informed that political interference is another rich source of corruption". Allegations have been made before us that some politicians resort to the device of securing the assistance of Goondas and bad characters who are given protection by the police.

A study conducted by the Indian Institute of Public Opinion at the instance of the Home Ministry regarding "The Image of the Police in India", showed the following conclusions:

Political interference is seen by the public as a major factor contributing to the poor image of the Police and manifests itself in the misuse and abuse of police powers and disregard of the law by the police.

Some of the typical situations or matters in which pressure is brought to bear on the police by political executive or other extraneous sources are listed below:

Arrest or non-arrest of a person against whom a case is taken up for investigating by the police.

Suppression of material evidence that becomes available during searches by the police. Its inclusion or non-inclusion in the charge sheet placed in the court on conclusion of investigation. Discretionary enforcement of law while dealing with public order situations, with emphasis on severity and ruthless in regard to persons opposed to the ruling party.

Transfer or suspension are used as weapons to make the officials to toe the line of the political masters. Almost all political parties, have done it, some with finesse, some crudely. Most of the time, the first casualty on the assumption of new Government, in the State, is the Chief of Police and the Chief Secretary. They are shifted to make room for more pliable officials. Many obliging subordinates officials develop such clout with the political leadership, that their seniors lean on them to retain their jobs. Their influence with the political leadership is so high that if any senior officials tries to control them, they get such an official shifted. The politically directed transfers seriously damage the discipline, morale, and chain of command.

Once the case is sent up to the court, it is for the prosecution agency to properly marshal the evidence, law and other aspects of the case.The efficient investigation alone, cannot lead to the offenders being brought to the book. It needs to be followed up, by equally efficient prosecution.

The UP Police Commission (1970-71 pages 512-517) noted that the performance of the prosecuting machinery was far from satisfactory.

The then Chief Justice of Allahabad High Court, Shri S K Verma deposed before the Commission saying: "At every level, the prosecution of the State cases is of poor quality and that is one of the reasons for the scandalous number of acquittals in the Districts". Another witness, a former Advocate General of UP told the Police Commission: "At most of the places today the District Government Counsel and the Assistant District Government Counsel are unsatisfactory."

One witness deposed as under: "It is a fact that appointment of the District Government Counsel and the Assistant District Government Counsel has in recent years become a matter of patronage by the Minister of local people. Both at the High Court and at the Sessions Court, there exists system of panel of lawyers, who attend to the overflow of work, which the Government Counsels cannot attend to personally. We have received innumerable complaints about the working of the panels of the Sessions and High Courts both from the Judges and the Bar. Generally brief-less lawyers are put on panels and failure of many Government cases are due to their inefficiency."

The observations of the Supreme Court are timely and they should be taken seriously, as a wake up call, to rectify the deficiencies in the prosecution as well as investigation of cases. Recommendations of several Police Commissions and the Law Commission, appointed after Independence have been pending with the State and Central Governments at least for the last three decades. It is time to dust those files, so that it is ensured that the guilty are brought to book and the guilty do not snook at the law and The Court. No Price is too big to ensure that justice is done and the faith of people is not eroded in the Criminal Justice System.

The selective grant of pardon to many convicted criminals in several States, like Haryana, Punjab, Andhara Pradesh, etc., has put a question mark on the political motive of the powers-that-be. Most pardons are based on political considerations.

A pardon is defined as forgiveness granted by a sovereign power for a crime and the penalty associated with it. Unfortunately, quite a few criminals who have been granted pardon for ghastly crimes include relatives of former Ministers, workers of political parties and other influential people.

Every country has a provision for pardon. In the US, the power of granting pardon in federal crimes is vested in the President by the American Constitution. Section 2 of Article II states that the President "shall have power to grant reprieves and pardons for offences against the United States, except in cases of impeachment."

Some people argue that pardons have been used more often for the sake of political expediency than to correct judicial error. One of the most famous pardons was granted by then President Gerald Ford to former President Richared Nixon on September 8, 1974, for the Watergate scandal. Polls showed a majority of Americans disapproved of it and Ford's public approval ratings plummeted subsequently. He was narrowly defeated in the presidential campaign, two years later. As President, Mr. Bill Clinton pardoned 140 people on his last day in office, including millionaire fugitive Marc Rich and his brother.

In Canada, pardons are decided by the National Parole Board under the Criminal Records Act, the Criminal Code and several other laws, after making suitable recommendations, and clemency is granted by the Governor-General of Canada or the Governor-in-Council. In England, the power to pardon is a royal prerogative – it depends on the monarch's mercy. In France, the President has the power to pardon and is the sole judge of the propriety of the decision. The right to grant clemency in Germany lies with the President.

In Italy, the President of the Republic can pardon or commute their punishment. Under the Constitution of Ireland, the President of Ireland can pardon convicted criminals. But the President cannot pardon people without the Government's consent; to do so would spark a constitutional crisis that may lead to the impeachment of the President.

The President of the Russian Federation has been vested with the right to pardon by Article 89 of the Constitution. The Pardon Committee manages the list of people eligible for pardon and directs them to the President for signing. While former President Boris Yeltsin frequently used the institution of pardon, his successor Vladimir Putin is much more discreet. He has not used this power yet.

So, it is seen that most countries have vested the power of pardon in their respective heads of state and that it has been mostly used to pander to sectional, personal or political interests.

The advocates of mercy fail to understand that if Mohammed Afzal Gurj is not hanged, terrorism will not end. Moreover, he is not the only person sentenced to death; there are 333 convicts awaiting execution, according to the recently released Prison Statistics of India, 2003. Fifty-six people have been given the death sentence in nine months, of whom only three are terrorists.

The Supreme Court, in its October 2006 judgement, has clarified the compelling grounds citing which the judiciary can be moved, challenging a decision of the President or a Governor to pardon a convict, reduce his prison term or even reject his mercy plea. It has ruled out grounds like religion, caste and political loyalty while the President or a Governor exercised his or her power to grant clemency to a convict. At the same time, it has laid doen guidelines for questioning the rationale behind the decision to pardon a condemned prisoner or remit his or her prison term.

The apex court has clarified that it is a well-settled legal principle that the Supreme Court and High Courts have a limited judicial scrutiny of exercise of clemency powers. And a convict can also question the rejection of his mercy plea. Exercise or non-exercise of the power to pardon a convict is not immune to judicial review, the bench has said. Thus, while the grant of relief to terrorists may be questioned before the Supreme Court, in turn, the accused and his well-wishers, too, may question the rejection of the mercy petition moved by him or his relatives.

The Supreme Court has observed: "The position, therefore, is undeniable that judicial review of the order of the President or the Governor under Articals 72 or Article 161, as the case may be, is available". Their orders can be challenged on the following grounds: That the order has been passed without application of mind; that the order is *mala fide*; that the order has been passed on extraneous or wholly irrelevant consideration; that relevant material have been kept out of consideration; that the order kept out of consideration; that the order suffers from arbitrariness.

28

The Crime Bursting Instrument

Normally, when people do not have trust in the State Investigating Agencies and when either the Government of India or State Governments or the Courts want an impartial investigation, they turn to CBI. Right or wrong, CBI is looked upon as an agency, which will deliver the goods, without fear or favour. In fact, there are more demands for a CBI inquiry rather than any other type of inquiries. The Central Bureau of Investigation was set by an Executive Order of the Government on 1st April 1963. The Delhi Special Police Establishment, (legal name of the CBI) was created in 1941. Its primary objective was, to deal with the corruption and economic offences, arising out of the Second World War, involving Federal Government employees and the federal funds. It was a very small organisation at that time, with a limited charter of duties.

The Central Bureau of Investigation is also the nodal police agency in India, for coordinating investigation on behalf of other Interpol Member countries with India and India's cases with other countries. The CBI is the only Central Government Agency, which has been credibly investigating cases entrusted to it, by the Constitutional Courts, that is the High Courts or the Supreme Court. However, where even Central or State Governments may not like to entrust cases to the CBI, the Constitutional Courts step in, to stem the rot. For instance, in the case of Bihar Fodder Scam, where the State Government opposed the CBI inquiry in 1996, it was the Supreme Court, which upheld High Court's Order, that the fodder scam be investigated by the CBI. The rest is a political history, where a serving Chief Minister and the President of the then Ruling Party, both in the Centre and State, had to leave office, under a cloud. It could not have been done, but for the direction of the Supreme Court and the High Court. Similarly, under the direction of Delhi High Court, CBI took up the investigation of JMM bribery case in 1996, which led to the conviction of a former Prime Minister and a former Home Minister. Of course, they were acquitted in appeal and the Government, in its wisdom, chose not to file appeal against the acquittal. The Taj investigation in August 2003, led to the Supreme Court ordering the registration of the cases against the Chief Minister of UP. According to some sources, the CBI investigation is the cause of break up of Mayawati's Coalition Government. It can be seen that CBI investigations have a major impact on the political and economic life of the nation, depending upon, who is being investigated.

The CBI is headed by a Director, who is of the rank of the Secretary to the Government of India. The other police ranks in CBI are Special Director/Addl. Director, Joint Director, Dy. Inspector. General of Police, Superintendent of Police, Deputy Superintendent of Police, Inspector, Sub-Inspector, Assistant Sub-Inspector, Head Constable and Constable, The total sanctioned police strength including all ranks is 5944. In addition, CBI has a sanctioned strength of 230 Law Officers, 194 Technical posts, 140 posts of Scientists in CFSL and 208 Group D posts.

The investigation of CBI cases is done only by officers of the rank of the Inspectors or Deputy Superintendents of Police, numbering about 1100. People below are only there to assist in the investigation and the people above, like the Superintendents of Police, DIsG, IsG, Special Directors or Additional Directors General of Police or Director or the Director General of Police are supervisory officers.

Law and order is a State subject. The basic jurisdiction to investigate crime lies with State Police. Besides, due to limited resources, and with nearly 30% vacancies in the ranks of Investigators and Prosecutors, who are the back bone of CBI cases, CBI cannot take up all cases, which come to it. The CBI can function in any State, with its consent and there have been instances in the past, where the CBI was asked to close its shop and not operate there. A draft CBI Act prepared and sent to the Government about two decades ago, is gathering dust in the Government cupboards. One main reason for the same is that, States do not want to have a super agency, over which they would have no control. The result is that, we do not have a Federal Law Enforcement Agency, for taking up any federal crimes. There is no concept of a federal crime in India. Despite all debate of zero tolerance to corruption, there has been talk of it. Only CBI is still dependent on the Government for all infrastructure. It has no independent status of its own. It is an information collecting wing of the Government. It has its master in CVC, who has been given the power, to supervise all cases of corruption. It is answerable to the Courts, as all its output and investigation results, are to go before the court. It has to depend on the Government, for getting its sanctions for infrastructure, as well as permission to prosecute the guilty. It cannot complain against the Government to the Courts or any body else, for any problem it may be facing. Despite Supreme Court holding that single directive, under which permission of the Government is required for taking up any case against the level of officials of Joint Secretary and above, the Central Vigilance Commission Bill, which has now become a law has restored it. Thus, there is a built-in insulation in the system to prevent any inquiry being launched, against the higher echelons of bureaucracy. It is a law passed by the Parliament. Unless the Supreme Court strikes the down the illegal section, as it did in the case of election laws, it will be in force.

In one year, well over 100 cases are entrusted to CBI by the Supreme and High Courts. Naturally with a strength, which is smaller than the strength of a single big District Police Force, it has a capacity of taking up about 1200 to 1300 cases per year, all over the country. Cases entrusted to it by the Courts, are given the highest priority, as they are generally time bound. CBI is a full time investigating agency, where the work load of one Investigating officer, is 2.5 cases per year of General Offences and 1.75 per Investigating Officer per year, of Economic Offences cases. A normal police station in the country handles over 80 to 100 cases per year. It is not that States cannot have, their own equally efficient investigating agency. It is because, at every step the political masters use the investigation of cases, to suit their needs. Madhumita sex and murder case in UP (May, 2003) is an unheard kind of parallel. The entire investigation team, including the Director General of Police was placed under suspension, ostensibly for not completing the investigation in time, but in reality in failing to save and adequately stonewall a case, against a former Minister, who was supporting the then Government. The CBI, to whom the case was referred to by the State Government solved it, with the help of the former Minister, who was in police judicial custody. The same police officers when they come on deputation to CBI, do a wonderful job. Pressure on CBI to take up more and more cases, whether by the public or Government or on the direction of the Court, is bound to increase. Unfortunately, the Government has no road map, as to what kind of and how strong or efficient the CBI it wants, at the end of five or ten years. With more liberalisation and more opening of economy, we can look forward to more scams and more defalcation. But if the present set up or approach continues, I apprehend that

CBI will find itself stretched beyond acceptable limits, to maintain the same level of efficiency. It is time that the Government took advance action.

Central Bureau of Investigation is always in news, sometimes for the right reasons and most often for wrong. People are generally not clear about the role of the Central Bureau of Investigation. After Independence, the jurisdiction of Delhi Special Police Establishment (DSPE) was extended to all the Union Territories, by the Union Government. Under the law, the jurisdiction of CBI (Legally DSPE,) can also be extended, to the States, but only with the consent of the State Governments concerned.

In view of the increasing corruption in Civil Services, the Government of India set up a Committee headed by Shri K Santhanam, to go into the whole gamut of circumstances, leading to corruption and make suitable recommendations for curbing it. It observed; "The tendency to subvert integrity in the public services, instead of being isolated and aberrative, is growing into a well-organised, well-planned racket. Corruption has increased to such an extent, that people have started losing faith, in the integrity of public administration" It recommended constitution of the Central Bureau of Investigation, on the pattern of the Federal Bureau of Investigation of The United States of America. The Government vide its resolution dated 1st April, 1963, envisaged a multi-dimensional role for the CBI. The CBI was constituted, not only for the investigation of the crimes, earlier handled by the DSPE, but also to take up investigation of important cases, relating to breach of Central Fiscal Laws, major frauds relating to Government of India departments, Public Joint Stock Companies, passport frauds, crimes on highseas, crimes on Airlines and serious crimes committed by organised gangs of professional criminals. It was only a cosmetic change by which, the name of the organisation was changed in Government records, but legally it was and is, the same position as earlier.

At Present the CBI can investigate only those offences, which are notified by the Central Government under section 3 of the DSPE Act. It can also take up investigation of cases, on the request of State Governments, with the approval of the Central Government. In actual practice, the CBI essentially takes up cases, which are substantially and essentially, against Central Government. employees or concerning affairs of the Central Govt. Cases, which are essentially and substantially against public servants of the State Governments or which are in respect of matters concerning a State Government, are investigated by the State Police irrespective of the fact that certain employees of the Central Government may also be involved as co-accused. Such cases, against the State government employees, are taken up only on the specific requests of the State Governments. The State Police has the full power to take up cases and lay traps, even in respect of Central Govt employees. However, normally the States, rarely take this action, but there is no bar on their taking action against Central Government employees.

Regarding corruption in India between 1996 and 2000, the CBI and the Central Vigilance Commission (eve) investigated 13,265 individuals for corruption. The CBI registered 2,256 cases under the Prevention of Corruption Act between 1998 and 2001. About 100 sanctions for prosecution against officers have been recommended by the CVC since 1990. Many high profile individuals including a former Vice Chairman of, DDA, a former Chairman of Central Board of Customs and Excise, a former Minister's PS and a Chairman of a State Public Service Commission and a host of lesser Government gods have been arrested. A few former Chief Ministers were arrested for being accessories or direct beneficiaries of corrupt practices. These days, the higher the officer, the higher the level of corruption. Nobody who is somebody, in the Government talks in terms of crores of Rupees. The days of hundreds or thousands, lakhs as bribe are over. The present position is that, size of the corruption problem is far worse than the exaggerations of the most brazen and most cynical. On May 7, 2003 the then Deputy Prime Minister L.K. Advani said that out of the 186 cases pending against IAS and IPS officers, the "overwhelming majority related to corruption charges". The former Prime Minister Atal Bihari Vajpayee said at a meeting of the National Integration Council in 1999: "People often perceive the bureaucracy as an agent of exploitation rather than a provider of service. Corruption has become a lowrisk and high reward activity."

A study by the Centre for Media Studies, Delhi, on corruption in urban services reveals, that nearly half of those who avail the services of the most frequently visited public departments of government in the country, have had first hand experience of giving bribes at one time or the other. Such is the pervasiveness of the phenomenon that many now dub babudom, as the steal frame. There have been a number of sting operations. The exposure by Tehalka.com of involvement of some top politicians and senior bureaucrats in shady arms deals, widely seen on television in march, 2001, was highly damaging for the image of the country as well as the Central Government and the political parties involved in it. Before the tapes were shown on television, there was a private screening of the same at a five star hotel in Delhi, to which I had been invited. As per the allegations in tape, the following is the detail, of who got what and got exposed: Bangaru Laxman paid Rs. 1 lakh. Jaya Jaitly, Samata chief, paid Rs. 2 lakh for the party. Brig. Anil Sehgal, Director, Directorate General of Ordnance and Supply (DGOS) paid Rs 40,000. Sashi Menon, Senior Section Officer (DGOS), Ministry of Defence, paid Rs. 52,000. Brigadier Iqbal Singh, Prospective Procurement Officer, Ordnance, Ministry of Defence; paid Rs, 50,000. Lieutenant Colonel Sayal (Retd), Defence middleman, formerly with the Directorate General of Ordnance and Supply, paid Rs, 80,000. Major General PSK Choudary, Additional DG, Weapons & Equipment, given Rs. 1 lakh and a gold chain. Major General SP Murgai (Retd), Additional Director General, Quality Assurancepaid Rs. 1.20 lakh. Narendra Singh, Additional Financial Advisor, Ministry of Defence, paid Rs. 10,000. H C Pant, Deputy Secretary, Ministry of Defence, paid Rs. 50,000. Surendra Singh Sulekha, Supplier of uniforms to the Ministry of Defence for the past 20 years paid Rs 1 lakh. L N Mehta, Additional Defence Secretary, given a gold chain. Raju Venkatesh, paid Rs. 10,000. Raghupati, paid Rs. 16,000. Suresh, paid Rs. 7,000.

In some cases after departmental inquiry or after calling for the explanations, matters were dropped. The then Government of the day, in its wisdom, set up a Commission of Inquiry to look into the issue and the two Commissions were on it for over three years. However, the present Central Government has decided, to set the legal process in motion, by asking the CBI to register criminal cases, which it has done. In another case of Cash on Camera and Audio Tapes, involving Jogi and newly elected MLAs of Chattishgarh, the same then Government, decided to ask the CBI to investigate the cases.

Many a times, people find fault with the CBI and criticize it incessantly, for acting only against the small fry and small fish, whereas the big fish, in the form of influential, high and mighty cock a snook at the law. The expectations of the people is that crooks, corrupt and criminals should be caught in the morning, tried in the after noon and sentenced to punishment by the evening. It is a reasonable expectations, on the part of the people, who are exposed to corruption at every level, whenever they have to deal with public officials. There is nothing wrong with their expectations. The problem arises, when CBI is not able to deliver for several reasons. First of all, it is not a constitutional or independent wing of the Governance, like Judiciary or Election Commission. No doubt, its output goes to the Court, who are the final authority, in deciding any case. But what can CBI do, if the Government of the day, chooses not to order investigation even into any serious malfeasance as pointed out above or is selective in its approach. In a Law (CVC) Bill passed by the Government and made effective since September, 2003, CBI cannot investigate cases, against the corrupt and dishonest public servants, who are of the rank of Joint Secretary and above. Forget about investigation, it cannot even inquire into the misconduct of any such official, without the permission of the Government. It almost amounts to asking a thief, whether his antecedents, work and undesirable activities may be inquired into. Incidentally this law, which existed in the form of a single directive, had been struck down by the Supreme Court, on 17th December, 1997. In the present Lok Sabha, nearly one fifth MP's are involved in one case or the other. If the law breakers are lawmaker, it is unfair to expect them to tighten noose around their neck, by having strict laws and independent agencies, to look into their conduct or criminal actions. It is human nature to want others to bend to your wishes. It is easy for the powerful politicians to do so, if they happen to get into trouble with the law. Recently Goa Government, withdrew its consent to the functioning of the CBI, as it found CBI's action unpalatable against one Cabinet Minister. The rot has spread cutting across party lines. However, a silver lining is the proactive role of the judiciary and a vigilant press. Ultimate solution for rooting out corruption lies in the political will and good governance and not viewing or examining every action, as to how it will affect vote bank politics. There is a need for a political consensus, to keep the criminals and corrupt out of the portals of powers. Then only, some salvation and relief is possible for the man, in the street.

After the end of second World War, the need for a Central Government agency, to investigate cases of bribery and corruption by Central Government employees was felt. The Delhi Special Police Establishment Act was, therefore, brought into force in 1946. This Act transferred the Superintendence of the SPE to the Home Department. Its functions were enlarged, to cover all departments, of the Government. of India.

The current name, Central Bureau of Investigation (CBI), given to DSPE was given, through a Home Ministry resolution of April 1963. Nowhere the word CBI is ever used in legal documents in Indian Courts. Initially, the offences that were notified by the Central Government related only to corruption by Central Government. servants. With the setting up of a large number of public sector undertakings, the employees of these undertakings have also been brought under CBI purview. Similarly, with the nationalisation of the banks in 1969, the Public Sector Banks and their employees also now fall within the ambit of the CBI.

Law and Order is a State subject and the basic jurisdiction to investigate crime lies with State Police. Besides, due to its limited resources and still more limited strength of less than 5000 with 30% vacancies, CBI takes up crimes and cases which are essentially against Central Government employees or concerning the affairs of Central Government or the cases in which the financial interests of the Central Government are involved or the cases relating to the breaches of Central Laws with which the Government of India is mainly concerned. Other cases taken up include big cases of fraud, cheating, embezzlement. Cases relating to companies, in which large funds are involved and similar other cases, when committed by organised gangs or professional criminals having ramifications in several States or cases having interstate and international ramifications and involving several official agencies where, from all angles, it is considered necessary that a single investigating agency should be incharge of the investigation. But this is subject to the consent and request of the State Governments to Central Government. CBI does not have an all embracing jurisdiction, unlike the FBI and the efforts to have a Federal Law Enforcement Agency or to treat certain offences as Federal Offences have been derailed by the State Governments. The CBI can take up the cases only at the request of the State Governments and not on its own.

The latest attack on the CBI or rather the Government was on 21st July, 2003, when the opposition alleged that CBI had been pressurised to dilute its chargesheet against Union Ministers, including the Deputy Prime Minister. It would be worthwhile to encapsulate the Babri Masjid demolition case:

December 6, 1992: First Information Report (FIR) No. 197/92 against unknown persons and 47 other cases were registered at Ram

Janam Bhoomi police station at Ayodhya. An FIR No.198/92 was also registered at Ram Jantar Bhoomi police station.

December 13, 1992: The FIR 197/92, relating to conspiracy, communal frenzy and rioting, transferred to the Central Bureau of Investigation (CBI).

August 27, 1993: The FIR 198/92, charge of conspiracy, did not figure in this case. It related to offences of inflammatory speeches, rioting, whipping up of communal frenzy and 47 other cases transferred to the CBI.

October 5, 1993: A composite chargesheet was filed by the CBI in both 197/92 and 198/92 eases against 40 accused in the Special Court of the Additional Chief Judicial Magistrate, Lucknow.

January 1, 1996: A supplementary chargesheet was filed by the CBI against nine more persons in Lucknow court.

September 9, 1997: Charges were framed against 49 accused by the Special Judge, Ayodhya Case, Lucknow. As many as 33 accused filed revision petition in Allahabad High Court.

February 2, 2001: Allahabad High Court upheld the order of September 9, 1997 of the Special Judge but held the notification of October 8, 1993 issued by the Uttar Pradesh Government in respect of case No. 198/92 setting up a Special Court, defective as there was no consultation with the High Court for issuing it. Cognisance, committal and order on framing charges in respect of 198/92 cited, were bad in law. The court held, that the defect could be rectified by issuing fresh notification by the State Government.

June 16, 2001: The CBI requested the Uttar Pradesh Government to issue a fresh notification, curing the technical defect of having not consulted the High Court. The State Government did not issue a fresh notification, to cure the defect, neither did it file a Special Leave Petition (SLP), challenging the High Court order before the Supreme court.

February to July 2002: Special Leave Petitions (SLP), pleading for issue of notification and revival of trial in the Ayodhya case, filed in the Supreme Court by Mohammad Aslam Bhure, Society for Justice, Kuldip Nayar and Mohammad Hashim.

September 2002: The Uttar Pradesh Government issued a notification specifying that Rae Bareli court would be the Special Court to try the case arising out of the FIR 198/92. This case, pending before the Lucknow court, will be transferred to Rae Bareli court.

November 2002: The Supreme Court upheld the Uttar Pradesh Government's notification on Rae Bareli Special Court.

May 31, 2003: The CBI filed a supplementary charge-sheet against Sh. L.K. Advani and seven others, including Murli Manohar Joshi, Uma Bharti, Vinay Katiyar and Ashok Singhal.

The CBI report contained the statements of 39 witnesses, documents and press reports relating to the investigation of case No. 198/92

The Opposition on July 21, 2003 tabled an adjournment motion, in the Parliament, alleging that the Central Bureau of Investigation had "dropped" the charges of conspiracy to demolish the Babri Masjid against the Deputy Prime Minister, L.K. Advani and some others. It led to stormy scenes in the Lok Sabha, which adjourned without transacting any business on Monday, 21st July. The opposition demanded that the Prime Minister should give an answer and also asked for the resignations of Mr. Advani and the Human Resource Development Minister, Murli Manohar Joshi. The Speaker however, rejected the Opposition demand and quoted from a "letter" from the Law Minister, Arun Jaitley, which stated thatthe subject matter was sub judice. Besides, "the CBI has not diluted any case, dropped any charge against the accused person. Section 120 B (relating to conspiracy) was never a charge in the Rae Bareilly chargesheet, the question of dropping it does not arise". The Speaker also added that: "Since the matter has not been dropped by the Government, the information with the (Opposition) members is not correct. Therefore, I do not agree to suspend the question hour". The law Minister said: "the entire premise that the CBI has diluted or dropped charges against Mr. Advani and others is factually incorrect... there has been no interference by the Centre, no dropping of charges by the CBI". He also added that the Congress had "withdrawn a record number of cases against its leaders in 1980, but the Vajpayee Government had not interfered in any way, in the Babri demolition case. In the Rae Bareilly court, it was for the judge to accept, add to, or delete charges made out by the CBI, it was for the court to decide not Parliament..., it would be unprecedented if parallel arguments on what charges should be framed are made in Parliament. That would negate the rule of law". The Congress says that the CBI filed two chargesheets on October 5, 1993 and January 11, 1996. Both, one including the charge of conspiracy, were considered together by the special court in Lucknow and "neither the High Court of Allahabad nor any other court had quashed the chargesheets. Those charges were based not just on FIRs, but on investigations by the CBI and they cannot be wished away.

There is a lot of merit in both sides. But the ideal forum to resolve the issue, is the Court, where the matter is pending. It would be better if the lawyers of both sides use their lung power there, which is the correct forum, for interpretation of law and taking legal action instead of Parliament. Otherwise the chances are, that Ayodhya case may derail the legislative work of the Parliament frequently.

There are certain holy cows in the country. If you say and do anything, or pronounce anything about them, it is considered blasphemy or contempt of the institution. Tehelka exposed the endemic corruption in the defence department. But what the Government of the day did, was to set up a Commission. When one judge heading the Commission resigned, another was appointed. This continued nearly for over three years. The truth and legal position is that Inquiry Commissions, in the first place have nothing to do with the law and justice. Among other things, they are not courts of law and hence cannot punish people. More than anything else, Governments are not required to act on any or all of their recommendations. Setting up a Commission of Inquiry, is the best and at the same time, a toothless way of tackling a problem. It is one way of postponing the handling of the problem for which, any Commission ostensibly might have been set up. Even after a Commission is set up and gives its report, the report can be conveniently confined to the cold storage. Vajpayee Government had set up a Commission, to review the Constitution, when it knew fully well, that it did not have the majority, to bring about the changes, however eminently suitable they may be for the country. Who benefits from such Commission? The obvious conclusion is, not the aggrieved party, but the personnel constituting such Commissions. Thus, the politics and games of Commissions goes on and on in the country, depending upon which side of the fence you are. Tehalka story was nothing except a revelation on corruption in defence procurements. It showed, how the defence ministry, one of the holy cows, was steeped in a cesspool of profound corruption.

The Tehalka expose showed a systemic decay, which was sought to be sheltered, under the excuse that any exposure of corruption in the army, will demoralise the army. However, nobody in right senses can claim, that showing somebody corrupt or dishonest will demoralise, those who are doing their job correctly. After viewing

Tehalka expose in a private hotel, I was so disgusted that I walked out of the show. When I was asked as to why I was leaving, I said the video showing, was much worse than imaginable reality. In reality, video had captured, what had already happened.

Generally, inquiries or Inquiry Commissions in our country are set up, to diffuse red-hot, unmanageable crises. These are temporary attention diverting techniques and not solutions. Once set up, a Commission can take, as much time as it wants, may be five to ten years to produce a report.

It is for the Government of the day to order investigation, even into any serious malfeasance, or be selective in its approach. Even otherwise, there are a lot of shackles on the functioning of the investigating agencies. Joints secretaries and above cannot be prosecuted without the permission of Central Government. This is one way to unleash them. It conveys the signal to the bureaucrats, that if you do, the political master's bidding, you can also share the dishonest gains and also be safe. Incidentally this law, which existed in the form of a single directive, had been struck down by the Supreme Court, on 17th December, 1997. However, a Public Interest Litigation has been filed against it and the matter is pending in the Supreme Court.

Being an MP or an MLA is considered, a kind of insurance against any action by the Government, especially if you are supporting the party in power. It becomes easy for the powerful politicians, to trade their support, for overcoming any troubles with the law. Recently, a jailed MP enjoyed all the trappings of his office and influence, while being in a judicial custody in Bihar. Supreme Court has taken cognisance of it and is taking step to ensure, that judicial custody is not misused by the high and mighty, who wield tremendous clout in the Government. CBI cannot function or take action against anybody, including a Central Government employee, unless the State Government gives consent to its functioning there. In October, 2004 Goa Government, withdrew its consent, to the functioning of the CBI, as it did not like CBI's action and searches against one of its Cabinet Minister. Politicians pay lip service that law is supreme. But they leave no opportunity to escape or disobey it, if it does not suit their overall interests.

The CBI has become the favourite whipping boy of the opposition, irrespective of the fact that, the same party, might have been in power in the past. Whatever action is not found palatable, becomes the subject matter of criticism. It is not to deny the right of the Parliament to censure or disapprove, any action of the Government or any Government agency. After all, it is the job of the opposition to oppose. Under the existing circumstances, even what CBI has achieved so far, is no mean achievement. As against the general conviction percentage of 6.5 per cent, CBI has a conviction rate of over 70 per cent. However, it is a fact that CBI has no control over the cases pending in the Courts. It is for the Government of the day, to make sure that justice is not only seen to be done, but also done promptly. Ultimately, the responsibility lies on the rulers of the day as to what kind of governance or CBI, they want to give to the country.

29

Diligent Diaspora

There are 20 million-Non-Resident Indians, who hold Indian passports and are People of Indian Origin in 110 foreign countries. This figure also includes citizens of Indian descent. According to a recent UN report, India is among the world's top 10 exporters of migrants. Indians are now second only to Mexicans, the next door country to the US, in migrating to the US. More than 2.45 lakh Indians have officially migrated to the US in 2001-2002. 20 per cent of our medical graduates, half of the IIT graduates and 85,000 skilled computer professionals leave the country every year, leading to a UN-estimated 'resource loss' of $2 billion to India.

Similarly, Indians are third in the record of top 10 nationalities who had migrated to New Zealand in 2001-02. In New Zealand, there are more than 60,000 Indians living today. There are close to 1 lakh Indians living in Australia. Over 5,000 Indians immigrated to Australia in 2001-2002 and the demand is going up, as Immigration generates more immigration. Approximately the number of Indians settled in various countries are as under:

Austria1	11,945,
Belgium	7,000,
Botswana	9,000,
Brunel	7,600,
Greece	7,000,
Guadelope	40,000,
Japan	10,000,
Lebanon	11,025,
Libya	12,400,
Madagascar	29,000,
Maldives	9,001,
Mozambique	20,870,
Norway	5,630,

Philippines	38,000,
Russia	16,044,
Seychelles	5,000,
Spain	29,000,
Sweden	11,000,
Switzerland	13,500,
Uganda	12,000,
Zambia	13,000,
Zimbabwe	16,700,

Country wise size of overseas Indian community (above 5,000 people)

Canada	8,51,000,
USA	16,78,765,
Jamaica	61,500,
Trinidad & Tobago	5,00,600,
Guyana	3,95,350,
Netherlands	2,17,000,
UK	22,00,000,
France	65,000,
Portugal	70,000,
Suriname	1,50,456,
Nigeria	25,000,
Israel	45,300,
Germany	35,000,
Kenya	1,02,500,
Italy	71,500,
Saudi Arabia	15,00,000,
Kuwait	2,95,000,
South Africa	10,00,000,
Yemen	1,00,900,
Mauritius	7,15,756,
Reunion Island	2,20,055,
Tanzania	90,000,

Qatar	1,31,000,
Bahrain	1,30,000,
UAE	9,50,000,
Oman	3,12,000,
Hong Kong	50,500,
Australia	1,90,000
Thailand	85,000,
Myanmar	29,02,00,
Malaysia	16,65,000,
Singapore	3,07,000,
Fiji	3,36,829,
New Zealand	55,000

Over 1,200 NRIs and persons of Indian origin (PIO) from 55 countries attended the first Pravasi Bharatiya Divas celebrated from January 9-11, 2003 in Delhi. The main objectives of the celebrations was to understand the sentiments of NRIs and PIOs about India and create a policy framework for a sustained and productive interaction. The objective of the event was to create a network of the Indian Diaspora across 110 countries and recognise the contribution made by them towards improving India's relationship, with the countries of their adoption. It was also expected that the celebrations will help in increasing the foreign direct investment (FDI) share of the NRI Indians resulting in a beneficial and interactive impact on the Indian economy. The term NRI or Non Resident Indians, has been jocularly, severally called Non-Returning Indian, Non Responsible Indian and Nerve-Racking Indian. The word NRI has an assortment of meanings and most of them are not very complimentary. When all is said and done an NRI is a person who has left India, but India never left him.

There is no uniform NRI identity. An NRI, who could be one whose great grandfather migrated to South Africa or other countries in 1900 in search of some job. Or he could be a relation, who went to the US recently to work. The official definition of an NRI is somebody, who has stayed away from India for over a year.

It is only in recent years, with the improved travel and communication that the older NRIs have begun to bridge the gap with India. However for many in the younger generation, India remains a mystery and a country, which is far behind the developed Western World. My own cousins, children are reluctant to come to India, on the ground that, the food available is not hygienic here. In fact, many NRI's prefer to foot the bill of their parents to visit them, rather than come to the country, where they feel that there are lot of hassles in getting even ordinary things done.

When a person goes abroad for earning his livelihood, it is for two reasons. The first one is that he is not able to get a job in India, suiting his qualifications. Secondly, he wants to make as much money abroad, as possible in the quickest possible time. Except for a few hundreds of Indians, who have become millionaire or multi-millionaire, all others are well off only to the extent, that they are living well with all the comforts, the money can buy. There is a kind of belief about the NRIs, that all of them are loaded with dough and are willing to invest in India. It is the same impression about the Western tourists coming to India, that he has unlimited and vast cash reserves at his disposal.

It is a good thing that the Government organised an NRI Mela or fair or gathering or by whatever name you may call it. The point is that if its objective was to get vast NRI investment in India, it would never succeed, unless we match our professings with actions to match not only NRIs, but an ordinary Indian's expectations. Our system has been made so corrupt and so complicated, that it has become a heaven for extortionists and racketeers. We want NRIs to invest money in India, but question arises as to where and what is the guarantee, that even their capital would be safe. There have been a number of cases where NRIs property and houses have been taken over by others and they have to run from pillar to post to retrieve as to what is their due. Sometimes, even that does not happen. Laws are the same for the NRIs as well as other Indians. People indulging in cheating are sure that no NRI can afford to be absent from his place of work for years together to fight the court case. One of my relations, living in Switzerland, invested Rs. 75 lakh in a company, only on reading some beautiful and coloured brochures. He was assured that he would be inducted into the board of the company. When he came to India for a week, the promoters, who had already received his money, refused to see him. About five years have passed and he is still to see the colour of his original investment. At his request, I asked the NRI Commissioner, to look into his problem and solve it. He replied that he had no authority. It was the baby of the SEBI. When I spoke to the concerned in SEBI, I was told that it being something concerning a Non Banking Financial Institution, it is in the purview of the Reserve Bank of India.

Obviously, the Prime Minister cannot give any sovereign guarantee, that the money would be safe. The next best thing is to put in place a system and a single window, with an overriding authority to redress the NRIs problem. In the present system, if an NRI has to invest money, he has to approach separate departments for purchase of land, electricity, water connection and licenses and permissions. No single department is willing to own up an NRI. The biggest problem, which both citizens and NRIs face, is that of corruption. How can the NRIs escape this dragnet, when right from getting down at the air port, they are confronted by corrupt customs and immigration officials and rapacious taxi drivers? After all it is the same Indians, who are handling their matters as well as that of the local citizens. If the Government of India wants foreign investment and all-round development of our country, they have to create a congenial atmosphere.

Corruption in the system is responsible for all ills. NRIs and foreigners would gladly invest in India, but what generally has prevented them is the corruption-ridden system. All of us should resolve to make the country free of corruption. To make India a corruption free country, a biggest mass movement of the stature of the freedom movement in country and the equally massive will on the part of the Government are required. It is possible only if the too much of red tapism in India is cut and the Government becomes both transparent and honest in its working. If it is not done, then the celebration of Indian Diaspora, would have been just another non event, which by next year would have been completely forgotten.

INDEX

G

H

I

N